CW00591243

How to access your on-line resources

Kaplan Financial students will have a MyKaplan account and these extra resources will be available to you online. You do not need to register again, as this process was completed when you enrolled. If you are having problems accessing online materials, please ask your course administrator.

If you are not studying with Kaplan and did not purchase your book via a Kaplan website, to unlock your extra online resources please go to www.en-gage.co.uk (even if you have set up an account and registered books previously). You will then need to enter the ISBN number (on the title page and back cover) and the unique pass key number contained in the scratch panel below to gain access.

You will also be required to enter additional information during this process to set up or confirm your account details.

If you purchased through the Kaplan Publishing website you will automatically receive an e-mail invitation to register your details and gain access to your content. If you do not receive the e-mail or book content, please contact Kaplan Publishing.

Your code and information

This code can only be used once for the registration of one book online. This registration and your online content will expire when the final sittings for the examinations covered by this book have taken place. Please allow one hour from the time you submit your book details for us to process your request.

Please scratch the film to access your unique code.

Please be aware that this code is case-sensitive and you will need to include the dashes within the passcode, but not when entering the ISBN.

CIMA

Subject BA4

Fundamentals of Ethics, Corporate Governance and Business Law

Study Text

CIMA Certificate in Business Accounting

KAPLAN PUBLISHING'S STATEMENT OF PRINCIPLES

LINGUISTIC DIVERSITY, EQUALITY AND INCLUSION

We are committed to diversity, equality and inclusion and strive to deliver content that all users can relate to.

We are here to make a difference to the success of every learner.

Clarity, accessibility and ease of use for our learners are key to our approach.

We will use contemporary examples that are rich, engaging and representative of a diverse workplace.

We will include a representative mix of race and gender at the various levels of seniority within the businesses in our examples to support all our learners in aspiring to achieve their potential within their chosen careers.

Roles played by characters in our examples will demonstrate richness and diversity by the use of different names, backgrounds, ethnicity and gender, with a mix of sexuality, relationships and beliefs where these are relevant to the syllabus.

It must always be obvious who is being referred to in each stage of any example so that we do not detract from clarity and ease of use for each of our learners.

We will actively seek feedback from our learners on our approach and keep our policy under continuous review. If you would like to provide any feedback on our linguistic approach, please use this form (you will need to enter the link below into your browser).

https://docs.google.com/forms/d/1YNo3A16mtXGTDIFJzgJhcu377QA4Q4ihUgfYvVKclF8/edit

We will seek to devise simple measures that can be used by independent assessors to randomly check our success in the implementation of our Linguistic Equality, Diversity and Inclusion Policy.

Published by: Kaplan Publishing UK

Unit 2 The Business Centre, Molly Millars Lane, Wokingham, Berkshire RG41 2QZ

Acknowledgements

We are grateful to the CIMA for permission to reproduce past examination questions. The answers to CIMA Exams have been prepared by Kaplan Publishing, except in the case of the CIMA November 2010 and subsequent CIMA Exam answers where the official CIMA answers have been reproduced. Questions from past live assessments have been included by kind permission of CIMA,

Notice

The text in this material and any others made available by any Kaplan Group company does not amount to advice on a particular matter and should not be taken as such. No reliance should be placed on the content as the basis for any investment or other decision or in connection with any advice given to third parties. Please consult your appropriate professional adviser as necessary.

Kaplan Publishing Limited and all other Kaplan group companies expressly disclaim all liability to any person in respect of any losses or other claims, whether direct, indirect, incidental, consequential or otherwise arising in relation to the use of such materials.

Kaplan is not responsible for the content of external websites. The inclusion of a link to a third party website in this text should not be taken as an endorsement.

Kaplan Publishing's learning materials are designed to help students succeed in their examinations. In certain circumstances, CIMA can make post-exam adjustment to a student's mark or grade to reflect adverse circumstances which may have disadvantaged a student's ability to take an exam or demonstrate their normal level of attainment (see CIMA's Special Consideration policy). However, it should be noted that students will not be eligible for special consideration by CIMA if preparation for or performance in a CIMA exam is affected by any failure by their tuition provider to prepare them properly for the exam for any reason including, but not limited to, staff shortages, building work or a lack of facilities etc.

Similarly, CIMA will not accept applications for special consideration on any of the following grounds:

- failure by a tuition provider to cover the whole syllabus
- failure by the student to cover the whole syllabus, for instance as a result of joining a course part way through
- failure by the student to prepare adequately for the exam, or to use the correct pre-seen material
- errors in the Kaplan Official Study Text, including sample (practice) questions or any other Kaplan content or
- errors in any other study materials (from any other tuition provider or publisher).

British Library Cataloguing in Publication Data

A catalogue record for this book is available from the British Library.

ISBN: 978-1-83996-215-8

Printed and bound in Great Britain

Contents

Introduction

How to Use the Materials

These Kaplan Publishing learning materials have been carefully designed to make your learning experience as easy as possible and to give you the best chances of success in your CIMA Cert BA Objective Test Examination.

The product range contains a number of features to help you in the study process. They include:

- a detailed explanation of all syllabus areas

- extensive 'practical' materials

- generous question practice, together with full solutions.

This Study Text has been designed with the needs of home-study and distance-learning candidates in mind. Such students require very full coverage of the syllabus topics, and also the facility to undertake extensive question practice. However, the Study Text is also ideal for fully taught courses.

The main body of the text is divided into a number of chapters, each of which is organised on the following pattern:

- **Detailed learning outcomes.** These describe the knowledge expected after your studies of the chapter are complete. You should assimilate these before beginning detailed work on the chapter, so that you can appreciate where your studies are leading.

- **Step-by-step topic coverage.** This is the heart of each chapter, containing detailed explanatory text supported where appropriate by worked examples and exercises. You should work carefully through this section, ensuring that you understand the material being explained and can tackle the examples and exercises successfully. Remember that in many cases knowledge is cumulative: if you fail to digest earlier material thoroughly, you may struggle to understand later chapters.

- **Activities.** Some chapters are illustrated by more practical elements, such as comments and questions designed to stimulate discussion.

- **Question practice.** The text contains exam-style objective test questions (OTQs).

- **Solutions.** Avoid the temptation merely to 'audit' the solutions provided. It is an illusion to think that this provides the same benefits as you would gain from a serious attempt of your own. However, if you are struggling to get started on a question you should read the introductory guidance provided at the beginning of the solution, where provided, and then make your own attempt before referring back to the full solution.

If you work conscientiously through this Official CIMA Study Text according to the guidelines above you will be giving yourself an excellent chance of success in your Objective Text Examination. Good luck with your studies!

Quality and accuracy are of the utmost importance to us so if you spot an error in any of our products, please send an email to mykaplanreporting@kaplan.com with full details, or follow the link to the feedback form in MyKaplan.

Our Quality Coordinator will work with our technical team to verify the error and take action to ensure it is corrected in future editions.

Icon explanations

Definition – These sections explain important areas of knowledge which must be understood and reproduced in an assessment environment.

Supplementary reading – These sections will help to provide a deeper understanding of core areas. The supplementary reading is **NOT** optional reading. It is vital to provide you with the breadth of knowledge you will need to address the wide range of topics within your syllabus that could feature in an assessment question. **Reference to this text is vital when self-studying.**

Test your understanding – Following key points and definitions are exercises which give the opportunity to assess the understanding of these core areas.

Illustration – To help develop an understanding of particular topics. The illustrative examples are useful in preparing for the Test your understanding exercises.

Study technique

In this section we briefly outline some tips for effective study during the earlier stages of your approach to the Objective Test Examination. We also mention some techniques that you will find useful at the revision stage. Use of effective study and revision techniques can improve your chances of success in the CIMA Cert BA and CIMA Professional Qualification examinations.

Planning

To begin with, formal planning is essential to get the best return from the time you spend studying. Estimate how much time in total you are going to need for each subject you are studying. Remember that you need to allow time for revision as well as for initial study of the material.

With your study material before you, decide which chapters you are going to study in each week, and which weeks you will devote to revision and final question practice.

Prepare a written schedule summarising the above and stick to it!

It is essential to know your syllabus. As your studies progress you will become more familiar with how long it takes to cover topics in sufficient depth. Your timetable may need to be adapted to allocate enough time for the whole syllabus.

Students are advised to refer to the CIMA website, www.cimaglobal.com, to ensure they are up-to-date.

Students are advised to consult the syllabus when allocating their study time. The percentage weighting shown against each syllabus topic is intended as a guide to the proportion of study time each topic requires.

Tips for effective studying

(1) Aim to find a quiet and undisturbed location for your study and plan as far as possible to use the same period of time each day. Getting into a routine helps to avoid wasting time. Make sure that you have all the materials you need before you begin so as to minimise interruptions.

(2) Store all your materials in one place, so that you do not waste time searching for items every time you want to begin studying. If you have to pack everything away after each study period, keep your study materials in a box, or even a suitcase, which will not be disturbed until the next time.

(3) Limit distractions. To make the most effective use of your study periods you should be able to apply total concentration, so turn off all entertainment equipment, set your phones to silent mode, and put up your 'do not disturb' sign.

(4) Your timetable will tell you which topic to study. However, before diving in and becoming engrossed in the finer points, make sure you have an overall picture of all the areas that need to be covered by the end of that session. After an hour, allow yourself a short break and move away from your Study Text. With experience, you will learn to assess the pace you need to work at. Each study session should focus on component learning outcomes – the basis for all questions.

(5) Work carefully through a chapter, making notes as you go. When you have covered a suitable amount of material, vary the pattern by attempting a practice question. When you have finished your attempt, make notes of any mistakes you made, or any areas that you failed to cover or covered more briefly. Be aware that all component learning outcomes are examinable.

(6) Make notes as you study, and discover the techniques that work best for you. Your notes may be in the form of lists, bullet points, diagrams, summaries, 'mind maps' or the written word, but remember that you will need to refer back to them at a later date, so they must be intelligible. If you are on a taught course, make sure you highlight any issues you would like to follow up with your lecturer.

(7) Organise your notes. Make sure that all your notes, calculations etc. can be effectively filed and easily retrieved later.

Progression

There are two elements of progression that we can measure: how quickly students move through individual topics within a subject; and how quickly they move from one course to the next. We know that there is an optimum for both, but it can vary from subject to subject and from student to student. However, using data and our experience of student performance over many years, we can make some generalisations.

A fixed period of study set out at the start of a course with key milestones is important. This can be within a subject, for example 'I will finish this topic by 30 June', or for overall achievement, such as 'I want to be qualified by the end of next year'.

Your qualification is cumulative, as earlier papers provide a foundation for your subsequent studies, so do not allow there to be too big a gap between one subject and another. For example, E1 Managing finance in a digital world builds on your knowledge of the finance function from certificate level and lays the foundations for E2 Managing performance and all strategic papers particularly E3 Strategic management and P3 Risk management.

We know that exams encourage techniques that lead to some degree of short term retention, the result being that you will simply forget much of what you have already learned unless it is refreshed (look up Ebbinghaus Forgetting Curve for more details on this). This makes it more difficult as you move from one subject to another: not only will you have to learn the new subject, you will also have to relearn all the underpinning knowledge as well. This is very inefficient and slows down your overall progression which makes it more likely you may not succeed at all.

In addition, delaying your studies slows your path to qualification which can have negative impacts on your career, postponing the opportunity to apply for higher level positions and therefore higher pay.

You can use the following diagram showing the whole structure of your qualification to help you keep track of your progress. Make sure you seek appropriate advice if you are unsure about your progression through the qualification.

Reproduced with permission from CIMA

Objective Test

Objective Test questions require you to choose or provide a response to a question whose correct answer is predetermined.

The most common types of Objective Test question you will see are:

- multiple choice, where you have to choose the correct answer(s) from a list of possible answers – this could either be numbers or text

- multiple response with more choices and answers, for example, choosing two correct answers from a list of five available answers – this could be either numbers or text

- number entry, where you give your numeric answer to one or more parts of a question, for example, gross profit is $25,000 and the accrual for heat and light charges is $750

- drag and drop, where you match one or more items with others from the list available, for example, matching several accounting terms with the appropriate definition

- drop down, where you choose the correct answer from those available in a drop down menu, for example, choosing the correct calculation of an accounting ratio, or stating whether an individual statement is true or false

- hot spot, where, for example, you use your computer cursor or mouse to identify the point of profit maximisation on a graph

- other types could be matching text with graphs and labelling/indicating areas on graphs or diagrams.

CIMA has provided the following guidance relating to the format of questions and their marking:

- questions which require narrative responses to be typed will not be used

- for number entry questions, a small range of answers will be accepted. Clear guidance will usually be given about the format in which the answer is required e.g. 'to the nearest $' or 'to two decimal places'

- item set questions provide a scenario which then forms the basis of more than one question (usually 2–4 questions). These sets of questions would appear together in the test and are most likely to appear in BA2 and BA3

- all questions are independent so that, where questions are based on a common item set scenario, each question will be distinct and the answer to a later question will not be dependent upon answering an earlier question correctly

- all items are equally weighted and, where a question consists of more than one element, all elements must be answered correctly for the question to be marked correct.

Throughout this Study Text we have introduced these types of questions, but obviously we have had to label answers A, B, C etc. rather than using click boxes. For convenience we have retained quite a few questions where an initial scenario leads to a number of sub-questions. There will be questions of this type in the Objective Test Examination but they will rarely have more than three sub-questions.

Guidance re CIMA on-screen calculator

As part of the CIMA Objective Test software, candidates are provided with a calculator. This calculator is on-screen and is available for the duration of the assessment. The calculator is available in Objective Test Examinations for BA1, BA2 and BA3 (it is not required for BA4).

Guidance regarding calculator use in the Objective Test Examinations is available online at: https://connect.cimaglobal.com/

CIMA Cert BA Objective Tests

The Objective Tests are a two-hour assessment comprising compulsory questions, each with one or more parts. There will be no choice and all questions should be attempted. The numbers of questions in each assessment are as follows:

BA1 Fundamentals of Business Economics – 60 questions

BA2 Fundamentals of Management Accounting – 60 questions

BA3 Fundamentals of Financial Accounting – 60 questions

BA4 Fundamentals of Ethics, Corporate Governance and Business Law – 85 questions

All questions are equally weighted. All parts of a question must be answered correctly for the question to be marked correct. Where questions are based upon a common scenario, each question will be independent, and answers to later questions will not be dependent upon answering earlier questions correctly.

Structure of subjects and learning outcomes

Each subject within the syllabus is divided into a number of broad syllabus topics. The topics contain one or more lead learning outcomes, related component learning outcomes and indicative syllabus content.

A learning outcome has two main purposes:

(a)   to define the skill or ability that a well prepared candidate should be able to exhibit in the examination

(b)   to demonstrate the approach likely to be taken in examination questions.

The learning outcomes are part of a hierarchy of learning objectives. The verbs used at the beginning of each learning outcome relate to a specific learning objective e.g.

Calculate the break-even point, profit target, margin of safety and profit/volume ratio for a single product or service.

The verb **'calculate'** indicates a level three learning objective. The following table lists the learning objectives and the verbs that appear in the CIMA Cert BA syllabus learning outcomes.

CIMA VERB HIERARCHY

CIMA place great importance on the definition of verbs in structuring objective tests. It is therefore crucial that you understand the verbs in order to appreciate the depth and breadth of a topic and the level of skill required. The objective tests will focus on levels one, two and three of the CIMA hierarchy of verbs. However, they will also test levels four and five, especially at the management and strategic levels.

Skill level	Verbs used	Definition
Level 3 **Application** How you are expected to apply your knowledge	Apply	Put to practical use
	Calculate	Ascertain or reckon mathematically
	Conduct	Organise and carry out
	Demonstrate	Prove with certainty or exhibit by practical means
	Prepare	Make or get ready for use
	Reconcile	Make or prove consistent/compatible
Level 2 **Comprehension** What you are expected to understand	Describe	Communicate the key features of
	Distinguish	Highlight the differences between
	Explain	Make clear or intelligible/state the meaning or purpose of
	Identify	Recognise, establish or select after consideration
	Illustrate	Use an example to describe or explain something
Level 1 **Knowledge** What you are expected to know	List	Make a list of
	State	Express, fully or clearly, the details/facts of
	Define	Give the exact meaning of
	Outline	Give a summary of

CIMA Cert BA resources

Access to CIMA Cert BA resources including syllabus information is available online at www.cimaglobal.com.

Additional resources

This Study Text is designed to be comprehensive and therefore sufficient to meet the needs of students studying this subject. However, CIMA recognises that many students also want to read around particular topic(s), either to extend their knowledge and understanding, or because it is particularly relevant to their work environment.

CIMA has therefore produced a related reading list for those students who wish to extend their knowledge and understanding, whether for personal interest or to help support work activities as follows:

BA1 – Fundamentals of Business Economics

Principles of Economics 3rd ed.	McDowell & Thom
Applied Economics 12th ed.	Griffiths & Wall
Mathematics for Economists: An Introductory Textbook 4th ed.	Pemberton & Rau

BA2 – Fundamentals of Management Accounting

Management and Cost Accounting	Colin Drury
Management Accounting	Catherine Gowthorpe

BA3 – Fundamentals of Financial Accounting

Financial Accounting – An Introduction	Pauline Weetman
Frank Wood's Business Accounting 1 & 2	Frank Wood & Alan Sangster

BA4 – Fundamentals of Ethics, Corporate Governance and Business Law

Students can find out about the specific law and regulation in their jurisdiction by referring to appropriate texts and publications for their country.

Managing Responsible Business	CGMA Report 2015
Global Management Accounting Principles	CIMA 2015
Embedded Ethical Values: A guide for CIMA Partners	CIMA Report 2014
Business Ethics for SMEs: A Guide for CIMA Partners	CIMA Report 2014
Ethics: Ethical Checklist	CIMA 2014
Ethics Support Guide	CIMA 2014
Acting under Pressure: How management accountants manage ethical issues	CIMA 2012

SYLLABUS GRIDS

BA4: Fundamentals of Ethics, Corporate Governance and Business Law

Syllabus overview

The learning outcomes in this subject reflect the professional standards to be demonstrated for the benefit of all stakeholders. With this in mind, the place of ethics and ethical conflict is an essential underpinning for commercial activity. Ethics is more than just knowing the rules around confidentiality, integrity and objectivity. It's about identifying ethical dilemmas, understanding the implications and behaving appropriately. It includes the role of corporate governance, corporate social responsibility and audit; and their increasing impact in the management of organisations.

Wherever business is conducted the legal and administrative framework underpins commercial activity. With this in mind the areas of contract law, employment law, administration and management of companies is considered.

Assessment strategy

There will be a two hour computer based assessment, comprising 85 compulsory objective test questions.

Syllabus structure

The syllabus comprises the following topics and weightings:

Content area		Weighting
A	Business ethics and ethical conflict	30%
B	Corporate governance, controls and corporate social responsibility	45%
C	General principles of the legal system, contract and employment law	15%
D	Company administration	10%
		100%

BA4A: Business ethics and ethical conflict (30%)

Learning outcomes

On completion of their studies, students should be able to:

Lead	Component	Level	Indicative syllabus content
1. Demonstrate an understanding of the importance of ethics to society, business and the professional accountant.	a. Explain the nature of ethics and its application to society, business and the accountancy profession.	2	• The importance of ethics.
	b. Apply the values and attitudes that provide professional accountants with a commitment to act in the public interest and with social responsibility.	3	• The nature of ethics and its relevance to society, business and the accountancy profession.
			• Values and attitudes for professional accountants.
	c. Explain the need for a framework of laws, regulations and standards in business and their application and why CIMA and IFAC each have ethical codes.	2	• Legal frameworks, regulations and standards for business.
			• The role of national 'Professional Oversight Boards for Accountancy' and 'Auditing Practices Boards'.
	d. Distinguish between detailed rules-based and framework/principles approaches to ethics.	2	• The role of international accounting bodies e.g. IFAC.
			• Rules-based and framework approaches to ethics.
	e. Identify the ethical issues significant to organisations and how CIMA partners with strategic bodies to assist its members with ethical tensions/synergies.	2	• Managing responsible businesses.
			• Organisational and personal values.
	f. Describe how personal and organisational policies and values promote behaviour.	2	
2. Explain the need and requirements for CIMA students and members in adopting the highest standards of ethical behaviour.	a. Explain the need to develop the virtues of reliability, responsibility, timeliness, courtesy and respect.	2	• The personal qualities of reliability, responsibility, timeliness, courtesy and respect.
	b. Explain the fundamental ethical principles.	2	• The fundamental ethical principles, and examples of their use for professional accountants in practice and professional accountants in business.
	c. Identify concepts of independence, scepticism, accountability and social responsibility.	2	
	d. Illustrate the threats and safeguards to the fundamental ethical principles.	2	• Continual Professional Development (CPD), personal development and lifelong learning.
			• Disclosure required by law (confidentiality).
			• The concepts of independence, scepticism, accountability and social responsibility.
			• The threats and safeguards approach to resolving ethical issues, including whistle-blowing, grievance, regulations and laws.

Lead	Component	Level	Indicative syllabus content
3. Explain the various means of regulating ethical behaviour, recognising different parties' perspectives towards ethical dilemmas.	a. Explain the relationship between the CIMA Code of Ethics and the law.	2	• The relationship between the CIMA Code of Ethics and the law.
	b. Describe the consequences of ethical behaviour to society, business, the profession and the professional accountant.	2	• The distinction between CIMA's Code of Ethics, contracts, and the responsibilities of students and members when they conflict.
	c. Identify conflicting perspectives of interest when dealing with stakeholders in society, business and the values of professional accountants.	2	• The consequences of unethical behaviour: reputation, financial, legal and regulatory; and the benefits of good ethical behaviour
			• The concepts of corporate and personal ethical stances, in relation to multiple stakeholders.
4. Identify ethical dilemmas and how they may be resolved.	a. Identify situations where ethical dilemmas and conflicts of interest occur, based on CIMA's ethical checklist.	2	• The nature of ethical dilemmas, tensions and synergies.
			• Conflicts of interest and how they arise.
			• Issues of corporate confidentiality.
			• CIMA's Ethical Checklist.

BA4B: Corporate governance, controls and corporate social responsibility (45%)

Learning outcomes

On completion of their studies, students should be able to:

Lead	Component	Level	Indicative syllabus content
1. Explain the role of corporate governance in meeting the concerns of society and investors over the management of corporations.	a. Describe corporate governance.	2	• The role and key objectives of corporate governance, agency theory.
	b. Explain the interaction of corporate governance with business ethics and company law.	2	• Objectivity and independence.
	c. Explain the purpose, definition of the Organisation for Economic Co-operation and Development (OECD) principles of Corporate Governance.	2	• The interaction of corporate governance, ethics and the law. • The purpose, definition and status of the OECD Corporate Governance Code.
	d. Describe IFAC's main drivers of sustainable corporate success.	2	• IFAC's drivers for sustainable organisational success.
	e. Illustrate CIMA's practical proposals for better corporate governance.	2	• CIMA's proposals for better reporting of corporate governance.
	f. Distinguish between detailed rules-based and principles-based approaches to governance.	2	• Rules and principles based approaches to governance.
2. Explain the impact of corporate governance on the directors and management structures of corporations.	a. Describe the role of the board and different board structures.	2	• The role of the board in establishing corporate governance standards.
	b. Explain the effects of corporate governance on directors' powers and duties.	2	• Types of board structures and the role of the board as independent, objective, sceptical and resourceful.
	c. Describe the types of policies and procedures that constitute 'best practice'.	2	• The impact of corporate governance on directors' powers and duties.
	d. Describe the respective committees and their roles and responsibilities with regards monitoring and controlling the actions of the Executive.	2	• Policies and procedures for 'best practice' in companies. • Audit committee – controls, monitoring and relationships. • Appointments Committee. • Remuneration Committee.
3. Explain the role of external and internal audit.	a. Identify the requirements for external audit and the basic processes undertaken.	2	• External audit. • Fair presentation.
	b. Explain the meaning of fair presentation.	2	• Distinction between external and internal audit.
	c. Distinguish between external and internal audit.	2	• Internal audit.
	d. Explain the purpose and basic procedures of internal audit; the need for financial controls and the purpose of audit checks and audit trails.	2	• Financial controls, audit checks and audit trails. • The role of internal audit in providing a service to management.
	e. Explain the role of internal audit in non-financial monitoring and control activities.	2	• How internal audit plays an important and value added service throughout the corporation both in financial and non- financial processes.
	f. Illustrate the added value internal audit provides to both the board and management of the corporation.	2	

Lead	Component	Level	Indicative syllabus content
4. explain the nature of errors and frauds.	a. Explain the nature of errors.	2	• Errors including those of principle, omission, and commission.
	b. Explain the nature of fraud.	2	• Types of fraud.
	c. Describe the different methods of fraud prevention and detection.	2	• Methods for prevention of fraud including levels of authorisation, documentation and staff organisation. • Methods of detection of fraud including spot checks, comparison with external evidence, reconciliations and control accounts.
5. Explain Corporate Social Responsibility (CSR) – a political and corporate perspective.	a. Describe the OECD general policies.	2	• The OECD general policies. • The role of international frameworks.
	b. Explain the role of national and international laws and regulations.	2	• The demands of stakeholders, maximising shareholder return and enhancing the supply chain.
	c. Describe conflicting demands of stakeholders.	2	• Issues within the supply chain.
	d. Identify issues with CSR and the supply chain.	2	
6. Explain the role of CSR within company reporting.	a. Describe the guidelines of reporting CSR within annual reports.	2	• Disclosure guidelines and sources of best practice.
	b. Identify synergies and tensions with CSR and brand management.	2	• The link between CSR and a company's brand.

BA4C: General principles of the legal system, contract and employment law (15%)

Learning outcomes

On completion of their studies, students should be able to:

Lead	Component	Level	Indicative syllabus content
1. Explain how the law determines the point at which a contract is formed and the legal status of contractual terms.	a. Identify the essential elements of a valid contract and situations where the law requires the contract to be in a particular form.	2	• The essential elements of a valid contract.
	b. Explain how the law determines whether negotiating parties have reached agreement and the role of consideration in making that agreement enforceable.	2	• The legal status of statements made by negotiating parties. Offers and acceptances and the application of the rules to standard form contracts using modern forms of communication.
	c. Explain when the parties will be regarded as intending the agreement to be legally binding and how an agreement may be avoided because of misrepresentations.	2	• The principles for establishing that the parties intend their agreement to have contractual force and how a contract is affected by a misrepresentation.
	d. Explain how the terms of a contract are established and their status determined.	2	• Incorporation of express and implied terms, conditions and warranties.
	e. Explain the ability of a company to contract.	2	• Corporate capacity to contract.
2. Explain the essential elements of an employment contract and the remedies available following termination of the contract.	a. Explain how the contents of a contract of employment are established.	2	• The express and implied terms of a contract of employment.
	b. Explain what policies and procedures may be present in the workplace.	2	• The rights and duties of employers and employees.
	c. Explain the distinction between unfair and wrongful dismissal and the consequences.	2	• Diversity, discrimination, anti-bribery, gifts, conflicts of interest, whistle-blowing, money laundering, disciplinary, data protection, social media, health and safety.
			• Notice and dismissal, redundancy.
			• Unfair and wrongful dismissal.

BA4D: Company administration (10%)

Learning outcomes

On completion of their studies, students should be able to:

Lead	Component	Level	Indicative syllabus content
1. Explain the nature, legal status and administration of business organisations.	a. Describe the essential characteristics of the different forms of business organisations and the implications of corporate personality.	2	• The essential characteristics of sole traders, partnerships, companies limited by shares and corporate personality.
	b. Explain the differences between public and private companies.	2	• 'Lifting the corporate veil' both at common law and by statute.
	c. Explain the purpose and legal status of the Articles of Association.	2	• The distinction between public and private companies.
	d. Explain the main advantages and disadvantages of carrying on business through the medium of a company limited by shares.	2	• Company registration and the advantages of purchasing a company 'off the shelf'.
			• The purpose and contents of the Articles of Association.
			• The advantages and disadvantages of a company limited by shares.

Information concerning formulae and tables will be provided via the CIMA website, www.cimaglobal.com.'

Business Ethics

Chapter learning objectives

Upon completion of this chapter you will be able to:

- explain the nature of ethics and its application to society, business and the accountancy profession

- apply the values and attitudes that provide professional accountants with a commitment to act in the public interest and with social responsibility

- explain the need for a framework of laws, regulations and standards in business and their application and why CIMA and IFAC each have ethical codes

- distinguish between detailed rules-based and framework/principles approaches to ethics

- identify the ethical issues significant to organisations and how CIMA partners with strategic bodies to assist its members with ethical tensions/synergies

- describe how personal and organisational policies and values promote behaviour

- explain the need to develop the virtues of reliability, responsibility, timeliness, courtesy and respect

- explain the fundamental ethical principles

- identify concepts of independence, scepticism, accountability and social responsibility

- illustrate the threats and safeguards to the fundamental ethical principles.

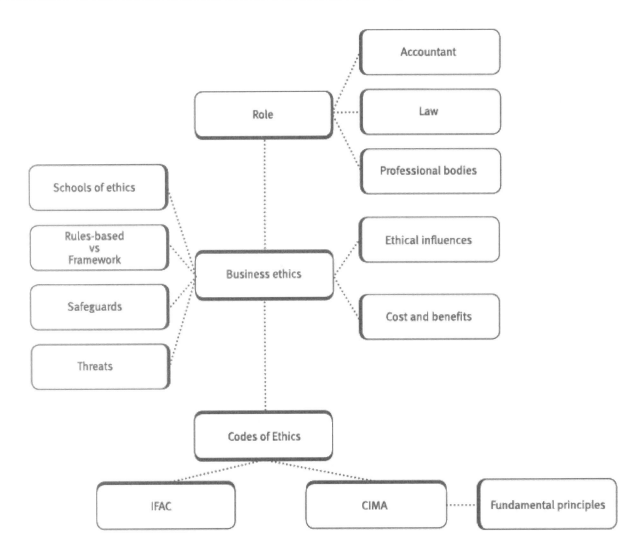

1   Introduction to business ethics

 Definition of Ethics

The Oxford English Dictionary defines ethics as the "moral principles that govern a person's behaviour of the conducting of an activity".

Ethics is thus concerned with how one should act in a certain situation, about 'doing the right thing' and is ultimately about morality – the difference between right and wrong.

Illustration 1

Ethical choices

Consider the following ethical dilemmas:

- You buy something in a shop and later discover that they have undercharged you for an item. Do you go back and tell them?

- You want a new designer label item of clothing but think it is too expensive. Would you buy a cheap fake copy if you saw one for sale while on holiday?

- Would you stop buying a particular product if you found out that the working conditions in the factories where they are made were far below 'acceptable' standards (such as low pay rates, excessive hours worked, use of child labour)?

Does the fact that you are a (student) member of a professional body affect your answers?

Schools of ethics

Virtue ethics, drawing on the work of Aristotle, holds that the virtues (such as justice, charity, and generosity) are dispositions to act in ways that benefit both the person possessing them and that person's society. This is the ethical school of the accountancy profession.

The second, deontological, defended particularly by Kant, makes the concept of duty central to morality: humans are bound, from a knowledge of their duty as rational beings, to obey the categorical imperative to respect other rational beings.

Thirdly, utilitarianism asserts that the guiding principle of conduct should be the greatest happiness or benefit of the greatest number.

2 Business ethics

Business ethics is the application of ethical principles to the problems typically encountered in a business setting.

Whether an action is considered to be right or wrong normally depends on a number of different factors, including:

- the consequences – does the end justify the means?

- the motivation behind the action

- guiding principles – e.g. 'treat others as you would be treated'

- key values – such as the importance of human rights.

Typical issues in business ethics

Some typical issues addressed in business ethics include:

- 'creative accounting' to misrepresent financial performance

- misleading advertising

- aggressive personal selling (e.g. insurance or double glazing)

- data protection and privacy

- the difference between corporate hospitality and bribery

- the difference between business intelligence and industrial espionage

- political contributions to gain influence

- corporate crime, including insider trading and price fixing

- employee issues, such as discrimination or unfair dismissal

- environmental issues and related social concerns

- marketing, sales and negotiation techniques

- product issues such as patent and copyright infringement, planned obsolescence, product liability and product defects

- using legal loopholes to avoid paying tax.

3 The role of the accountant in promoting ethical behaviour

A management accountant's role is to provide the crucial information that forms the basis of decision-making within an organisation. If work is undertaken badly or in bad faith there can be wide-ranging consequences. Unethical behaviour can affect not only the accountant (perhaps resulting in disciplinary action against the employee or by CIMA), but may also affect the jobs, financial viability and business efficacy of an organisation in which the accountant works. Management accountants in the public sector are also dealing with tax-payers' money which, if poorly stewarded, might be wasted or misused.

At many business meetings, or on many Boards of Directors, it is only the professional accountant who belongs to a profession and therefore has a duty to act in the public interest.

Public interest refers to the common well-being or general welfare of society. Professional accountants must consider this, as they have a wider duty to act in the best interests of the public at large, as well as to the business and its owners.

The professional accountant therefore has a special role in promoting ethical behaviour throughout the business.

4 Ethical influences

Each of us has our own set of values and beliefs that we have evolved over the course of our lives through our education, experiences and upbringing. We all have our own ideas of what is right and what is wrong and these ideas can vary between individuals and cultures.

There are a number of factors that affect ethical obligations.

(i) The law

For example, deceptive advertising is illegal and violators of this law are liable to large fines, court action and/or loss of goodwill. Legislation hopefully makes it very clear what is acceptable as a minimum standard. However, ethics is more than just obeying the law. For example, using legal loopholes to minimise a global firm's tax bill may not be illegal but is increasingly viewed as unethical.

(ii) Government regulations

For example, regulations set standards on issues such as unfair competition, unsafe products, etc. Failure to comply with these regulations could lead to criminal charges, or fines etc. Unfortunately, some firms will still find ways to get round such regulations.

Artificial sweeteners

In 1970 cyclamates (a type of artificial sweetener) were banned in the USA following evidence that they were carcinogenic.

Following the ban a major US food manufacturer still sold 300,000 cases of cyclamate sweetened food overseas instead.

(iii) Ethical codes

Many organisations have codes that clearly state the ethical standards and principles an employee or member should follow.

Generally, written codes clarify the ethical issues and principles but leave the resolution to the individual conscience.

Ethical codes are usually followed if written down and enforced – say by disciplinary procedures. However, many companies have 'unwritten' codes of practice and/or have no method of enforcement.

(iv) Social pressure

Many people draw their values from what they see other people doing, whether on the news or people they know. However, social pressure can change, just as society changes.

Many protest groups and activists hope to change public values with the long term hope that new values become reflected in law. A good example of this is the change in discrimination laws over the last hundred years.

(v) Corporate culture

Corporate culture is defined as "the sum total of all the beliefs, attitudes, norms and customs that prevail within an organisation" or "the way we do things around here".

Ideally we want a culture that supports and encourages ethical behaviour.

For example, if everyone else is exaggerating expense claims or covering up mistakes, then this can quickly become a norm of behaviour that new employees soon adopt.

Of particular importance is the example set by senior management – sometimes referred to as the 'tone at the top'.

(vi) Personal policies and values

An individual's personal characteristics such as gender, age and religious beliefs can also play a part in their approach to ethics.

5   The costs and benefits of business ethics

It can be argued that the primary purpose of a business is to try and earn a profit. In a company, for instance, the directors have been employed in order to earn the owners of the business a return on their investment.

Some have concluded from this that going beyond the legal minimum standard of behaviour is contrary to the directors' duty to make money and that behaving ethically increases costs and reduces profits.

For example:

- Increased cost of sourcing materials from ethical sources (e.g. Fairtrade products or free range eggs).

- Having to turn away business from customers considered to be unethical (e.g. an 'ethical' bank may choose not to invest in a company that manufactures weapons).

- The management time that can be taken up by planning and implementation of ethical practices.

However, as well as the moral argument to act ethically, there can be commercial benefits to firms from acting ethically:

- Having good ethics can attract customers.

    This can be because good ethics tend to enhance a company's reputation and therefore its brand. Given the choice, many customers will prefer to trade with a company they feel is ethical.

- Good ethics can result in a more effective workforce.

    A reputation for good business ethics is likely to involve good working conditions for employees, allowing the business to attract a higher calibre of staff.

Avoiding discrimination against workers is likely to give the company access to a wider human resource base.

Ethics programmes can cultivate strong teamwork and improve productivity.

- Ethics can give cost savings.

Avoiding pollution will tend to save companies in the long run – many governments are now fining or increasing taxes of more polluting businesses.

- Ethics can reduce risk.

Many firms have failed due to unethical practices within them.

Approaches to ethics in practice

Imagine you are a company that runs a large chain of supermarkets. You have identified an opportunity to expand into country G. This expansion will create large numbers of local jobs and is expected to earn you significant profits.

Local officials in country G have made it clear that, in order to gain the appropriate planning permissions, you will need to pay them money as inducements (bribes). This is common practice for officials in country G, though it is illegal in your home country. What should you do?

The answer depends on your approach to ethics.

Consequentialists would argue that your decision depends on the consequences of paying the bribes.

If you were **egoist** (looking at your own needs), you would probably pay the bribes as you would still stand to earn a significant profit from the venture.

If you are a **utilitarian** company, you may also consider paying the bribe as doing so will not only mean that you can earn large profits, but will provide jobs for many locals. Paying the bribe will therefore be for the greater good. (However, it is worth noting that whatever the organisation may think about bribery, under UK law it is an illegal act.)

Pluralists would look at ensuring that the needs of none of the stakeholders are seriously compromised by paying the bribe. In this case, while the payment will involve some loss to our shareholders, paying the bribe will still allow us to expand into country G, benefiting everyone.

Relativists would look at the context of the decision to pay the bribe. In this case, bribery is a commonly accepted part of doing business in country G. Therefore, we can be flexible with our approach and may consider paying the bribe.

Absolutists would look at whether paying the bribe was fundamentally incorrect. In this case, bribery is illegal in our home country. An absolutist would therefore be likely to conclude that paying bribes to officials in country G would also be inappropriate, as doing so is always wrong.

6 The role of law in ethics

Legal and disciplinary frameworks do provide an effective means of challenging serious wrong-doing. They can provide deterrents to bad practice, through punishment and censure and remedies for some of the damage that results, for example by means of compensation. However, these means of controlling behaviour set the threshold for what amounts to unacceptable accounting practice at a fairly high level.

Thus, relying solely on the law and disciplinary frameworks to 'police' accounting ethics is not the most desirable way of preventing and detecting undesirable practices. Law by nature can be inflexible, therefore causing difficulty when trying to apply it to cases of ethical misconduct.

7 The role of professional bodies

There are a number of professional bodies, both international and national, that are relevant to the professional accountant's work.

The International Federation of Accountants (IFAC)

The International Federation of Accountants (IFAC) is an international body representing all major accountancy bodies across the world.

The role of the IFAC is to protect the public interest by developing high quality international standards, promoting strong ethical values and encouraging quality practice.

IFAC's International Ethics Standards Board for Accountants (IESBA)

IFAC's International Ethics Standards Board for Accountants (IESBA) is an independent standard-setting board that develops and issues, in the public interest, high-quality ethical standards and other pronouncements for professional accountants worldwide.

Through its activities, the IESBA develops the Code of Ethics for Professional Accountants, which establishes ethical requirements for professional accountants.

The board also provides adoption and implementation support, promotes good ethical practices globally, and fosters international debate on ethical issues faced by accountants.

The Financial Reporting Council (FRC)

The Financial Reporting Council (FRC) is the UK's independent regulator responsible for promoting high quality corporate governance and reporting to foster investment.

The main areas where most accountants experience the work of the FRC are in terms of accounting and auditing standards:

- The Board of the FRC issues UK versions of International Standards on Auditing where appropriate, taking advice from the Audit & Assurance Council (part of the FRC)

- The Board of the FRC also issues UK versions of International Financial Reporting Standards where appropriate, taking advice from the Accounting Council (part of the FRC).

The Conduct Committee

The Conduct Committee is part of the FRC and provides independent oversight of professional disciplinary issues, together with oversight of the regulation of accountants and actuaries in the UK and Republic of Ireland.

The Conduct Committee

The Conduct Committee's responsibilities include overseeing:

- Monitoring of Recognised Supervisory and Recognised Qualifying bodies

- Audit Quality Reviews

- Corporate Reporting Reviews

- Professional discipline

- Oversight of the regulation of accountants and actuaries.

8   Codes of Ethics

Each profession has its own specific code of ethics which form part of the identity of the profession i.e. the medical profession – sanctity of life.

Accountants have the ethical responsibility to be objective, independent in their representation of the accounts. These ethical principles create solidarity of the profession that society accepts within in its universalistic morality. Therefore, to maintain the benefit which accrue from the profession (status and financial benefits) it is the responsibility of the professional to ensure it acts within the ethical principles of the profession and ensuring the Public Interest is paramount within the ethical dimension of decision making both personally and within the organisation the professional is working. However, it is not the role of the individual accountant to work outside the law, therefore, in discerning the correct decision or action to take the rule of law should always take precedence.

Corporate codes of ethics

Most companies (especially if they are large) have approached the concept of business ethics by creating a set of internal policies and instructing employees to follow them. These policies can either be broad generalisations (a corporate ethics statement) or can contain specific rules (a corporate ethics code).

There is no standard list of content – it will vary between different organisations. Typically, however, it may contain guidelines on issues such as honesty, integrity and customer focus.

Many organisations appoint Ethics Officers (also known as Compliance Officers) to monitor the application of the policies and to be available to discuss ethical dilemmas with employees where needed.

The International Federation of Accountants (IFAC)

In June 2005, IFAC published their Code of Ethics for Professional Accountants which was prepared by the International Ethics Standards Board of the International Federation of Accountants. That Committee was charged with developing and issuing **high-quality ethical standards and other pronouncements for professional accountants around the world**. This reflected what has been seen as a growing crisis of confidence in accounting ethics internationally, following financial scandals with global implications. The Code has been revised over the years with the most recent version being issued in 2018.

IFAC is an umbrella organisation for accounting standards worldwide, the Code and its principles are shared by accounting bodies globally.

CIMA

In 2006, the CIMA Code of Ethics for Professional Accountants' was launched. Revised codes were issued in 2010, 2015 and 2020.

The CIMA Code reflects the standards CIMA expects of its members and students and is aligned with global standards across the profession. It reflects its status as a Chartered Institute and as a basis for any complaints or cases under CIMA's disciplinary procedures.

The CIMA Code of Ethics aims to:

(i)   identify the nature of the personal responsibility that the management accountant takes on as part of the price for getting a reasonable salary and status

(ii)   provide guidance on how to identify the practical situations where particular care might need to be taken because of the ethical pitfalls involved

(iii)   provide general guidance on how to address those difficult questions.

It is split into three parts with a list of definitions at the end:

Part 1 – Complying with the Code

This covers an introduction and the fundamental principles of professional ethics for professional accountants. It also provides a conceptual framework that should be used to identify, evaluate and apply safeguards to eliminate threats to compliance with the fundamental principles.

Part 2 – Professional Accountants in Business (including CGMA designation holders)

This part was developed in co-operation with the American Institute of CPAs (AICPA).

It covers issues such as potential conflicts, preparation and reporting of information, acting with sufficient expertise, financial interests and inducements.

Part 3 – Professional Accountants in Public Practice

This covers particular issues identified as being of relevance to accountants in public practice such as professional appointment, conflicts of interest, second opinions, fees and other types of remuneration, marketing professional services, gifts and hospitality, custody of client assets, objectivity in all services and independence in assurance engagements.

The Code establishes ethical requirements for professional accountants and applies to all member firms or bodies of IFAC. Any such firm or **body may not apply less stringent standards than those stated in this Code**.

There is an override, should any firm or body be prohibited by law or regulation in complying with any parts of the Code. The expectation is that all parts of IFAC Code will be complied with otherwise. Professional accountants need to familiarise themselves with any differences if there are any, but to comply with the more stringent requirements and guidance unless prohibited.

9   Fundamental principles

CIMA's code lists five fundamental principles with which its members are expected to comply.

The fundamental principles are introduced in Section 110.

Extract from CIMA Code of Ethics

110.1 A1 There are five fundamental principles of ethics for professional accountants:

(a) **Integrity** — to be straightforward and honest in all professional and business relationships

(b) **Objectivity** — not to compromise professional or business judgments because of bias, conflict of interest or undue influence of others.

(c) **Professional competence and due care** — to:

    (i) Attain and maintain professional knowledge and skill at the level required to ensure that a client or employing organisation receives competent professional service, based on current technical and professional standards and relevant legislation; and

    (ii) Act diligently and in accordance with applicable technical and professional standards.

(d) **Confidentiality** — to respect the confidentiality of information acquired as a result of professional and business relationships.

(e) **Professional behaviour** — to comply with relevant laws and regulations and avoid any conduct that the professional accountant knows or should know might discredit the profession.

 More on fundamental ethical principles

Section 111 – Integrity

Integrity implies fair dealing and truthfulness.

Members are also required not to be associated with any form of communication or report where the information is considered to be:

•   materially false or to contain misleading statements

•   provided recklessly

•   incomplete such that the report or communication becomes misleading by this omission.

Section 112 – Objectivity

Accountants need to ensure that their business/professional judgement is not compromised because of bias or conflict of interest.

However, there are many situations where objectivity can be compromised, so a full list cannot be provided. Accountants are warned to always ensure that their objectivity is intact in any business/ professional relationship.

Section 113 – Professional competence and due care

There are two main considerations under this heading:

1   Accountants are required to have the necessary professional knowledge and skill to carry out work for clients.

2   Accountants must follow applicable technical and professional standards when providing professional services.

Appropriate levels of professional competence must first be attained and then maintained. Maintenance implies keeping up to date with business and professional developments, and in many institutes completion of an annual return confirming that continuing professional development (CPD) requirements have been met.

Where provision of a professional service has inherent limitations (e.g. reliance on client information) then the client must be made aware of this.

Section 114 – Confidentiality

The principle of confidentiality implies two key considerations for accountants:

1   Information obtained in a business relationship is not disclosed outside the firm unless there is a proper and specific authority or unless there is a professional right or duty to disclose.

2   Confidential information acquired during the provision of professional services is not used to personal advantage.

The need to maintain confidentiality is normally extended to cover the accountant's social environment, information about prospective clients and employers and also where business relationships have terminated. Basically there must always be a reason for disclosure before confidential information is provided to a third party.

The main reasons for disclosure are when it is:

1   permitted by law and authorised by the client

2   required by law, e.g. during legal proceedings or disclosing information regarding infringements of law

3   there is professional duty or right to disclose (when not barred by law), e.g. provision of information to the professional institute or compliance with ethical requirements.

Section 115 – Professional behaviour

Accountants must comply with all relevant laws and regulations.

There is also a test whereby actions suggested by a third party which would bring discredit to the profession should also be avoided.

An accountant is required to treat all people contacted in a professional capacity with courtesy and consideration. Similarly, any marketing activities should not bring the profession into disrepute.

Ethics in action: Professional competence

Written by the CIMA professional standards team and based on realistic situations, the following is a practical guide to using the CIMA Code of Ethics to guide good decision-making.

The scenario:

You are working at a small business on a finance training scheme. You have been there for one year and have completed the Operational Level of the CIMA Professional Qualification.

You work in a team of three: you, your manager, and a third-year graduate trainee. Your team should have more people, but recent budget cuts led to losing two members of your team, and those who remain are under significant pressure to deliver work quickly. Your line manager finds you in the office one afternoon and asks you to complete some complicated revenue calculations before you leave for the day. You don't feel confident doing this. It's a new type of work that you have briefly touched upon in your studies, but you have no practical experience. It will take hours, and the other members of the team will be going home very soon.

Ethical issues and guidance

CIMA's Code of Ethics (the Code) applies to students as well as members and should be used as a resource in helping you decide on the best course of action.

The fundamental principle of professional competence and due care (Section 113 of the Code) requires that members and students "attain and maintain professional knowledge and skill at the level required to ensure that a client or employing organisation receives competent professional service". In this scenario you are concerned that you do not have the professional knowledge to complete the task competently.

It is vital that you are open and honest about this, rather than trying to complete work you are not qualified for, which will open up the business to risk and also mean you are in contravention of the Code.

The Code goes on in Section 260.6 A7 to highlight a number of threats to the professional competence and due care principle. The relevant threats to this situation include "insufficient time for properly performing or completing the relevant duties" and "insufficient experience, training or education". The Code suggests a number of ways to safeguard against these threats in Section 260.6 A8, which include performing additional research, obtaining assistance from someone with the necessary expertise, and consulting with superiors within the organisation.

You should highlight your concerns to your line manager, citing the CIMA Code of Ethics and your obligations as a CIMA student to follow this. You should express your concern that you have not completed this type of work before and therefore do not feel sufficiently qualified to complete the work alone. You should also highlight that you don't think this work is achievable in the suggested time frame, as the work will need to be rushed and this could increase the risk of mistakes being made.

You could suggest that you work on the calculations together with the more experienced third-year trainee when they come into the office the next day. This will mean that the work is overseen by someone with more experience, and you can use the opportunity to gain some experience, which might allow you to complete this work on your own in the future. If you frame it in a positive way and suggest a solution, it is likely to come across better to your line manager than if you simply focus on the reasons you cannot do what you have been asked. Highlight the fact that working with someone on this will both reduce the risk of errors being made and allow you to develop skills that will be helpful in the future for managing the workload across the team.

If your line manager isn't willing to listen to your concerns and insists you should complete the work, you should think about whether there is someone you could talk to. This could be a mentor or someone responsible for the trainee programme. They may be able to speak to your manager on your behalf to reiterate the points made about your lack of experience and offer some practical solutions to help get the work done whilst also supporting your development.

After you have dealt with this situation, you could ask to schedule some time with your line manager or another relevant person to discuss your training at the company to ensure that you are gaining the practical experience you need to complement the exams you are taking. Through being proactive in having these discussions, you may find that your line manager is open to ensuring your development continues even as the business is going through a difficult time.

This article appeared in Financial Management, February 2020.

10   Threats and safeguards

Conceptual framework approach

- The circumstances in which management accountants operate may give rise to specific threats to compliance with the fundamental principles.

- It is impossible to define every situation that creates such threats and specify the appropriate mitigating action.

- A conceptual framework that requires a management accountant to identify, evaluate and address threats to compliance with the fundamental principles, rather than merely comply with a set of specific rules which may be arbitrary, is, therefore, in the public interest.

Threats

To apply the fundamental principles of the code (integrity, objectivity, professional competence and due care, confidentiality, and professional behaviour), you first need to be able to identify and evaluate existing or potential threats to them. If a threat exists that is anything other than trivial, you will need to take action to remove the threat or reduce it to an acceptable level.

Although it is impossible to define all the situations that could create a threat to the fundamental principles, the code does identify five categories of common threat:

- **Self-interest threats** can occur as a result of your own or your close family's interests – financial or otherwise. These threats often result in what is commonly called a 'conflict of interest' situation. Working in business, a self-interest threat could result from concern over job security, or from incentive remuneration arrangements. For those in practice it might be the possibility of losing a client or holding a financial interest in a client.

- **Self-review threats** occur when you are required to re-evaluate your own previous judgement, for example if you have been asked to review and justify a business decision you made, or if you are reporting on the operation of financial systems that you were involved in designing or implementing.

- **Familiarity threats** can be present when you become so sympathetic to the interests of others as a result of a close relationship that your professional judgement becomes compromised. Sometimes this can result from long association with business contacts who influence business decisions, long association with colleagues, or from accepting gifts or preferential treatment from a client.

- **Intimidation threats** occur when you are deterred from acting objectively by actual or perceived threats. It could be the threat of dismissal over a disagreement about applying an accounting principle or reporting financial information, or it could be a dominant personality attempting to influence the decision making process.

- **Advocacy threats** can be a problem when you are promoting a position or opinion to the point that your subsequent objectivity is compromised. It could include acting as an advocate on behalf of an assurance client in litigation or disputes with third parties. In general, promoting the legitimate goals of your employer does not create an advocacy threat, provided that any statements you make are not misleading.

Safeguards

So what should you do if there is a threat (or potential threat), to the principles of the code?

CIMA's code of ethics has a 'threats and safeguards' approach to resolving ethical issues. This means that if you are in a situation where there might be a threat to any of the code's fundamental principles you should first assess whether the threat is significant. If it is, you should to take action to remove or mitigate it.

The CIMA code does not describe all the safeguards that could be implemented, but instead gives general guidance for handling ethical issues, both for accountants working in business and for those in practice.

Safeguards include, but are not restricted to:

- educational, training and experience requirements for entry into the profession

- continuing professional development requirements

- corporate governance regulations

- professional standards

- professional or regulatory monitoring and disciplinary procedures

- external review of the reports, returns, communications or information produced by a member and carried out by a legally empowered third party.

- the employing organisation's systems of corporate oversight or other oversight structures

- the employing organisation's ethics and conduct programmes

- recruitment procedures in the employing organisation emphasising the importance of employing high calibre competent staff

- the employing organisation's grievance procedures

- strong internal controls

- appropriate disciplinary processes

- leadership that stresses the importance of ethical behaviour and the expectation that employees will act in an ethical manner

- timely communication of the employing organisation's policies and procedures, including any changes to them, to all employees and appropriate training and education on such policies and procedures

- consultation with another appropriate professional. The nature of the safeguards to be applied will vary depending on the circumstances. In exercising professional judgement, a member should consider what a reasonable and informed third party, having knowledge of all relevant information, including the significance of the threat and the safeguards applied, would conclude to be unacceptable.

Ethical threats and safeguards

Ethical threat	Safeguard
Conflict between requirements of the employer and the fundamental principles For example, acting contrary to laws or regulations or against professional or technical standards.	• Obtaining advice from the employer, professional organisation or professional advisor • The employer providing a formal dispute resolution process • Legal advice
Preparation and reporting on information Accountants need to prepare/report on information fairly, objectively and honestly. However, the accountant may be pressurised to provide misleading information.	• Consultation with superiors in the employing company • Consultation with those charged with governance • Consultation with the relevant professional body

Having sufficient expertise Accountants need to be honest in stating their level of expertise – and not mislead employers by implying they have more expertise than they actually possess. Threats that may result in lack of expertise include time pressure to carry out duties, being provided with inadequate information or having insufficient experience.	• Obtaining additional advice/training • Negotiating more time for duties • Obtaining assistance from someone with relevant expertise
Financial interests Situations where an accountant or close family member has financial interests in the employing company. Examples include the accountant being paid a bonus based on the financial statement results which he or she is preparing, or holding share options in the company.	• Remuneration being determined by other members of management • Disclosure of relevant interests to those charged with governance • Consultation with superiors or relevant professional body
Inducements with intent to improperly influence behaviour Refers to incentives being offered to encourage unethical behaviour. Inducements may include gifts, hospitality, entertainment, donations, preferential treatment, employment opportunities or inappropriate appeals to loyalty. Objectivity and/or confidentiality may be threatened by such inducements.	• Do not accept the inducement! • Inform relevant third parties such as senior management and professional association (normally after taking legal advice) • Consider amending or terminating the business relationship with the offeror
Inducements with no intent to improperly influence behaviour This requires the exercise of professional judgement as to whether there is no intent. An example is a routine meeting which is held by inviting the accountant to lunch. If such an inducement is trivial and inconsequential, any threats created will be at an acceptable level.	• Being transparent with senior management about offering or accepting an inducement • Registering the inducement in a log maintained by the employing organisation of the member or the counterparty

Confidential information	
Accountants should keep information about their employing company confidential unless there is a right or obligation to disclose, or they have received authorisation from the client.	• Disclose information in compliance with relevant statutory requirements, e.g. money laundering regulations
However, the accountant may be under pressure to disclose this information as a result of compliance with legal processes such as anti-money laundering/terrorism – in this situation there is a conflict between confidentiality and the need for disclosure.	
Whistleblowing Situations where the accountant needs to consider disclosing information, where ethical rules have been broken by the client.	Follow the disclosure provisions of the employer. Otherwise disclosure should be based on assessment of: legal obligations, whether members of the public will be adversely affected, gravity of the matter, likelihood of repetition, reliability of the information, reasons why employer does not want to disclose

Ethics in action: When gifts put you at risk

Written by the CIMA professional standards team and based on realistic situations, the following is a practical guide to using the CIMA Code of Ethics to guide good decision-making.

The scenario:

You're an accountant in a small finance department at a stationery company. It's early December, and you come into work one day to find a large gift basket of festive food has been delivered from a consultancy firm, XYZ Consulting, whom you recently worked with on a project to introduce a new piece of accountancy software.

You check with your line manager, Alex, and she confirms that it's totally fine to accept the gift. A week later, a tender goes out for another consultancy project, this time focusing on redesigning a website. Alex asks you to tell the procurement manager that you would favour XYZ Consulting again, even though you're concerned they may not have enough experience in this area to do a good job. Alex tells you that the managing director of XYZ Consulting has mentioned that they have a box at a top football team's stadium that they might be open to inviting you both to if your firm continues to offer business to XYZ Consulting.

What should you do?

Ethical issues and guidance

Gifts and hospitality can be a normal part of doing business, but checks and balances need to be in place to ensure that they do not influence your integrity or the fair business process.

In this scenario, you would be right to question whether XYZ Consulting is attempting to influence your business decisions by offering gifts and hospitality.

The first place to start would be checking whether there are any internal policies relating to gifts and hospitality. Most companies will have a policy that includes a monetary limit on what is considered acceptable and may also have a prohibition against accepting gifts or hospitality during the tender process. Depending on the policy, the gift basket may have been acceptable. However, it is likely the offer of further hospitality should additional business be awarded to XYZ Consulting is unacceptable.

Even if there is no internal policy in place, you are still right to be concerned. The fact that Alex has told you what you should say could be a threat to your integrity and objectivity, both fundamental principles of the CIMA Code of Ethics.

The Code specifies under the principle of integrity that you must be "be straightforward and honest in all professional and business relationships. … Integrity also implies fair dealing and truthfulness". If you do what Alex has asked and are not truthful about your concerns regarding XYZ Consulting's experience, you will not be applying the principle of integrity.

Furthermore, under the principle of objectivity, there is "an obligation on all professional accountants not to compromise their professional or business judgment because of bias, conflict of interest or the undue influence of others".

Section 230 of the Code of Ethics deal with gifts and hospitality for members working in business. The need to consider local law and custom is highlighted, as in some jurisdictions the offering of gifts and hospitality in certain situations will be considered bribery.

In some areas of the world, a gift is customary and there is the risk of offending potential partners if you refuse it. Some businesses may seek to exploit these customs, especially if the business is cross-border. It can be difficult to determine whether something is a genuine gift or is intended to influence decision-making.

> Here's where an internal policy comes in handy. Being able to say, "I'm sorry, but our company policy prevents me from accepting this" may save face all round and help you sidestep a potentially embarrassing situation.
>
> You should begin by bringing up your concerns with Alex and make it clear that you will not lie about your impression of XYZ Consulting. You should highlight your concerns about XYZ Consulting, both in terms of their ability to do the new consultancy work and also the fact that they appear to be attempting to influence you through sending gifts and offering hospitality.
>
> You can use any internal policies along with the fact you are bound by the CIMA Code of Ethics to support your arguments. It may be that Alex is also a CIMA member, or a member of another professional body, and raising the fundamental principles may act as a reminder that she also should consider this.
>
> If Alex is unwilling to see your point of view, you may feel it is necessary to escalate further within the organisation. If there is no policy on internal gifts and hospitality, you could suggest that this might be an opportunity to introduce one to avoid any confusion in the future. It's not necessarily just the policy on gifts and hospitality that can help — it may be that a procurement policy will contain certain requirements of firms wishing to tender for work.
>
> **This article appeared in Financial Management, December 2019.**

11 Rules-based and framework approaches to ethics

There are two different approaches to formulating a code of ethics:

- a rules-based approach
- a framework approach.

Rules-based ethics

A rules-based approach to ethics is sometimes referred to as a compliance approach. It explicitly sets out what individuals can and cannot do, and specifies the sanctions that will be imposed for non-compliance.

A rules-based approach works because it instils a sense of fear. Individuals comply because they are required to and because they fear the consequences. However, the main disadvantage of this approach is the fact that the rules cannot cover every particular situation and rules may become out of date as circumstances change.

Rules based approach

Rules tend to be characterised by three things:

1   In theory, you are either inside a rule (compliant) or have broken it. This sometimes provides a harsh divide which is often more about the precise interpretation of the rule than the human activity it regulates.

2   Because of these attempts to make sharp distinctions in rules (so people know where the boundaries of self-preservation lie), there is always argument about the precise meaning of rules.

3   Rules require enforcement by an objective party to decide on things like interpretation and to ensure that breach of the rule has a consequence.

These factors make rules expensive, the source of contention and inflexible. Moreover, in ethics, rules seldom are capable of encompassing the rather difficult questions about behaviour that are involved, without becoming incredibly complicated. The Code-based approach blends the mandatory requirement to take account of the Code with a principles or values-based approach.

Framework approach

A framework approach to ethics provides a set of principles to help individuals arrive at the correct decision. It attempts to instil the idea of the 'correct' thing to do.

Its main advantage is that it can be applied more easily to new developments in business practice or to unique cases. However, its disadvantage is that it is left to the member to decide how best to deal with an ethical question within the framework laid down.

It is also much more difficult to monitor compliance than in a rules-based approach.

Framework approach

There has been a change in public and private attitudes to the performance of duties over the last five years that has moved against the idea of just doing what you can get away with towards continually striving to do the right thing. It is mirrored in the changes in management accounting trends from variance accounting, through activity-based to lean accounting. In management, it is reflected in the idea of performance management, rather than the management of labour. In public life, it is reflected in the change from a culture of trust and deference to those with authority, to a requirement for standards in public life and accountability.

The management accountant finds him or herself pushed by all three strands. Trends in management accounting look towards a more transparent approach to representing the life cycle of accounts. As an employee, the accountant is not there just to do a job and go home, but to do it well and continually improve. Ultimately, whether or not the accountant is employed in the public sector, the role of the accountant is to perform a public function in providing the truthful and independent account of finances that will be the basis of judgements by owners, shareholders, regulators, the government and so on.

The Seven Principles of Public Life

The publicly employed accountant is explicitly subject to the 'The Seven Principles of Public Life' issued by the Committee of Standards in Public Life, which arose out of the perceived crisis in public ethics of the 1990s in the United Kingdom. The Committee of Standards in Public Life is a body that was set up by the UK Government. The principles are reflected to a great extent in the professional standards for all accountants.

Selflessness

Holders of public office should act solely in terms of the public interest. They should not do so in order to gain financial or other benefits for themselves, their family or their friends.

Integrity

Holders of public office should not place themselves under any financial or other obligation to outside individuals or organisations that might seek to influence them in the performance of their official duties.

Objectivity

In carrying out public business, including making public appointments, awarding contracts, or recommending individuals for rewards and benefits, holders of public office should make choices on merit.

Accountability

Holders of public office are accountable for their decisions and actions to the public and must submit themselves to whatever scrutiny is appropriate to their office.

Openness

Holders of public office should be as open as possible about all the decisions and actions that they take. They should give reasons for their decisions and restrict information only when the wider public interest clearly demands.

Honesty

Holders of public office have a duty to declare any private interests relating to their public duties and to take steps to resolve any conflicts arising in a way that protects the public interest.

Leadership

Holders of public office should promote and support these principles by leadership and example.

Given the trends towards less trust and more desire for accountability, it is therefore of little surprise that management accountants are now expected to do more than merely follow the rules.

12 Contrasting compliance driven and principles based codes

The following table, contrasting the characteristics of a compliance-driven framework versus one primarily driven by values, principles and ethics.

Feature	Framework	Compliance (Rules)
Objective	Prevention	Detection
Approach	Principles	Law based
Motivation	Values driven	Fear driven
Standards	Implicit	Explicit
Measure	Principles (values)	Rules
Choices	Judgement	Obedience/disobedience
Enforceability	Discretionary	Mandatory

An example of applying the different approaches above would be a company which has a strong rules-based culture, where individuals clearly have a sense of what they can and cannot do (letter of the law, black and white, mandatory, explicit) and what will happen if they do not (fear-driven, requires obedience, mandatory). However, if an employee is faced with a situation not covered by the 'rule book' they will be required to use their own judgement as to what to do. In most instances, the decision they take will be the right one but any potential for the wrong decision being made will be reduced if the employee has guiding values and principles which will underpin that difficult decision-making. So, an ethical framework of guidance is likely to be more wide-ranging in its applicability than a fully rules-based one.

A key aspect of compliance is measurement in addition to 'ticking boxes' that all is well. This, of course, is difficult with ethical issues which tend not to be conveniently black and white. There is therefore a need to develop and use proxy indicators by those assuring themselves that individuals are acting in a proper fashion.

In a wider context, the same is true in the public and private sectors, where organisations equally, as though they were individuals, seek to build trust with their employees, customers, suppliers, shareholders and all others who have a legitimate interest in how they perform.

But the essential question remains: Is trust better engendered by principled behaviour based on 'doing it because it is the right thing to do' or because the individual, the company or the public body has to?

13 Personal development and life-long learning

Every professional person has a duty in maintaining their role of acting in public interest by keeping themselves up to date professionally, that is technically as well developing their competencies to be better informed. It is also essential in a dynamic area of practice, where failure to keep oneself aware of developments may fundamentally undermine basic professional competence and leave the accountant open to accusations of negligence.

This has grown in importance as the pace of change develops and the role of the professional accountant grows more complex. It is now regarded as one of the fundamental principles in the CIMA 'Code of Ethics' (see Appendix for the complete code), where the professional accountant has the duty to maintain professional knowledge and skill at the level required to ensure that a client or employer receives competent professional service based on current developments in practice, legislation and techniques.

The concept of competent professional service is thus based not only on attaining professional competence but also in maintaining it. This requires a continuing awareness of up-to-date developments in the profession. This can be met through continuing professional development. CIMA has developed the CIMA Professional Development framework which addresses both the requirements on members and the institute regarding CPD, and the ways in which CIMA is supporting members in their professional development.

Personal qualities

Members of the profession need, or need to develop, certain qualities and virtues in order to meet the expectations of CIMA and the public, served in the wider context. In upholding the highest standards of ethical behaviour, members are contributing to the promotion of the integrity of CIMA's qualification and supporting CIMA's purpose.

The underlying reason has been explained earlier, in the context of 'virtue ethics'. The professional attitude being encouraged provides the ethical compass and personal motivation to act in accordance with the values of the profession and to make ethically sound decisions in everyday practice.

The particular qualities and virtues sought are reliability, responsibility, timeliness, courtesy and respect. These are taken from 'Approaches to the Development and Maintenance of Professional Values, Ethics and Attitudes in Accounting Education Programs,' published by the International Accounting Education Standards Board.

Reliability

This is the concept of being able to be trusted by others and to be dependable through the ability to deliver what and when it has been agreed with another. It is linked to the idea of providing a consistent approach to work, both in quality and in dependability. It is fairly clear that an unreliable accountant would almost certainly also be falling short of other basic standards of professional competence.

Responsibility

This is the concept of being accountable for one's actions and decisions. This also entails an individual's assumption of authority for making decisions. A responsible accountant addresses the decision-making processes that he or she needs to engage with and is willing and able to personally answer for those decisions. A management accountant is in a position of responsibility because he or she is being employed for his or her expertise in making professional judgements and will need to be able to explain and answer for their exercise to colleagues who may or may not share that expertise.

Timeliness

This is the concept of delivering in a timely manner without delay and meeting the expectations of others. The practical implications of poor timekeeping are self-evident, however there is a further reflection of the ethics of diligence in addressing tasks and responsibility in prioritising and managing work.

Courtesy

This is the virtue of demonstrating politeness and good manners towards others. While respect for clients and others is regarded as appropriate and professional, the increasing seriousness with which unacceptable forms of address (racist, sexist, homophobic and the like) are being tackled by law mean that it underpins a more fundamental set of societal values.

Respect

This is the virtue demonstrating an attitude of esteem, deference, regard or admiration of others in dealing with them, especially where their attitudes might differ. It is not to be mistaken for undue deference, merely that the accountant should listen to others, take account of their views and ideas, and if for no other reason than these may provide a broader base for making informed judgements.

Like a number of these qualities, it is easy to see reasons why respect might be practically useful and help avoid problems that might lead to sanction or censure, but the utility of respecting people is not the reason why you should respect them; it is not simply a case of respecting those who you think might have something useful to say, like each of these qualities they are aspects of professionalism to be cultivated for their own sake.

14 Independence

It is in the public interest, and required in CIMA's Code of Ethics that members of assurance engagement teams and their firms (and when applicable extended network firms too) be independent of the assurance clients. An audit should be performed with an attitude of professional scepticism which includes a questioning mind and being alert to conditions which may indicate fraud or error.

There are two key attributes to independence used in connection with the assurance engagement:

1   Of mind

It is required that the professional accountant has a state of mind that permits a conclusion to be expressed without being affected by influences that would compromise their professional judgement.

This allows the individual to act with integrity and exercise objectivity and professional scepticism. Bias is an insidious thing, and sometimes we are not fully aware of the influencing factors on our mind. Second opinions of close judgement calls can often help, but the accountant is ultimately responsible for his or her decisions. Keeping a clear, professional attitude and focusing on objective information, rather than over-relying on intuitions is a useful means of maintaining some independence of mind.

2   In appearance

This is a test reliant on the view that a reasonable and informed third party would conclude that a member of the assurance team's integrity, objectivity or professional scepticism was compromised if significant facts and circumstances were avoided or overlooked. The accountant often exercises judgements that have impacts on people's jobs, pay and progression. It is therefore of paramount importance that the exercise of professional judgement not only be just, but manifestly and undoubtedly be seen to be so.

It is impossible to define all situations where independence might be compromised, so it is in the public interest to prepare a conceptual framework requiring firms and member of assurance teams to identify, evaluate and address threats to independence. This can be based on identifying relationships between all the parties. For any threats so identified, safeguards can be introduced to eliminate or significantly reduce them to an acceptable level.

15 Accountability, social responsibility and professional scepticism

Accountability

The concept of accountability is that of the professional accountant being responsible to someone and for something or an action, and being able to explain those actions. It is an important aspect of the profession and of leadership in the wider business environment.

It is acknowledged that the professional accountant through CIMA, as a Chartered Institute, is accountable to the public in performing a public interest duty. That accountability is monitored by the FRC in the United Kingdom through the Conduct Committee and the Accounting Council.

Accountability is also to every client and employer too for whom the professional accountant is providing services. If that accountability fails then the client or employer can seek redress through complaint or disciplinary procedures.

Social responsibility

The professional accountant has a wider role in fulfilling their public duty, which is to be aware of their social or corporate responsibility. This is their role within the community, be it defined as their profession, their firm or place of work, where their place of work or home is located or howsoever the individual cares to define community.

Corporate Social Responsibility (CSR) is the outward manifestation of an ethical policy. CSR policies state the nature of the interaction between the company and its stakeholder base, employees, customers, suppliers and so forth (covered in more detail in Chapter 5). These CR policies need to be factored into risk management, which the better companies will report on in their reporting, internally and externally.

Typically, this is in relation to stakeholders listed as shareholders, employees, customers, suppliers and the wider community, to whom the company pays taxes and with whom it has a relationship as part of society. In upholding the principles of CIMA's 'Code of Ethics', the individual has a social responsibility to behave with integrity, courtesy, respect and with due care.

Professional scepticism

The application of an appropriate degree of professional scepticism is an essential skill for accountants, especially for those working in assurance and audit. Professional scepticism is an attitude of mind that ensures auditors are prepared to challenge management's assertions, and be alert to possible misstatements in the financial statements due to error or fraud. Auditors initially approach an audit without a strong belief that either the financial information is misstated or that management are other than honest and truthful. But if an auditor obtains information suggesting that the financial information could be misstated, they will step up their enquiries and look for more audit evidence to resolve issues, especially if they are concerned about the accuracy of the evidence or the integrity of those providing it.

A sceptical mind-set will be influenced by an individual's personality, their experience, their education and training, and by the culture of the firm where they work. It is through professional development and experience that an auditor learns the 'right' level of scepticism to be applied in different circumstances.

Professional accountants must recognise that scepticism is an integral part of their work and is closely interrelated to the fundamental concepts of independence and objectivity. Ethical Standards address the issue of auditors placing too much trust in their clients through requirements such as rotation of audit firms and partners and staff, and the prohibition of certain non-audit services, but ultimately it is the responsibility of individuals to perform their work with an appropriate degree of scepticism and challenge.

16   Ethical conflict: confidentiality

The following are circumstances where professional accountants are or may be required to disclose confidential information or when such disclosure may be appropriate:

(a) **Disclosure is permitted by law and is authorised by the client or the employer:**

An example of this might be personal data. Personal data held by an accountant (for example, bank details of an individual) is covered by data protection legislation. This gives rise to particular responsibility on the accountant to maintain that data accurately and not to disclose it, except for the purposes it was disclosed. There are, however, some exceptions. One important one is that the person to whom that data pertains may have been given an authorisation for disclosure to third parties for marketing purposes. This would still need authorisation by the employer, but falls within the category of permissible disclosure.

(b) **Disclosure is required by law, for example:**

    (i)   Production of documents or other provision of evidence in the course of legal proceedings – numerous pieces of legislation allow investigative bodies, ranging from the national taxation authorities through to the police, the power to gain access to documents in the process of investigation. Strictly speaking, such access is limited to circumstances where the investigating agency has specific authorisation by a court, normally in the form of a warrant. In such circumstances, there is a duty to disclose that overrides any others.

    (ii)   Disclosure to the appropriate public authorities of infringements of the law that come to light – accountants are under some professional and ethical responsibility to disclose information which they believe tend to show illegal activity. This is a problematic area because such disclosures frequently run in the face of what an employer considers to be a duty of trust and confidence. A misplaced belief that an employer is doing wrong, which leads to an unauthorised disclosure will often end up as an acrimonious employment dispute.

Public interest disclosure legislation in the United Kingdom provides a means by which these two issues can be balanced. The accountant should first draw their manager's attention to the wrongdoing, or if it is inappropriate in the circumstances, a senior manager's attention may be drawn to it. If there is no adequate response or there is serious malfeasance which the accountant believes may be 'covered up', they may alert a professional body or an agency such as the police. Going to press is a risky and inadvisable course of action and carries with it few of the protections that are offered to those disclosing to professional bodies. In such circumstances, it is advisable to contact CIMA's Ethics Helpline. Members and students of CIMA can contact the Ethics Helpline for advice on whether and how to make a public interest disclosure. CIMA's Ethics Helpline can help any member or student facing an ethical conflict.

(c) **There is a professional duty or right to disclose, when not prohibited by law:**

    (i)   To comply with the quality review of a member body or professional body

    (ii)   To respond to an inquiry or investigation by a member body or regulatory body

    (iii)   To protect the professional interests of a professional accountant in legal proceedings; or

    (iv)   To comply with technical standards and ethics requirements.

All these examples in (c), above, relate to the regulation and disciplinary functions of CIMA and the profession more generally. It is important that disclosures are not only those necessary for the achievement of purpose of the inquiry but that they also cover all relevant aspects of the subject matter being inquired into. Partial disclosure is tantamount to deception and may give rise to disciplinary or legal penalties or consequences.

Disclosure is generally a question of professional discretion, as much as the application of rules. In identifying whether confidential information can be disclosed, it is necessary to consider whether any parties would be harmed by such disclosure, whether all relevant information is known and substantiated, and the type of disclosure and to whom it is to be made.

Ethics in action: Confidentiality within the organisation

Written by the CIMA professional standards team and based on realistic situations, the following is a practical guide to using the CIMA Code of Ethics to guide good decision-making.

The scenario

You work at WeMakeStuff, a large manufacturing company which makes all types of gadgets and widgets for the modern family. As the financial director for the widget division, you have overall responsibility for signing off on contracts with a value above £100,000.

You are approached by the group compliance officer, who tells you that a report has been made via the confidential Speak Up hotline that members of the procurement team have been colluding with suppliers to increase the value of contracts, with both sides taking a cut of the additional profits.

The group compliance officer asks you to help with the investigation by providing a list of all contracts signed in the last year and contracts in the process of negotiation within your division.

However, several contracts are highly confidential, related to a new area of business development. Only you, key members of the finance and procurement teams, and the CEO are aware of the details of these contracts.

You are unsure as to whether you can share the information about these contracts with the group compliance officer.

Can you share the contracts?

Ethical issues and guidance

The key issue here is what information you can and should share with a member of staff to support an internal investigation into possible misconduct and fraud.

Under the fundamental principle of confidentiality in the CIMA Code of Ethics, you have a duty to "maintain confidentiality of information within the firm or employing organisation". The Code specifies that you may disclose information which would normally be kept confidential when required by law, or to comply with an inquiry or investigation by a professional or regulatory body.

However, this specific example involves an internal investigation. You should consider the risks of disclosure as well as the implications of refusing to disclose the information.

Refusing to disclose the details of these contracts could jeopardise the ability of the compliance team to investigate the reports. Colluding with suppliers could constitute serious fraud, and it is certainly possible that legal action will be taken against the employees should the internal investigation substantiate the claims.

If you refuse to share the information with the group compliance officer or provide an incomplete list by leaving out the confidential contracts, you could create the risk that the alleged fraud may continue, putting the organisation at greater risk of losing money and future legal action being taken.

You should also consider that handing over the information does mean disclosing confidential information to a wider group of employees.

However, the group compliance officer and their team will be well aware of the importance of maintaining confidentiality, given the nature of their roles. You should specify when providing this information that it should be shared with only essential members of staff, explaining that it is commercially sensitive.

You may also wish to alert the CEO that you are sharing this information, although you should consider discussing this with the group compliance officer first to ensure that this would not compromise the investigation if, for example, the CEO is in any way implicated in the wrongdoing.

This article appeared in Financial Management, October 2020.

17   CGMA Report on Managing Responsible Business

Two of the world's most prestigious accounting bodies, AICPA and CIMA, have formed a joint venture to establish the Chartered Global Management Accountant (CGMA®) designation to elevate and build recognition of the profession of management accounting. This international designation recognises the most talented and committed management accountants with the discipline and skill to drive strong business performance. CGMA designation holders are either CPAs with qualifying management accounting experience or associate or fellow members of the Chartered Institute of Management Accountants.

Definitions (as used in the survey by CGMA)

Responsible business:

- is about an organisation's commitment to operating in a way that is economically, socially and environmentally sustainable

- means ensuring this commitment prevails while still upholding the interests of various stakeholder groups.

Business ethics:

- is the application of values such as integrity, fairness, respect and openness to organisational behaviour

- apply to all strategic and operational aspects of business conduct, including sales and marketing techniques, accounting practices and the treatment of suppliers, employees and customers

- may also be termed "business principles", and are usually set out in a code of ethics or similar policy document.

Ethical performance

- is the extent to which an organisation's behaviour aligns with its stated ethical values and commitments.

Ethical management information

- allows an assessment of the organisation's ethical performance, such as the efficacy of relevant policies and procedures, occurrence of breaches of relevant policies or codes, stakeholder opinion and other metrics

- may include specific ethics information, such as the number of employees attending ethics training or calls to an ethics helpline, as well as routine management and risk information

- will often originate from multiple sources within the business, and can be either quantitative or qualitative.

Integrated reporting

- describes an approach to corporate reporting. It is based on both financial and nonfinancial information that demonstrates the linkages between an organisation's strategy, governance and financial performance as well as the social, environmental and economic context within which it operates.

Ethical issues within organisations

- Security of information
- Safety and security in the workplace
- Discrimination
- Conflicts of interest
- Bribery
- Environmental
- Supply chain
- Responsible marketing
- Human rights
- Whistleblowing
- Fairness of remuneration.

18 Embedding ethical values: A guide for CIMA partners

CIMA and the Institute of Business Ethics have jointly produced two new guidance documents, the first of which is 'Embedding ethical values – a guide for CIMA partners'. The purpose of this guide is twofold: for organisations that don't yet have an ethical policy or equivalent, it provides the right resources and support to draw up a code or policy document. For organisations that already have a code in place, this guide directs to resources which helps address what else can be done to embed ethical values and make the code effective.

Below are extracts from the guide.

How does a company start to ensure that business behaviour reflects ethical values?

If an organisation wants to take ethics seriously, it first needs to identify the core values to which it is committed and wishes to be held accountable.

Core ethical values are those regarded by a company as non-negotiable – they form the foundation for a set of corporate ethical standards and commitments and the organisation's approach to corporate responsibility.

Commonly used value words found in introductions/preambles to codes of ethics include: responsibility, integrity, honesty, respect, trust, openness, fairness and transparency. Organisations may also articulate a set of business values, such as quality, profitability, efficiency, reliability and customer service.

Why produce a code?

Codes of ethics are critical to preventing misconduct and should not be developed merely as a reaction to a reputation crisis. They provide guidance for all employees on what is expected of them and how to act responsibly in different circumstances. Critically codes should be live documents that are referred to regularly by management to promote and support an ethical culture.

Is having a code enough?

Simply drawing up and publishing a code is never enough to influence behaviour and decision-making. Ethical values must be strongly embedded in an organisation's culture. To be effective the code should be supported by a programme of communication and training as well as leadership example. Ethical commitments need to be reflected through core business activities and policies and processes e.g. recruitment, appraisal, tendering, marketing, speak up etc. The organisation also needs to establish a monitoring programme which will assure its governing body that it is living up to its values.

Board agrees that a statement of corporate values and code of ethics is required

Board asks a senior manager to develop the statement of values and corporate code of ethics

Senior manager consults with board members and employees at all levels about core values	Consults other business/experts on best practice	Consults with employees and other stakeholders to find out what ethical challenges and issues are material	Collates existing company policies on ethical issues	Works out an implementation programme

Senior manager produces first draft of values statement and corporate code of ethics and implementation programme

Circulates for comment to senior management	Has comparisons made with other company statements and codes	Organises cross company and all level 'focus' groups to comment on the draft	Considers standardising against an outside benchmark

Final (draft) version goes to the board

When approved, a programme of familiarisation and integration is set in motion

Ethical issues incorporated into all company training programmes	Regular reports to the board on how the code is working	Annual reporting process is put in place and a committee of the board is given overall oversight of the policy

Based on Developing a Code of Business Ethics guide, p16, IBE, 2003

Ethical Values

Code of Ethics	Communication and Awareness Campaigns	Training and Reinforcement	Supporting Context and Culture	Monitoring and Accountability

Embed values ⟶ influence behaviour

Good practice:

- Root the code in core values e.g. trust, integrity
- Give a copy to all staff
- Provide a way to report breaches in a confidential manner
- Include ethical issues in corporate training programmes
- Set up a board committee to monitor the effectiveness of the code
- Report on the code's use in the annual report
- Make conformity to the code part of a contract of employment
- Make the code available in the language of those staff located overseas
- Make copies of the code available to business partners, including suppliers
- Make a named individual responsible for code implementation
- Review code in light of changing business challenges
- Make sure senior staff 'walk the talk'.

Poor practice:

- Just pinning the code to the notice board
- Failing to obtain board commitment to the code
- Leaving responsibility for the code's effectiveness to HR or any other department
- Failing to find out concerns of staff at different levels
- Failing to feature the code in induction training and management development activities
- Having no procedure for revising the code regularly
- Making exceptions to the code's application
- Failing to follow up on breaches of the code's standards
- Unhelpful example by corporate leaders
- Neglecting to have a strategy to integrate corporate values and standards into the running of the business
- Treating the code as confidential or a purely internal document
- Making it difficult for staff to have direct access to the code or the person who is responsible for it.

19 Test your understanding questions

Test your understanding 1

Are these statements true or false?

A   Professional accountants are expected to have regard to the public interest in performing their duties

B   Professional accountants are not expected to have regard to the public interest in performing their duties

C   Ethical values describe what an entity does, not how it does business

D   Ethical values describe how entity does its business, not what it does

Test your understanding 2

Are these statements true or false?

A   A rules based approach provides a set of principles

B   A framework approach explicitly sets out what individuals can or cannot do

C   'The Seven Principles of Public Life' govern only professional accountants

D   The CIMA 'Code of Ethics' includes reference to how a professional accountant can raise a concern about unprofessional or unethical behaviour

Test your understanding 3

Are these statements true or false?

A   An ethically based code is based on principles

B   A compliance based code is a rules-based framework

C   A characteristic of a compliance based code is that it takes a tick box approach

D   Compliance with legislation is mandatory

Test your understanding 4

Are these statements true or false?

A   The five qualities and virtues sought by CIMA are reliability, accountability, fairness, responsibility and timeliness

B   The five qualities and virtues sought by CIMA are reliability, responsibility, timeliness, courtesy and respect

C   The professional accountant is not bound by the principles of confidentiality after the end of the relationship with a client or employer

D   The professional accountant is bound by the principles of confidentiality after the end of the relationship with a client or employer

Test your understanding 5

Are these statements true or false?

A   Professional accountants are expected to exercise professional scepticism

B   Professional accountants are not expected to exercise professional scepticism

C   The IFAC code is mandatory for all member firms or bodies of IFAC

D   The IFAC code is a guide for all member firms or bodies of IFAC

Test your understanding 6

Which of the following is incorrect?

A   The IFAC Code of Ethics takes a rules-based approach

B   The CIMA Code of Ethics takes a framework-based approach

C   Company codes of ethics can take a framework-based or a rules-based approach

D   Code of ethics are often based on core values or principles

Test your understanding questions 7–9 are reflective questions and should be discussed or thought over. Answers to these have not been provided.

Test your understanding 7

Consider your work and, separately, everyday life. In what circumstances do you find the following compromised?

A   Objectivity

B   Courtesy

C   Confidentiality

D   The appearance of independence

Test your understanding 8

In relation to 7, above, consider whether each is because of:

A   Something you have done

B   Something you have failed to do

C   Something you believe in

D   Something outside your control

Test your understanding 9

Drawing on the discussions above, consider how and whether application of the ethical principles outlined might help you identify problems, and whether they might help you avoid them if you put them into practice.

Test your understanding answers

Test your understanding 1

A **True.** Professional accountants, whether practicing in public or private practice have a leadership role and are expected to behave and act in the public interest. This is laid down in the Royal Charter which governs CIMA – the Chartered Institute of Management Accountants.

B **False.**

C **False.**

D **True.**

Test your understanding 2

A **False.** This applies to a framework approach.

B **False.**

C **False.** The Seven Principles of Public Life apply to all holders of public office.

D **True.**

Test your understanding 3

A **True.**

B **True.**

C **True.**

D **True.**

Test your understanding 4

A **False.**

B **True.**

C **False.**

D **True.**

Test your understanding 5

A   **True.**

B   **False.**

C   **True.**

D   **False.**

Test your understanding 6

A

The CIMA and IFAC Codes both take a framework-based approach.

Test your understanding 7

There is no suggested solution.

Test your understanding 8

There is no suggested solution.

Test your understanding 9

There is no suggested solution.

Ethical Conflict

Chapter learning objectives

Upon completion of this chapter you will be able to:

- explain the relationship between the CIMA Code of Ethics and the law

- describe the consequences of unethical behaviour to the individual, the profession and the society

- identify conflicting perspectives of interest when dealing with stakeholders in society, business and the values of professional accountants

- identify situations where ethical dilemmas and conflicts of interest occur and apply CIMA's ethical check list to ethical dilemmas.

1 The relationship between ethics and the law

Ethical Codes vs Legislation

If the question of ethics is 'what to do for the best?' then the next natural question is 'why should I take responsibility for deciding what to do?' In effect, the key issues for all accountants are the linked questions of who should take responsibility for doing the right things and who picks up the pieces when it all goes wrong.

If there are problems of global or national significance that arise from a systematic failure, which in turn pressurises the individual into facing unpleasant choices, shouldn't the government or the profession step in to deal with the problem? The answer has to be 'yes'. This is why some aspects of professional conduct are regulated not by the profession, but by law.

The corporate and social responsibility agenda means that adherence to the ethics of the professions that support the business and the more general promotion of professionalism in the workplace is of paramount importance in the determination of the culture of organisations.

Laws do not, of themselves, help you out of general ethical problems. For example, you might feel that it is unethical to obey an immoral law. However, such difficulties do not arise in management accounting. If there is a conflict between a professional duty, such as confidentiality, and statute law, the CIMA Code explicitly states that the law is to be preferred. In the hierarchy of obligations, law overrides everything.

Ethical Codes v Contracts

But what about other legal obligations? Surely the contract you sign with your employer is a legal obligation and the contracts with clients have legal effects? Of course this is true. However, voluntarily assumed legal obligations are exactly that. You have made a choice to enter into that obligation. You have a choice not to comply with a contractual obligation and take instead the penalty for breach of that contract. This might be the appropriate course of action when performing the contract would bring you into serious breach of the CIMA Code.

Contractual duty vs professional duty

An example of where you might break with a contractual duty is where your employer instructed you to act in a way that is professionally unacceptable. Another might be where you are directed to follow a corporate policy that was devised to apply to general situations, but which you feel is inappropriate in a particular context because there are special ethical considerations.

From a purely ethical standpoint, if you are confronted by a choice of breach of professional ethics and a breach of your contract of employment, you are ultimately supposed to favour your profession over your employer.

CIMA support

A difficult situation can arise when you are expected to do something which is part of a contract with an outside client. Often, the management accountant has no direct relationship with the client. However, the repercussions of refusing to act in a certain way on your employer's client relationships can be considerable. Often, clients will simply take their business elsewhere, if they feel that your employer will not accommodate them. It may not cause a direct confrontation between you and your employer, but if clients won't work with your employer because of you, there is always the chance that you may feel that it is you who will be the first in line for redundancy!

Often, you will be trying to do the right thing, not for you, but for someone else. Resolving ethical conflict seldom has much more reward to the individual than the feeling that you know you have done the right thing. However, the accountant is not on his or her own. CIMA provides support for individuals faced with ethical conflict situations and the law 'helps' accountants and employers to make the right choice, often by imposing personal liability for the individual who acts unprofessionally or forces another to do so.

2 Consequences of unethical behaviour

The personal consequences of unethical behaviour can be dire, as typically it will entail a loss of reputation. For the individual, a loss of reputation may result in loss of earning potential, job, professional status, position in the community and so forth. For a professional body, a significant loss of reputation, if it were brought into disrepute, would undermine its credibility and, ultimately, potentially its loss of Chartered Institute status. For a corporation, loss of public confidence is likely to result in the failure and dissolution of the organisation.

In the wider context, when such unethical behaviour is identified there is a greater damage, as trust is undermined not only in the people and organisations directly affected but also in similar bodies or institutions on the fear that they also may be targeted or affected by scandal. This is the trust that society bears for its organisations.

Often however, the true economic and human consequences of unethical behaviour are diffuse and hard to pinpoint. Like a lot of 'victimless crimes', the indirect global effects of one person who is discourteous, slow and unreliable might be minimal, but the impact on the profession of a few thousand practitioners who are like that can be considerable, as the legal profession would have to acknowledge.

Volkswagen scandal

In 2015 Volkswagen became embroiled in one of the biggest corporate scandals of recent years.

The German car maker had been installing "defeat devices" – software that allows cars to cheat in emissions tests, making them appear cleaner than they actually are.

Volkswagen admitted to cheating the tests deliberately and revealed that 11 million cars worldwide were fitted with the device. The scandal caused much anger particularly amongst customers of Volkswagen. In 2017, a US federal judge ordered Volkswagen to pay a $2.8 billion criminal fine for "rigging diesel-powered vehicles to cheat on government emissions tests". As of June 2020, the scandal had cost Volkswagen $33.3 billion in fines, penalties, financial settlements and buyback costs.

3 Ethical dilemmas and conflicts of interest

Introduction

There is an expectation in wider society that professional accountants have a leadership role in ensuring that companies, institutions, public bodies and all types of organisations where they work will behave ethically in carrying out their activities. Demonstrating such leadership by example can be achieved only if the individual professional concerned is sensitive enough to spot and to tackle ethical dilemmas. Without an 'inner guide' to ethical behaviour an individual may easily trip up.

For instance, a leader who fails to follow company procedures by deciding to appoint a friend to the board of the company is vulnerable to accusations of a conflict of interest if the appointment fails, or if there is a lack of transparency in making the appointment in the first instance. Governance procedures can add rigour to the appointment process, but it should be natural instinct to realise that business cannot be run without a core ethical values.

All individuals need to be able to recognise an ethical dilemma and deal with it appropriately. Pressures challenge personal integrity as well as business skills, which is why ethical acumen is an essential ingredient for a professional accountant.

Identifying ethical dilemmas

In identifying ethical dilemmas, it is important to understand how they arise.

Conflict can arise from any number of sources, however common ones include:

- societal values
- professional values
- personal values
- corporate values.

Individuals will recognise tensions if they are asked to condone the behaviour by their company which they feel to be wrong or inappropriate. If the tension is too great, they will leave the company. Before doing so, however, they may try to speak up, to voice their concerns. An example is where an employee is asked to 'overlook' improprieties carried out by their company, which would be counter to their professional code.

There are also tensions between corporate values and the values of society. If companies or individuals are deemed by society to be behaving or conducting their business inappropriately, then laws will be introduced to enforce minimum levels of behaviour. Such laws are wide ranging in order to cover the wide ranging activities of a business from employment practices to disposal of products in an environmentally friendly way, to banning cartels and unfair competitive activities and fraud, and the prevention of bribery and corruption.

Ethical dilemmas arise in many guises within an organisation – from those related to strategy and policy as faced by those running the organisation to those faced by middle managers or individuals in the course of their work. Dilemmas can occur at all levels.

How to identify an ethical dilemma

Behaving ethically or choosing how one wants to undertake business and achieve business goals is discretionary. Therefore, companies, as represented by the board, may or may not choose to encourage ethical behaviour by their staff.

Dilemmas arise when the boundaries of right and wrong are not clear; when an individual is faced with two options – the choice between making a better choice, or the least wrong. The individual must choose what to do. What makes ethical decisions hard is that they often are such unpalatable choices.

It is clear that what is not an ethical dilemma is when there is a choice between what is good for me and what is prescribed by professional standards. Doing what I want for my own reasons is not a professional choice but a personal preference, and therefore has no place in ethical reasoning.

Personal compromises include when friendships, families, loyalties and affiliations to organisations, political and other belief systems are involved. None of these are relevant to decision-making, except when they so strongly colour your perceptions that they make you incapable of objective judgement or where they so taint the outside perception of you that others think that you lack objectivity.

 Dilemmas

Here are some examples of dilemmas which might occur:

- My wife has just got a great job as managing director of a successful business, which also happens to be one of my biggest clients. Does it matter?

- I have taken over a new account from my manager. In re-evaluating their work, I have come across a significant error, which nobody seems to have picked up on. I don't want to jeopardise my relationship with my manager. What should I do?

- I have had a client for many years who has always taken me for dinner after her year end to celebrate and say thank you. This year she says she's done rather well so she's offered to take me golfing for the weekend in St Andrews. Should I accept?

- Our firm has taken out an advert in the local paper to promote our services. However, it says that we are experts in tax and none of the partners have that expertise. I feel uncomfortable, but what can I do?

- Our firm is being taken over and there is talk of redundancies being made. I've been asked to review the accounting policies and see if I could 'make things look more favourable'; it was implied that my job would depend upon it. What should I do?

- I'm tendering for new business, and I bumped into the current accountants at a conference. They said they wouldn't be re-tendering for the business because of 'certain difficulties' with the client, but when pressed said that the information was confidential. What should I do?

In response to each of these instances, the CIMA Code gives guidance on how to avoid conflicts of interest and threats to independence, and how to deal with confidential issues.

Conflicts of interest

Individuals can often find that they face a conflict of interest between their professional and business lives. In such instances, it is important to follow guidelines laid down in the Code of Ethics. Some instances are obvious, others are subtle so the individual needs to be sensitive in spotting them.

Illustration 1: Conflicts of interest

Steve is the Management Accountant at the Head Office of EnviroServices Group. One of his best friends, Dan, works in another part of the group. They've been friends since university, their wives are also great friends and their families have been on holiday together once or twice. Steve and Dan often talk about work when their wives aren't listening, keeping each other abreast of developments in the respective parts of the group, although neither of them puts pressure on the other to divulge any sensitive information.

Restructuring is taking place throughout EnviroServices. Steve is a member of an internal working party mandated to ensure that the internal communications policies and practices of the group fully support the changes that will take place in the course of the restructuring. As a member of the working party, Steve is privy to plans for the restructuring. This is price-sensitive information available only to a few people apart from top management. This includes information about the proposed selling off of one part of the group, which is no longer seen as core business. It is the part of the group where Dan works.

There are bound to be redundancies, especially at Dan's middle manager level. When Steve and Dan had last got together, he'd been talking about moving his house, taking on a substantial new mortgage in the process, in order to be able to send his daughter to a special school for children with learning disabilities.

In this situation Steve may feel that there is a conflict of interest between his friendship with Dan and his role as a member of the internal working party.

Steve must follow the CIMA Code of Ethics in dealing with this conflict of interest.

Conflicts of interest are not wrong in themselves, but they do become a problem when a professional continues to engage in a course of action being, aware of that conflict. When you think you may have a conflict of interest, it is always a sensible idea to declare it. It is normal that an individual will withdraw from a course of dealing when a conflict arises.

Ethics in action: 'Just make something up!'

Written by the CIMA professional standards team and based on realistic situations, the following is a practical guide to using the CIMA Code of Ethics to guide good decision-making.

The scenario:

You work for a consulting company. You have been asked to take the lead on producing the organisation's annual integrated report, and your name will appear on the report as the lead author.

In addition to the financial data, you have been asked to collate information from a number of departments on the broader performance of the organisation. Investors, customers, and employees are all expecting more from business when it comes to acting in the interests of wider society, so you ask the COO to provide information on environmental and social indicators. He emails back telling you to "just make something up — say we reduced plastic usage in the offices and donated some money to save the bees or whatever".

The COO is much more senior than you and is known to be a tricky person to work with. You worry that if you push back, he will be angry and you might be passed over for a promotion you are hoping to achieve next year.

What should you do?

Ethical issues and guidance

In this scenario, a senior colleague is asking you to falsify information in the organisation's annual report.

The CIMA Code of Ethics makes it clear that you must not produce misleading reports. Under the fundamental principle of integrity, the Code states: "A professional accountant shall not knowingly be associated with reports, returns, communications or other information where the accountant believes that the information:

(a)   Contains a materially false or misleading statement

(b)   Contains statements or information provided recklessly; or

(c)   Omits or obscures required information where such omission or obscurity would be misleading."

Whilst at first glance this may not seem as serious as falsifying financial reports, you should consider the possible implications of misleading stakeholders by misrepresenting the company's environmental performance.

Increasingly, stakeholders are holding organisations to account when it comes to environmental data. Clients may have criteria for selecting consultancy firms, such as only working with organisations which have made a commitment to achieving net-zero. An integrated report is likely to be a key piece of evidence potential partners use to verify performance.

If you were to include false or misleading information in the integrated report, this could have serious negative impacts down the line should a stakeholder find out about it. There could potentially be legal ramifications. It could also have a serious impact upon the reputation of your organisation, were it discovered that the information provided is inaccurate.

You may wish to consider whether anyone else in the organisation could provide you with truthful information you could include. Even if there isn't a sustainability team, other employees may be involved in relevant activities. For example, there might be an employee environmental group that has organised initiatives in specific offices focused on reducing plastic use, or employees may have used volunteering days to support local causes.

If nothing is happening currently, try to find out whether there are plans for the future which you could mention — for example, has the organisation or any specific department committed to reducing carbon emissions?

You could look at last year's report to see what has been said previously. If the company is adopting integrated reporting for the first time, there may be nothing wrong with simply including a section that describes the company's intention to begin sustainability practices and be in a position to report on these next year. This is something positive to give to stakeholders right now and sets the scene for development internally.

As a professional management accountant, you may be in a position to influence the future direction of the organisation by encouraging the COO and CEO to do more on sustainability, highlighting the demand from a range of stakeholders when making the business case. You could ask your manager to give you the responsibility of developing an internal sustainability strategy that is supported by suitable processes, or work with colleagues to form an employee-led sustainability group.

You may wish to discuss your concerns with your manager, who might be able to provide support in deciding the best approach to take, especially given the COO's potentially volatile personality. Whatever happens, your name must not appear on any report which you know or suspect includes false or misleading information.

This article appeared in Financial Management, September 2020.

Resolving ethical dilemmas/conflicts

The code is clear that the professional accountant should respond to an ethical conflict. Inaction or silence may well be a further breach of the code.

A professional accountant may be called upon to resolve a dilemma in the application of the CIMA Code of Ethics' Fundamental Principles.

CIMA's Ethical Checklist

CIMA is committed to upholding the highest ethical and professional standards and to maintaining public confidence in management accounting. CIMA members and students are required to comply with the CIMA Code of Ethics and to adopt its five fundamental principles to their working lives.

CIMA's Ethical Checklist provides an approach for when dealing with issues.

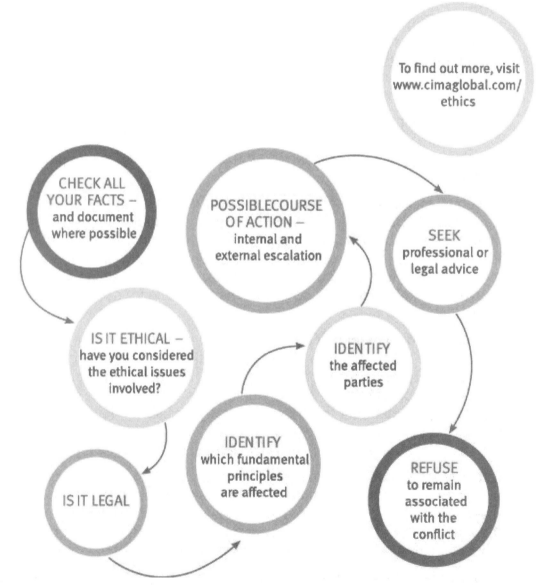

http://www.cimaglobal.com/Global/Images/standards-and-ethics/ethics_checklist_web_June2015_update.pdf

Guidance is given in the Code in Section 210.

Ethical Conflict Resolution

210.1 – If an ethical conflict is encountered, a member should take steps to best achieve compliance with the rules, fundamental principles and law.

210.1 A1 An ethical conflict arises when a member encounters one or both of the following:

(a)   Obstacles to following an appropriate course of action due to internal or external pressures

(b)   Conflicts in applying relevant professional and legal standards.

For example, a member suspects a fraud may have occurred, but reporting the suspected fraud would violate the member's responsibility to maintain the confidentiality of their employer's confidential information.

210.1 A2 In weighing alternative courses of action, a member might consider factors such as the following:

(a)   Relevant facts and circumstances, including applicable rules, laws, or regulations.

(b)   Ethical issues involved.

(c)   Established internal procedures.

210.1 A3 A member should be prepared to justify any departures they believe are appropriate in applying the relevant rules, fundamental principles and law.

210.1 A4 If a member is unable to resolve the conflict in a way that permitted compliance with the applicable rules, fundamental principles and law, the member may have to address the consequences of any violations.

210.1 A5 Before pursuing a course of action, a member might consult with appropriate persons within the organisation that employs the member.

210.1 A6 If a member decides not to consult with appropriate persons within the employing organisation, and the conflict remains unresolved after pursuing the selected course of action, the member should consider either consulting with other individuals for help in reaching a resolution or obtaining advice from an appropriate professional body or legal counsel. The member also should consider documenting the substance of the issue, the parties with whom the issue was discussed, details of any discussions held, and any decisions made concerning the issue.

210.1 A7 If the ethical conflict remains unresolved, the member will in all likelihood be in violation of one or more rules or fundamental principles if they remain associated with the matter creating the conflict. Accordingly, the member should consider their continuing relationship with the specific assignment or employer.

You need to act quickly when facing an ethical dilemma. The longer you leave it, the more chance there is for repercussions for the organisation, yourself and the standing of the profession. CIMA's Code of Ethics can help you identify and deal with situations where professional integrity may not exist.

CIMA is committed to upholding the highest ethical and professional standards and to maintaining public confidence in management accounting. CIMA members and students are required to comply with the CIMA Code of Ethics and to adopt its five fundamental principles to their working lives.

1   Check all your facts – and document where possible

–   Identify all relevant facts.

–   Do not rely on word of mouth, or assumptions. Is it really your problem?

–   Can anybody else help?

2   Is it ethical – have you considered the ethical issues involved?

–   Does it feel right?

–   How would you feel if you saw it in a newspaper?

–   How would you feel about your peers, friends, family knowing about it?

–   Have you referred to the CIMA Code of Ethics?

–   Have you referred to your internal Code of Ethics/Conduct and other internal policies?

3   Is it legal?

–   Is the issue in question regulated by the law – national and international?

–   Does it comply with rules, policies, standards and contracts imposed by relevant regulators/bodies and by your employer?

4   Identify which fundamental principles are affected

–   Integrity

–   Objectivity

–   Professional competence and due care

–   Confidentiality

–   Professional behaviour.

5   Identify the affected parties

–   Who are the individuals, organisations and key stakeholders affected?

–   In what way are they affected?

–   Are there conflicts between different stakeholders?

–   Understand the effects of non-action – to the organisation, to yourself and to society.

6   Possible course of action – internal and external escalation

–   Escalate internally; consider grievance procedures.

–   Document every action you take to resolve the conflict.

–   Escalate externally to auditor, legal advisors, professional body.

7   Seek professional or legal advice

–   Your internal whistle-blowing or speak up helpline.

–   Legal advisors.

–   CIMA ethics helpline: free to members and students.

8   Refuse to remain associated with the conflict

–   If resolution seems unlikely, disassociate yourself from the issue – in writing if necessary.

–   Legal advice may be needed if this affects your employment status or if you are implicated in any way with the issue.

7 actions to consider when facing pressure to act unethically

Pressure to act in an unethical way can come from unexpected sources and can take you by surprise, but there are steps you can take to deal with the threat. This article gives some practical suggestions.

During the course of your professional life as a member or a registered student, you may face occasions where you are pressured by those around you to cross an ethical line. This may be pressure to ignore, condone, or even participate in illegal activity such as money laundering or fraud.

Often, the reasons for crossing these lines are framed as being down to necessity, expedience, or practicality. Pressure to behave unethically is not always obvious or immediately intimidatory. It can be insidious, and if left unchecked, can become pervasive.

Typical scenarios raised on the CIMA Ethics Helpline include internal fraud, e.g. work colleagues fiddling their expenses, amending accounts to cover up bad management decisions or mistakes, and applying pressure to manipulate company accounts to give a false representation of a company's financial health.

If you are asked (or expected) to do something you feel uncomfortable with, it can be particularly difficult to push back if you are working in a high-pressure environment or in a work culture that prioritises results over and above the manner in which the results are achieved. You may have a manager or client who demands that you take a particular course of action, or you may be working as part of a team where unethical work practices are normalised. You may want to raise concerns but are apprehensive about the way in which these will be received.

You may have your own personal commitments, family, and other considerations that make pushing back a risk. You may not be comfortable with confrontation, or the pressure may be coming from someone more senior than you. Alternatively, it may be more intangible: It may be the culture of the organisation that pushes you to engage in unethical behaviour without anyone expressly telling you to do so.

Here are tips to help if you ever find yourself being pressured into unethical conduct:

Know your business's culture

Often, people consider how best to respond to pressure to behave unethically after the situation has occurred, but by that point you are already in the thick of it. It can be useful to prepare yourself before such dilemmas occur.

Before taking a job or engagement, it is helpful to have an understanding of your employer's or client's business culture and the behaviour that is expected of employees — and build that understanding once you are in a position. Be sure to do your research before taking a position and ask questions throughout the interview process.

Understand your professional obligations

Be confident you understand your obligations under your professional body's code of ethics so that you can apply them when pushing back. It will then be easier to resist undue pressure and maintain these standards in times of stress.

Section 280 of Part 2 of the CIMA Code of Ethics addresses pressure to breach the rules or fundamental principles.

The Code recognises that "pressure exerted on, or by, a member might create an intimidation or other threat to compliance with one or more of the fundamental principles or the rules". In particular, Section 280.3 (a) is clear that a member shall not allow "pressure from others to result in a breach of compliance with the rules". Advisory clauses in the Code give examples of the types of pressure members might face and where they might come from, and provide suggestions for how a member can approach these circumstances.

When pushing back, as a CIMA member it may be useful to highlight the professional obligations that exist to reinforce your position, explaining the consequences associated with breaching these obligations. Drawing attention to CIMA's indicative sanctions guidance can be a further way to push back against pressure to act unethically if pressured to do so by another CIMA member.

Put the facts into context

It is important to understand the facts in context before you diagnose the problem. For example, have you spotted a practice that has remained unchecked for some time, or are you being asked to do something unusual for which there is no precedent? Are others being asked to look the other way, or is it just you? Is the pressure coming from senior managers or your own colleagues? Understanding the motivation for the pressure will be an important part of your solution.

The Code requires you to be objective, and objectivity can be a useful tool in keeping emotion out of the situation when dealing with pressure. Management will be more receptive to an issue if you describe the problem based on the facts, the risks to the business, and propose a solution.

Raise the issue with your line manager

When you are ready to take action, the best approach is to raise the issue with your line manager. Problems arise when your manager is unreceptive or indeed if they are the perpetrator of the unethical practice. Talking to the right people can help you think through a dilemma. Someone at a similar level in the organisation may have gone through something similar and so can share useful insights. There may be someone else in a senior position at your organisation who is able to support your position and intercede on your behalf. You may have a mentor or career coach who can provide useful guidance. It may even be a colleague whom you trust and who just listens.

You may also wish to consider obtaining external guidance or advice. CIMA's ethics helpline and inbox can direct you to useful resources and help you decide on a strategy that suits your particular situation.

Point out potential reputational damage

A useful tactic for pushing back when pressured to act unethically can be to point out the potential reputational damage to a business. You could ask your senior decision-makers, "How would this look if it ended up on the front page of tomorrow's newspaper or went viral on social media?"

For companies with a public profile, there may well be a public interest in your work, and unethical or illegal activity could lead to a very public scandal with far-reaching consequences.

Reminding others of reputational risks and associated fallout as a means of highlighting the consequences of unethical behaviour is an important part of pushing back.

Consider further action

Identifying, evaluating, and addressing threats are covered in Section 120 of the Code.

Sometimes it is not possible to reduce a threat, particularly if the pressure continues. In these circumstances it may be necessary to disassociate. You may be able to have your name removed from a misleading report (see Subsection 111 – Integrity – of the Code), or you may comply with a management decision you are uncomfortable with if you can secure a commitment to a review of business practice to prevent it from happening again. Unfortunately, the ultimate disassociation is resignation, and you may feel that this is your only option if you consider your position to be untenable.

If you are unable to solve a serious threat, you may feel that you have no choice but to report it more widely. It may be appropriate to inform all the directors of a business of a situation where you are being pressured by one individual. You may also consider Section 200.11 of the Code, "Communicating With Those Charged With Governance". Ultimately, you may feel that you have no alternative but to become a whistle-blower. Larger employers may have a confidential "speak-up" helpline, and the Protect advice line offers expert and confidential advice on how best to raise your concern and your protection as a whistle-blower.

Always keep records

How you proceed will ultimately be determined by many factors, but you should always be sure to keep contemporaneous records to document the actions you take. These will be invaluable resources to anyone providing you with support and/or any appropriate third parties that may end up intervening. CIMA recommends that you document:

- The facts.
- Courses of action considered.
- The advice you gave.

Make sure you follow up any conversations you have with an email confirming the advice you gave. Keeping accurate and up-to-date records of your steps will save you a lot of trouble moving forward. You may never use them — however, it's better to have them should your decisions be challenged.

This article appeared in Financial Management, June 2022.

4 Business ethics for SME's: A guide for CIMA partners

Alongside 'Embedding ethical values' discussed in chapter 1, CIMA and the Institute of Business Ethics have produced a second guidance document, 'Business Ethics for SMEs', which explores what business ethics means for small to medium-sized business enterprises and how they can introduce and support high standards of business practice. Although both guides are aimed at CIMA partners, they are also relevant to members or students who seek to embed ethical values to their organisation or want to find out more about introducing a Code of Ethics.

Below is an extract:

Owners and managers can often encounter ethical challenges.

Examples include:

- Do I meet a deadline with my customer and ship out products even though I know there is a possibility they might be faulty, or do I openly discuss my difficulties with the customer?

- How do I ensure that my employees do their work properly and do the right thing?

- How do I deal with my employees' desire to balance their work obligations with their personal ones?

- How do I respond when securing an important contract seems to require the payment of a kickback?

- Do I delay payment to suppliers and the Inland Revenue when my cash flow is currently limited?

Some benefits of making ethical values explicit

- Increased employee loyalty, higher commitment and morale as well as lower staff turnover

- Reputational benefits (customers and suppliers)

- Attraction of 'high-quality' staff

- More open and innovative culture

- Generation of goodwill in the communities in which the business operates

- Decreased cost of borrowing and insurance

- Supports employees to act ethically and raise concerns which reduces integrity risks.

Business values may include

- Customer service
- Quality
- Innovation
- Reliability
- Efficiency
- Value for money.

Ethical values may include

- Integrity
- Honesty
- Openness
- Respect
- Fairness
- Responsibility.

Examples of business ethics issues

- Bullying and harassment
- Use of social media
- Paying suppliers on time
- Health and safety
- Conflicts of interest
- Tax avoidance
- Religious practices in workplace.

 Ethics and CIMA

Going downhill fast

CIMA's ethics manager shares the true story of a CIMA member who contacted the institute's ethics helpline for advice. His problem stemmed from allowing what seemed, on the face of it, a minor issue to snowball into a job-threatening situation.

Andrew was the management accountant of a small firm that was part of a plc. His boss, Chris, was the firm's CEO. Several months ago Chris has approached him with a query about the month-end figures that Andrew has produced, saying that they must be wrong. At the time there was a certain amount of confusion, because their firm had just taken over another small company, so Andrew adjusted them as instructed.

Next month Chris questioned the numbers again, and Andrew duly changed them once more. This happened at several more month-ends until he began to suspect that Chris's reasons for changing the numbers might not be valid – and that the business was simply not performing. He raised the issue with his boss, who assured him that he would sort everything out. Relieved that Chris recognized that the matter needed to be dealt with, Andrew dropped it.

At the end of the firm's financial year, Chris announced that he had, as promised, found a solution to the problem of the ongoing adjustments. Unfortunately, this was very different from what Andrew was expecting. Chris proposed that he own up to the discrepancies, admit that they were the result of a simple error and then resign to prevent any further questions from being asked. In return for carrying the can, Andrew would receive a glowing reference – on the understanding, of course, that he kept quiet about the whole affair.

Shocked and unsure about what to do, Andrew contacted CIMA's ethics helpline. He had gone from accepting a small month-end adjustment to his figures to finding himself about to lose a job. Our guidance to Andrew was that he should consider taking the problem to more senior people in the group, since raising it with Chris wasn't an option. Andrew had some concerns about the possible repercussions of doing this, particularly because Chris was well respected in the group, and he was worried that his version of events would not be believed. The lack of an internal grievance or whistle blowing procedure made it hard for him to predict how his case would be handled.

Given all these factors, Andrew questioned whether quitting was an acceptable solution. A good reference had been promised, but was this pledge worth anything coming from Chris? And how would he explain to any future employer why he had left? And what would happen if a colleague were to complain to CIMA about his lack of competence? If this were to happen, he could potentially lose his membership. Even worse, lying to accept responsibility that wasn't his would be another breach of CIMA's code of ethics. If discovered, this would also have consequences for his membership.

After further discussion, Andrew identified a potential ally (a financial controller) at group level. He arranged a meeting through a trusted colleague in order to minimize the chances of discovery by Chris.

We suggested that Andrew should speak to the institute's legal advice line for expert guidance on his legal obligations and employment rights, and also to the whistle-blowing advice line for free, confidential, independent advice on raising his concerns.

Andrew spoke to the financial controller and Chris was eventually forced to resign. But Andrew's ongoing compliance with his boss's wishes was enough to have tarnished his reputation. A few months later he resigned of his own accord.

Andrew's case is a reminder of how crucial it is to use your professional judgment, heed the warning signs and establish the facts at the first sign of an ethical dilemma. Armed with these and CIMA's code of ethics, you can decide whether or not you need to act and, if so, what that action should be.

So how exactly do you know when an ethical dilemma is an ethical dilemma? As Oscar Wilde observed: 'Morality, like art, means drawing a line someplace.' When the amount of money is not material, the report is only for internal purposes or when no one else seems to think there's an issue, how can you be sure where that line is?

Taking time to consider the situation from all angles will help you to know for sure. In the code of ethics, the line is where a threat to our fundamental principles is anything more than trivial. Although the changes that Andrew made to the numbers in that first month might not have been material, the pattern that they established was. If he had stood up to Chris the first time he was asked to adjust the figures, the situation might never have developed.

This article appeared in Financial Management, November 2007.

Nike

Nike is one of the famous franchises in the world that sells sportswear for all ages. But is mostly famous for their athlete shoes and apparel and Nike is also one of the major manufacturers of sport equipment as well. The slogan for Nike is "Just Do It". Nike was founded in January 1962 in Oregon, United States by Philip Knight and Bill Bowerman. Nike has somewhere around 700 or more retail outlets spread all over the world, and has approximately 45 offices outside the United States. And it employs 30,000 people all over the world. Nike had a revenue excess of $16 billion in 2007. Nike's factories are mostly located in Asian countries like Pakistan, India, Malaysia, China, Indonesia, Philippines, Taiwan, Vietnam and Thailand.

The primary stakeholders of the company would be the shareholders, business partners, the employees, and the customers/consumers. What the shareholders and the investors want from the company is that the company achieves its profits, the employees of the expect work satisfaction, pay along with good supervision and the customers are concerned with quality, safety and availability of services when they require it. And when any primary stakeholder group is not satisfied the organisation's progress becomes questionable.

The secondary stakeholders of the company would be the community. Most companies like Nike exist under a charter or licenses and operate within the limits of safety laws, environmental protection and other laws and regulations. The socially responsible organisations like Nike should consider the effect of their actions upon all stakeholders. What all of these stakeholders want from the company is that the company is ethically and socially responsible and when this secondary stakeholder group becomes dis-satisfied, the reputation of the company gets tarnished (for example, the debate of sweatshops tarnished the reputation of Nike).

Issues faced by Nike:

- Child labour and the sweat shop problem

- Workers given a very low wage, and overtime in countries like Vietnam, China and Indonesia under a subcontract

- Poor working conditions, squalid working conditions and forced labour in the factories that manufacture their products

- Environmental damage done to society by air and water pollution, noise, and change in the climate due to pollution. (Stockdale & Crosby, 2004).

There are different kinds of guiding principles that can prevent Nike type scandals, and this is what the company did:

PR campaign

Nike decided to use a PR campaign so that it was able to repair its social image due to the sweatshop debate. The PR campaign covered the following actions:

Employment Practices

The management of Nike took a look at its employment practices; they made sure that the company was following the policies on recruitment, training, health, safety and welfare. The management of the company also oversaw their environmental practices – to make sure that the company follows procedures that are responsible in terms of waste disposal and avoidance and energy inputs.

Training Plan

They conducted and designed a training program for the employees. The management remembered that training and development programs are not universal solutions to every need of the company. Effective job designs, selection, placement and other activities of the HR department are also very important.

Assessing Performance

They set targets and identified performance measure standards. If performance is to be rated accurately, the performance of the company would require the management to assess each and every relevant performance dimension.

Ethical Responsibility

The management of Nike understood that ethical responsibility is needed within the company because it is the obligation of organisation's management to make decisions and take actions that will grow the welfare and interest of the society and the organisation. It would include activities and commitments that are related to human rights, governance and ethics, development, working conditions of the employees, community involvement, customer satisfaction, relations with the company's suppliers and customers and lastly respect for diverse cultures and different people.

5 Test your understanding questions

Test your understanding 1

Which of the following are possible consequences to the accounting profession if unethical behaviour is widespread?

(i)   The introduction of legislation.

(ii) Loss of its reputation.

(iii) Loss of its chartered institute status.

A   (i) and (ii) only

B   (ii) and (iii) only

C   (i) and (iii) only

D   (i), (ii) and (iii)

Test your understanding 2

Which statements are true or false?

A   Unethical behaviour will lead to financial loss

B   Codes of ethics are voluntary

C   Governance refers to how an organisation is run

D   Social responsibility refers to a company's relationship with its shareholders

Test your understanding 3

Which of the following is not an example of a familiarity threat?

A   Accepting gifts or preferential treatment from a client

B   Having a close business relationship with a client

C   Having a close family relationship with a director of a client

D   A former partner of the company being a director of the client

Test your understanding 4

An old friend has asked you to tender for accounting work. You are keen to assist. From an ethical as well as a business perspective, what is the most appropriate action for you to take?

A   Tender for the work

B   Suggest to your friend that they approach more than one company to create a competitive tender

C   Suggest to your friend that they assign the work to a different company instead

D   Ask a colleague to handle the client

Test your understanding answers

Test your understanding 1

D

They are all possible outcomes.

Test your understanding 2

A **False.** Unethical behaviour may have consequences when it is highlighted. Not all ethical behaviour is highlighted.

B **True.** A company may require its employees to comply with its code of ethics as part of the employee's contract of employment, but it is a voluntary decision of a company to set up a code of ethics initially.

C **True.** This is the generic manner in which the term governance is used.

D **False.** A company's social responsibility is a wider responsibility to ALL stakeholders of the company, not just the shareholders.

Test your understanding 3

B

Having a close business relationship with a client is an example of a self-interest threat.

Test your understanding 4

D

Accountants need to demonstrate both independence of mind and independence in appearance. You should therefore declare the potential conflict of interest and ask a colleague to handle the client.

3

Corporate Governance

Chapter learning objectives

Upon completion of this chapter you will be able to:

- describe corporate governance

- explain the interaction of corporate governance with business ethics and company law

- explain the purpose, definition of the Organisation for Economic Co-operation and Development (OECD) principles of Corporate Governance

- describe IFAC's main drivers of sustainable corporate success

- illustrate CIMA's practical proposals for better corporate governance

- distinguish between detailed rules-based and principles based approaches to governance

- describe the role of the board and different board structures

- explain the effects of corporate governance on directors' powers and duties

- describe the types of policies and procedures that constitute 'best practice'

- describe the respective committees and their roles and responsibilities with regards monitoring and controlling the actions of the Executive.

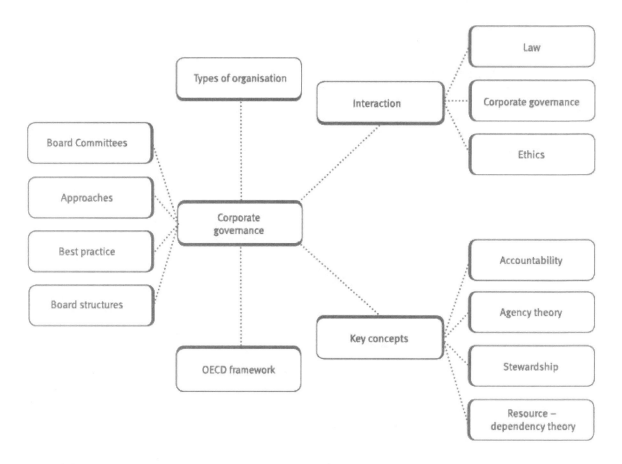

1 Introduction

This chapter deals with corporate governance which is contained in Section B of the syllabus.

You will be introduced to the concept of an 'organisation' within this chapter. This will be developed further in Chapter 8 which looks in more detail at the characteristics of particular types of organisations such as companies.

The rest of the chapter will look at the concept of corporate governance including its purpose and examples of policies and procedures.

2 Organisations

What is an organisation?

Defining an organisation is difficult as there are many types of organisations which are set up to meet a variety of needs, such as clubs, schools, companies, charities and hospitals.

What they all have in common is summarised in the definition produced by **Buchanan and Huczynski**.

 'Organisations are social arrangements for the controlled purpose of collective goals.'

What is an organisation?

Consider the three aspects of Buchanan and Huczynski's definition in more detail:

(a) 'Collective goals' – organisations are defined by their goals. The main goal of a school is to educate pupils. It will therefore be organised differently to a company that aims to make profits.

(b) 'Social arrangements' – someone working alone cannot be classed as an organisation. Organisations are structured to allow people to work together towards a common goal. Usually, the larger the organisation, the more formal its structures.

(c) 'Controlled performance' – an organisation will have systems and procedures in place to ensure that group goals are achieved. For a company this could involve setting sales targets, or periodically assessing the performance of staff members.

Different types of organisations

Different organisations have different goals. We can therefore classify them into several different categories.

Profit-seeking organisations

Profit-seeking (or commercial) organisations see their main objective as maximising the wealth of their owners.

There are three common forms that a commercial company can take:

- **Sole traders** – the organisation is owned and run by one person.

- **Partnerships** – the organisation is owned and run by two or more individuals.

Note that in both of these organisations, the owner of the business is not legally separate from the business itself. If a partnership is sued by a customer, the customer is actually suing the owner of the business.

- **Limited liability companies** – a company has a separate legal identity to its owners (who are known as shareholders). The owner's liability is limited to the amount they have invested into the company.

  In the UK, there are two types of limited company:

  Private limited companies (with 'Ltd' after their name) – these tend to be smaller businesses, often owned by a few shareholders. Shares cannot be offered to the general public.

  Public limited companies (with 'plc' after their name) – these can be much larger businesses. Shares can be offered to the general public, meaning that there can be millions of different shareholders. This makes it easier for the company to raise finance, enabling further growth.

Not for profit organisations

Not-for-profit organisations (NFPs) do not see profitability as their main objective. Instead, they seek to satisfy the particular needs of their members or the sectors of society that they have been set up to benefit.

NFP's examples
NFPs include the following: - government departments and agencies (such as HM Revenue and Customs) - schools - hospitals - charities (such as the Red Cross, Oxfam and Doctors Without Borders) - clubs.

Public sector organisations

The public sector is the part of the economy that is concerned with providing basic government services and is controlled by government organisations.

Public sector organisations
The organisations that make up the public sector vary from country to country, but generally include: • police • military • public transport • primary education • healthcare for the poor.

Private sector organisations

The private sector consists of organisations that are run by private individuals and groups rather than the government.

Private sector
The private sector will therefore normally include: • businesses • non-governmental organisations • charities and • clubs. Within these will be both profit-seeking and not-for-profit organisations.

Non-governmental organisations (NGOs)

A non-governmental organisation is one which does not have profit as its primary goal and is not directly linked to the national government.

NGOs often promote political, social or environmental change within the countries they operate.

NGOs
Some of the largest NGOs operate in the humanitarian sphere and include: • Oxfam • the Red Cross • World Vision • Amnesty International.

Co-operatives

Co-operatives (or mutuals) are organisations that are owned and democratically controlled by their members – the people who buy their goods or services.

They are organised solely to meet the needs of the member-owners, who usually share any profits.

> **Co-operatives**
>
> In the UK, the largest example of a co-operative is the Co-operative Group, which has over 5.5 million members and operates in diverse markets, such as banking, travel and groceries.

3 What is corporate governance?

Definition of corporate governance

The Financial Reporting Council defines corporate governance as follows:

> The purpose of corporate governance is to facilitate effective, entrepreneurial and prudent management that can deliver the long-term success of the company.

Corporate governance is the system by which companies are directed and controlled. Boards of directors are responsible for the governance of their companies. The shareholders' role in governance is to appoint the directors and the auditors and to satisfy themselves that an appropriate governance structure is in place. The responsibilities of the board include setting the company's strategic aims, providing the leadership to put them into effect, supervising the management of the business and reporting to shareholders on their stewardship. The board's actions are subject to laws, regulations and the shareholders in general meetings.

The aim of corporate governance initiatives is to ensure that companies are run well in the interests of their shareholders and the wider community.

In response to major accounting scandals (e.g. Enron), regulators sought to change the rules surrounding the governance of companies, particularly publically owned ones.

There are different codes and practices around the world but they tend to cover similar areas:

- The role of the board of directors.

- The reliability of financial reports and the relationship between the company and its auditors.

- The interest of the company's shareholders in the company.

Importance of corporate governance

- In most developed countries, listed companies are required to operate systems of corporate governance laid down either by statute or by professional organisations (such as the Securities and Exchange Commission (SEC) in the US or the Financial Conduct Authority (FCA) in the UK).

- The requirements are often given the support of the stock exchanges, in that they are built into listing rules.

- The development of corporate governance codes is closely associated with the UK, hence this is a model to discuss best practice.

- The UK Corporate Governance Code follows a principles-based approach and is endorsed by the London Stock Exchange. The US system has been much more legislative with the introduction of the Sarbanes-Oxley Act of 2002.

Development of corporate governance

- Governance regulations have developed largely as a result of a series of corporate failures in the 1980s and early 1990s.

- The corporate governance themes that began to emerge from these collapses were:

  - poorly-run companies, especially companies with a board of directors dominated by a single chairman/chief executive figure, and companies with 'greedy' or 'fat cat' directors (demonstrating the agency problem of a company failing to operate in the best interests of its shareholders)

  - poor financial reporting, raising questions about auditing and internal control systems, and

  - an apparent lack of interest by the major investment institutions in the performance of the companies in which they invested.

- Since then the UK Corporate Governance Code has been developed further.

Company collapses

Several issues or problems appear to emerge when there is a corporate governance 'scandal' and a company has collapsed.

- The company has not been well-run by its board of directors.

- In many cases, there has been an individual who has dominated the board and exerted excessive influence on decision-making by the board. In many cases, this individual held the positions of both chairman of the board and chief executive officer.

- A board of directors might have lacked sufficient breadth of knowledge and experience to appreciate the problems the company was in and the risks it faced.

- Companies were being run in the interests of the executive directors, who received high remuneration packages and generous bonuses, but the rewards were not being given for the achievement of objectives that were in the best interests of the shareholders. The interests of the directors were not properly aligned with those of the shareholders.

- Financial reporting was unreliable and the published accounts did not seem to give any indication of the true financial position of the company. In some cases there was a suspicion that the auditors were not sufficiently independent of the company and so not fulfilling their responsibilities adequately. Alternatively, the auditors were accused of doing their job badly or of being misled by the company's directors and management. (In 2002 audit firm Arthur Andersen collapsed from the consequences of its involvement in the Enron scandal.)

- Whenever a company collapsed unexpectedly, there have been suspicions that the internal control system was ineffective. There usually appears to have been inadequate risk management generally.

- Questions have also been asked about major institutional shareholders, and whether they could have done more to identify problems in companies and persuade or force the directors to make improvements.

Maxwell Communications Corporation

Robert Maxwell was born in to extreme poverty in Czechoslovakia in 1923. By the time of his death (accident or murder was never established) in 1991 he was a media mogul, having built a publishing empire that spanned the world. In the weeks that followed his death however, news emerged of the state of his company's finances.

After the Second World War he set up Pergamon Press publishing scientific journals. It became very profitable and he turned his attention to politics, later becoming a Member of Parliament for the Labour Party. His relationship with the Party was an uneasy one since anyone who criticised him was confronted in the courts. This was when signs emerged of his dishonesty.

In 1969, Maxwell agreed a takeover bid for Pergamon by Leasco (an American financial and data processing group). The profits of Pergamon were questioned by Leasco and eventually talks fell apart as a Department of Trade and Industry (DTI) enquiry ensued. Inspectors found that the profits depended on transactions with Maxwell family private companies. The DTI concluded that Maxwell 'is not a person... who can be relied upon to exercise proper stewardship of a publicly quoted company'.

In 1980 Maxwell took over the troubled British Printing Corporation renaming it Maxwell Communications Corporation. In 1984 he bought Mirror Group Newspapers (MGN) and Macmillan publishers, which put his company further into debt. In 1991 he floated MGN as a public company desperate to raise cash that would save the Group from bankruptcy (with debts over £2 billion). After Maxwell's death it transpired that he had taken money from the pension funds to keep the companies afloat and boost the share price.

Enron

In December 2001, US energy trader Enron collapsed. Enron was the largest bankruptcy in US history. Even though the United States was believed by many to be the most regulated financial market in the world, it was evident from Enron's collapse that investors were not properly informed about the significance of off-balance sheet transactions. US accounting rules may have contributed to this, in that they are concerned with the strict legal ownership of investment vehicles rather than with their control. By contrast, International Accounting Standards follow the principle of 'substance over form'. There were some indications that Enron may have actively lobbied against changing the treatment in US financial reporting of special purpose entities used in off-balance sheet financing. Overall, there was a clear need for greater transparency and trust in reporting.

The failure of Enron also highlighted the over-dependence of an auditor on one particular client, the employment of staff by Enron who had previously worked for the auditors, the process of audit appointments and re-appointments, the rotation of audit partners and how auditors are monitored and regulated.

As a consequence of the failure of Enron and WorldCom, the United States has introduced Sarbanes-Oxley legislation to address many of the criticisms of reporting and auditing practice. In their comments on the failure of Enron, the Association of Certified Chartered Accountants recommended the need for global financial markets to have a global set of principles-based financial reporting standards and a global code of corporate governance, arguing that legalistic, rules-based standards encourage creative, loophole-based practice.

Former chief executive Kenneth Lay died in 2006 before he could stand trial. Enron's former chief financial officer Andrew Fastow was sentenced in late 2006 to six years in prison for stealing from Enron and devising schemes to deceive investors about the energy company's true financial condition. Lawyers have to date won settlements totalling $US 7.3 billion from banks including JPMorgan Chase, Bank of America, Citigroup, etc.

WorldCom

WorldCom filed for bankruptcy protection in June 2002. It was the biggest corporate fraud in history, largely a result of treating operating expenses as capital expenditure.

WorldCom (now renamed MCI) admitted in March 2004 that the total amount by which it had misled investors over the previous 10 years was almost US$75 billion (£42 billion) and reduced its stated pre-tax profits for 2001 and 2002 by that amount.

WorldCom stock began falling in late 1999 as businesses slashed spending on telecom services and equipment. A series of debt downgrades had raised borrowing costs for the company, struggling with about US$32 billion in debt. WorldCom used accounting tricks to conceal a deteriorating financial condition and to inflate profits.

Former WorldCom chief executive Bernie Ebbers resigned in April 2002 amid questions about US$366 million in personal loans from the company and a federal probe of its accounting practices. Ebbers was subsequently charged with conspiracy to commit securities fraud, and filing misleading data with the Securities and Exchange Commission (SEC). Scott Sullivan, former chief financial officer, pleaded guilty to three criminal charges.

The SEC said WorldCom had committed 'accounting improprieties of unprecedented magnitude' – proof, it said, of the need for reform in the regulation of corporate accounting.

Wirecard

Wirecard, a payment processor and financial services provider based in Germany, is suspected to have engaged in a series of accounting fraudulent activities to inflate its profit by creating forged and backdated contracts.

In 2019, KPMG was brought in to perform a special audit into the irregularities and found that Wirecard's long-time auditor EY failed to verify the existence of cash reserves in what appeared to be fraudulent bank statements. The special audit report published by KPMG in April 2020 stated that they could not verify that profits reported from 2016 to 2018 were genuine.

In June 2020, it was announced that €1.9bn of cash balances were missing, the chief executive was arrested, EY refused to sign off the 2019 accounts and the company filed for insolvency.

EY have been criticised for failing to detect the fraud which has been ongoing for a number of years, and in particular, why the auditor failed to obtain confirmation from the bank of the cash held on behalf of Wirecard which is a standard audit procedure and could have revealed the fraud much sooner.

There is also criticism of how the German accounting regulator, BaFin, dealt with allegations against Wirecard. Despite allegations lodged against the company, BaFin took little action against the company before its eventual collapse and even filed a criminal complaint against two FT journalists who reported the whistleblower allegations about the company.

Carillion

In 2018, construction company Carillion collapsed after building up debts of £1.5 billion. The company was a major contractor for the UK government with contracts to build hospitals and schools as well as facilities management and ongoing maintenance. It was the second largest construction company in the UK and employed more than 43,000 people worldwide. The company took on too many projects and failed to realistically price the contracts resulting in huge cost overruns and losses being made. In December 2017 the major banks refused to lend more money to Carillion and in 2018 the company went into compulsory liquidation. This caused significant problems, not just for the shareholders who will receive nothing, but also for the significant number of employees who lost their jobs, the government contracts that were in progress that would not be completed, and for the suppliers who would not be paid.

One of the issues highlighted by Carillion was that of executive pay. Executive directors were earning significant amounts of money despite running the company into the ground. In 2016, the former chief executive director earned more than £2 million. The head of corporate governance at the Institute of Directors said that the collapse of Carillion suggests a lack of effective governance. Directors' remuneration allowed them to benefit despite the collapse of the company as there were no clawback conditions. The company could only request clawback from directors if there was gross misconduct or misstatement of financial results. The directors also received payoffs despite being responsible for the collapse.

The collapse of Carillion has also returned focus to the big accounting firms and their part in allowing companies to fail by not having raised the alarm much earlier.

4 Governance, ethics and company law

Clearly there is an overlap between business ethics, company law and corporate governance. In many jurisdictions company law is made up of ethical principles and standards of behaviour which legislators and courts have thought appropriate to codify as law.

	Compliance requirements	Penalties
Law	The law must always be obeyed.	Penalties for infringement of the law may be civil or criminal.
		Civil remedies may allow the company to recover funds from directors who breach their legal obligations.
		A fine and/or imprisonment might result from certain criminal infringements.

	Compliance requirements	Penalties
Corporate governance	In the UK the stock exchange rules require listed companies to comply with the UK Corporate Governance Code. If a listed company does not comply, it must specify the provisions with which it has not complied, and give reasons for its non-compliance. Unlisted companies are under no obligation to comply, although it is considered best practice to do so.	There are no formal penalties for non-compliance. However, the company may suffer loss of reputation and receive bad publicity.
Ethics	It is said that ethics begin where the law ends. If an action is legal, individuals generally have freedom of choice as to their conduct. However, good ethical behaviour may be above that demanded by the law. CIMA students and members are expected to follow the code of ethics published by CIMA.	An individual who behaves unethically may suffer loss of reputation, dismissal from their job and sanctions may possibly be imposed by their professional body.

Why does the law need to be supplemented?

It may be questioned therefore, if the law is so stringent, why has it proved necessary to have an additional body of rules and standards known as corporate governance? Why is it that the law has not prevented directors from paying themselves excessive salaries and/or involving their companies in major scandals?

The answer lies in the fact that, in many instances, the law provides for internal regulation of the activities of directors by:

(i) requiring directors to fully disclose their dealings to the shareholders and

(ii) by giving the shareholders the power to regulate the activities of the directors through their control of the company's constitution and, of course, by giving the shareholders the ultimate power, of appointing and dismissing the directors.

Why then does the law need to be supplemented? The short answer is that quite clearly these rules have not proved watertight, and in a number of high-profile instances directors have been able to circumvent the law. In general, this has happened for the following main reasons.

Firstly, persons and institutions who invest in shares in public limited companies mainly do so in order to achieve good capital growth, a good return on their investment in the form of dividends or a combination of the two. If that is what the investor is receiving, then he or she is less likely to be interested in the way that the company is being managed. In any event, the investors, particularly institutional investors, will be likely to have invested in a large number of companies throughout the world. It appears unrealistic in the extreme therefore, to suppose that fund managers will have the time to actively participate in the internal affairs of all the companies in which they invest.

Secondly, shares in public companies are potentially held by hundreds or even thousands of shareholders. It follows that shareholders in any particular company tend to be a disparate body, not united by any common objectives other than good returns on their investments. Such a group is likely to be difficult to organise behind a coherent policy and thus in a poor position to take on a relatively small powerful group like a board of directors. Even the ultimate power to remove directors may be difficult to use in practice. For example, it may be that the shareholders are concerned that if the market becomes aware of internal conflict within the company, that may have a detrimental effect on the share price. Additionally it may be that dismissing directors can be expensive in the extreme. Many directors of public companies would be entitled to large compensation payments in the event of their removal.

5 Key concepts

Accountability

Accountability means that people in a position of power can be held to account for their actions, i.e. they can be compelled to explain their decisions and can be criticised or punished if they have abused their position.

Accountability is central to the concept of good corporate governance – the process of ensuring that companies are well run.

The directors are accountable to the shareholders for the way in which they run the company.

 ### Agency theory

Agency theory is a group of concepts describing the nature of the agency relationship deriving from the separation between ownership and control.

Agency theory and corporate governance

Agency theory can help to explain the actions of the various interest groups in the corporate governance debate.

Agency theory and corporate governance

Examination of theories behind corporate governance provides a foundation for understanding the issue in greater depth and a link between an historical perspective and its application in modern governance standards.

- Historically, businesses were owned and managed by the same people. For economies to grow it was necessary to create a different business model which would encourage people to invest even in risk-taking ventures. This led to the development of the limited liability company which enabled people to invest in the knowledge that if the business failed they might lose their investment but not all of their assets. Also, stock markets were introduced enabling investors to freely market their shares.

- Limited liability – the concept that shareholders are legally responsible for the debts of the company only to the sum of the nominal value of their shares.

- Stock market – the "market" in which publicly held shares are issued and traded.

- Delegation of running the firm to the agent or managers.

- Separation of goals between wealth maximisation of shareholders and the personal objectives of managers. This separation is a key assumption of agency theory.

- Possible short-term perspective of managers rather than protecting long-term shareholder wealth.

- Divorce between ownership and control linked with differing objectives creates agency problems.

Stewardship

Stewardship is the responsibility to take good care of resources. A steward is a person entrusted with management of another person's property, for example, when one person is paid to look after another person's house while the owner goes abroad on holiday. The steward is **accountable** for the way he or she carries out their role.

This relationship, where one person has a duty of care towards someone else is known as a '**fiduciary relationship**'.

A **fiduciary relationship** is a relationship of 'good faith' such as that between the directors of a company and the shareholders of the company. There is a 'separation of ownership and control' in the sense that the shareholders own the company, while the directors make the decisions. The directors must make their decisions in the interests of the shareholders rather than in their own selfish personal interests.

In essence the directors are stewards of the company.

Resource-dependency theory

Resource-dependency theory is the study of how the external resources of organisations affect the behaviour of the organisation. The theory was formalised by Jeffrey Pfeffer and Gerald Salancik in 1978.

The ideology of resource dependence theory can be summarized as follows:

- Organisations depend on resources.

- These resources ultimately originate from an organisation's environment.

- The environment, to a considerable extent, contains other organisations.

- The resources one organisation needs are thus often in the hands of other organisations.

- Resources are a basis of power.

- Legally independent organisations can therefore depend on each other.

In the context of corporate governance, directors are responsible for developing appropriate strategies to exploit these resources in order to ensure the survival of their own organisation.

6   The OECD Principles of Corporate Governance

The OECD consists of 38 countries who want a free market economy with one set of rules for corporate governance.

Although there have always been well run entities as well as those where scandals have occurred, the fact that scandals do occur has led to the development of codes of practice for good corporate governance.

Often this is due to pressures exerted by stock exchanges. In 1999 the Organisation for Economic Co-operation and Development, OECD, assisted with the development of their 'Principles of Corporate Governance.' These were intended to:

- assist member and non-member governments in their efforts to evaluate and improve the legal, institutional and regulatory framework for corporate governance in their countries.

- provide guidance and suggestions for stock exchanges, investors, corporations, and other parties that have a role in the process of developing good corporate governance.

The OECD principles were first published in 1999 and were revised in 2004 and 2015. Their focus is on publicly traded entities. However, to the extent they are deemed applicable, they are a useful tool to improve corporate governance in non-traded entities.

There are six principles, each backed up by a number of sub principles.

The principles in detail

The six principles:

(i) **Ensuring the basis for an effective corporate governance framework**

The corporate governance framework should promote transparent and fair markets, and the efficient allocation of resources. It should be consistent with the rule of law and support effective supervision and enforcement.

(ii) **The rights and equitable treatment of shareholders and key ownership functions**

The corporate governance framework should protect and facilitate the exercise of shareholders' rights and ensure the equitable treatment of all shareholders, including minority and foreign shareholders. All shareholders should have the opportunity to obtain effective redress for violation of their rights.

(iii) **Institutional investors, stock markets and other intermediaries**

The corporate governance framework should provide sound incentives throughout the investment chain and provide for stock markets to function in a way that contributes to good corporate governance.

(iv) **The role of stakeholders in corporate governance**

The corporate governance framework should recognise the rights of stakeholders established by law or through mutual agreements and encourage active co-operation between corporations and stakeholders in creating wealth, jobs, and the sustainability of financially sound enterprises.

(v) **Disclosure and transparency**

The corporate governance framework should ensure that timely and accurate disclosure is made on all material matters regarding the corporation, including the financial situation, performance, ownership and governance of the company.

(vi) **The responsibilities of the board**

The corporate governance framework should ensure the strategic guidance of the entity, the effective monitoring of management by the board, and the board's accountability to the company and the shareholders.

The status of the OECD principles

- The principles represent a common basis that OECD Member countries consider essential for the development of good governance practice.

- They are intended to be concise, understandable and accessible to the international community.

- They are not intended to be a substitute for government or private sector initiatives to develop more detailed 'best practice' in governance.

7 IFAC's main drivers of sustainable corporate success

The Professional Accountants in Business (PAIB) Committee published a paper to support the global accountancy profession in responding to changing expectations of society, financial markets, and organisations, and promotes the value of professional accountants in business to their organisations.

The paper lists eight drivers of sustainable organisational success which provide the basis for understanding how the global accountancy profession needs to support the development of professional accountants, so that they can help organisations achieve sustainable value creation.

Customer and stakeholder focus

- Understanding and satisfying customer or service-user needs.
- Aligning all parts of an organisation to these needs.

Effective leadership and strategy

- Providing ethical and strategic leadership focused on sustainable value creation.
- Facilitating key performance drivers, including strong corporate values, ethical culture, and organisational structures and processes.

Integrated governance, risk and control

- Deploying effective governance structures and processes with integrated risk management and internal control.
- Balancing performance and conformance in governance.

Innovation and adaptability

- Innovating processes and products to improve reputation and performance.
- Adapting the organisation to changing circumstances.

Financial management

- Ensuring financial leadership and strategy support sustainable value creation.
- Implementing good practices in areas such as tax and treasury, cost and profitability improvement, and working capital management.

People and talent management

- Enabling people and talent management as a strategic function.
- Applying talent management to the finance function so it better serves the needs of the wider organisation.

Operational excellence

- Aligning resource allocation with strategic objectives and the drivers of shareholder and stakeholder value.

- Supporting decision making with timely and insightful performance analysis.

Effective and transparent communication

- Engaging stakeholders effectively to ensure that they receive relevant communications.

- Preparing high-quality business reporting to support stakeholder understanding and decision making.

8   CIMA's practical proposals for better corporate governance

CIMA was a contributor to Report Leadership which was a multi-stakeholder group that aimed to challenge established thinking on corporate reporting.

Report Leadership published a report on simple practical proposals for better reporting of corporate governance.

http://www.cimaglobal.com/Documents/Thought leadership docs/ Governance/Report-Leadership-Corporate-Governance-Report. pdf

The proposals were:

1   Tone from the top

Communicating the chairman's views on good governance and the culture of the board.

2   How the board works as a team

Showing how the board 'fits together' with a complementary set of skills, experience and personal characteristics.

3   The key actions of the board and its committees

Linking the activities of the board to the year's key corporate events.

4   Board effectiveness

Using board evaluations to communicate board performance and priorities.

5   Communication and engagement with shareholders

Explaining how the information needs of the shareholders have been met during the year.

9   Board structures

There are two kinds of board structure, unitary and two-tier (dual) boards.

Two-tier boards

These are predominantly associated with France and Germany. Using Germany as an example, there are two main reasons for their existence:

- Codetermination: the right for workers to be informed and involved in decisions that affects them. This is enshrined in the Codetermination Act (Germany) 1976.

- Relationships: banks have a much closer relationship with German companies than in the UK. They are frequently shareholders, and other shareholders often deposit their shares and the rights associated with them with their banks.

This creates a backdrop to creating structures where these parties are actively involved in company affairs, hence the two-tier structure.

Lower tier: management (operating) board:

- responsible for day-to-day running of the enterprise

- generally only includes executives

- the CEO co-ordinates activity.

Upper tier: supervisory (corporate) board:

- appoints, supervises and advises members of the management board

- strategic oversight of the organisation

- includes employee representatives, environmental groups and other stakeholders' management representatives (these NEDs are not considered to be 'independent NEDs')

- the chairman co-ordinates the work

- members are elected by shareholders at the annual general meeting (AGM)

- receives information and reports from the management board.

Advantages of a two-tier board

- Clear separation between those that manage the company and those that own it or must control it for the benefit of shareholders.

- Implicit shareholder involvement in most cases since these structures are used in countries where insider control is prevalent.

- Wider stakeholder involvement implicit through the use of worker representation.

- Independence of thought, discussion and decision since board meetings and operation are separate.

- Direct power over management through the right to appoint members of the management board.

Problems with a two-tier board

- Dilution of power, confusion over authority and hence a perceived lack of accountability. (NB Due to co-determination, there is a right for many different stakeholders to be involved in decisions which affect them).

- Isolation of supervisory board through non-participation in management meetings.

- Agency problems between the boards where one will be acting on behalf of another e.g. the Management Board meetings excluding the Supervisory Board resulting in confusion over authority.

- Increased bureaucracy which may result in slower decisions being made.

- Lack of transparency over appointment of supervisory board members leading to inefficient monitoring and governance.

Additional advantages of a unitary board

Issues specific to the unitary board tend to relate to the role of NEDs.

- NED expertise: the implied involvement of NEDs in the running of the company rather than just supervising.

- NED empowerment: they are as responsible as the executives and this is better demonstrated by their active involvement at an early stage.

- Compromise: less extreme decisions developed prior to the need for supervisory approval.

- Responsibility: a cabinet decision-making unit with wide viewpoints suggests better decisions.

- Reduction of fraud, malpractice: this is due to wider involvement in the actual management of the company.

- Improved investor confidence: through all of the above.

10   The development of corporate governance codes

The development of corporate governance codes is closely associated with the UK, therefore this model is used to illustrate best practice.

Report	Focus	Outcome
Cadbury (1992)	Board of directors	Chairman/CEO role should be split, and Chairman independence necessary
	Institutional investors	Need for greater dialogue
	Audit and accountability	Good communication and disclosure
	Formed part of stock exchange listing rules – **comply or explain**	
Greenbury (1995)	Directors' remuneration	Reporting balance between salary and performance
Hampel (1998)	Deal with criticisms of previous reports	Consolidation in a **Combined Code**
Turnbull (1999)	Need for directors to review internal control systems and report on them	Framework for establishing systems of internal control
Higgs (2003)	Role of non-executive directors (NEDs)	Specific guidelines regarding NEDs and their role
Tyson (2003)	Recruitment and development of NEDs	Additional guidance
Smith (2003)	Auditors and audit committee	Relationship between auditors and the company and the role of the audit committee
Sir David Walker & the FRC (2010)	Complete review of Corporate Governance following the financial crisis 2008 – 2009	The Code was found to be 'fit for purpose' and the name changed to 'UK Corporate Governance Code'. This was last updated in 2018.

11 Best Practice – policies and procedures

The UK Corporate Governance Code

In the UK for listed companies, the most important issues of best practice are contained in the UK Corporate Governance Code. This was first issued in 1998 and has been updated at regular intervals since then, most recently in 2018.

The UK Corporate Governance Code can be seen in full on the FRC website at

https://www.frc.org.uk/Our-Work/Codes-Standards/Corporategovernance/UK-Corporate-Governance-Code.aspx

The Code is not a rigid (or enforced) set of rules. Instead it consists of principles (main and supporting) and provisions. In the UK all companies quoted on the stock exchange have to comply with the FCA listing rules and these include a requirement that all companies include in their annual report:

- a statement of how the company has applied the main principles set out in the Code; and

- a statement as to whether the company has complied with all relevant provisions set out in the Code.

The main principles of the Code are:

Board leadership and company purpose

- A successful company is led by an effective board whose role is to promote long-term sustainable success thereby generating value for shareholders and contributing to wider society.

- The board should establish the company's purpose, values and strategy. The directors should lead by example and promote the desired culture.

- The board should ensure that the necessary resources are in place for the company to meet its objectives. The board should establish a framework of effective controls to enable risk to be assessed and managed.

- The board should ensure effective engagement with, and encourage participation from shareholders and stakeholders.

- The board should ensure that workforce policies and practices are consistent with the company's values. The workforce should be able to raise matters of concern.

Board roles

The chair's role

- Leads the board of directors.
- Enables flow of information and discussion at board meetings.
- Ensures satisfactory channels of communication with the external auditors.
- Ensures effective operation of board sub-committees.
- The chair should be independent to enhance effectiveness.

The chief executive's role

- Ensures the effective operation of the company.
- Head of the executive directors.
- Clear division of responsibilities between the chair and chief executive.

Executive directors

The executive directors have responsibility for running the company on a day to day basis.

Non-executive directors (NEDs)

The NEDs monitor the executive directors and contribute to the overall strategy and direction of the organisation. They are usually employed on a part-time basis and do not take part in the routine executive management of the company.

NEDs will:

- participate at board meetings.
- bring experience, insight and contacts to assist the board.
- sit on sub-committees as independent, knowledgeable parties.

Division of responsibilities

- The chair leads the board and is responsible for its overall effectiveness.
- The chair should ensure effective contribution of all board members.
- The chair should ensure that directors receive clear, accurate and timely information.
- The board should be balanced so that no individual or small group of individuals can dominate board decisions.

- NEDs should have sufficient time to meet their board responsibilities and should hold management to account.
- The board should ensure it has the policies, processes, information, time and resources it needs to function effectively and efficiently.

Composition, succession and evaluation

- Appointments to the board should be subject to a formal, rigorous and transparent procedure.
- An effective succession plan should be maintained for board and senior management.
- Appointments and succession should be based on merit and objective criteria and should promote diversity.
- The board and its committees should have a combination of skills, experience and knowledge.
- Annual evaluation of the board should consider its composition, diversity and how effectively members work together to achieve objectives.

Audit, risk and internal control including audit committees

- The board should establish formal and transparent policies and procedures to ensure the independence and effectiveness of internal and external audit functions and satisfy itself on the integrity of financial and narrative statements.
- The board should present a fair, balanced and understandable assessment of the company's position and prospects.
- The board should establish procedures to manage risk, oversee the internal control framework, and determine the nature and extent of the principal risks the company is willing to take in order to achieve its long-term strategic objectives.

Remuneration

- Remuneration should be designed to promote the long-term sustainable success of the company. Executive remuneration should be aligned to the company purpose, values and long-term strategy.
- The board should establish formal and transparent procedures for developing the policy for executive directors' remuneration.
- No director should be involved in setting their own pay.
- Directors should exercise independent judgment and discretion when authorising remuneration, taking account of company and individual performance, and wider circumstances.

Sarbanes-Oxley (SOX)

In 2002, following a number of corporate governance scandals such as Enron and WorldCom, tough new corporate governance regulations were introduced in the US by SOX.

- SOX is a rules-based approach to governance.

- SOX is extremely detailed and carries the full force of the law.

- SOX includes requirements for the Securities and Exchange Commission (SEC) to issue certain rules on corporate governance.

- It is relevant to US companies, directors of subsidiaries of US-listed businesses and auditors who are working on US-listed businesses.

Measures introduced by SOX

Measures introduced by SOX include:

- All companies with a listing for their shares in the US must provide a signed certificate to the SEC vouching for the accuracy of their financial statements (signed by CEO and CFO).

- If a company's financial statements are restated due to material noncompliance with accounting rules and standards, the CEO and chief finance officer (CFO) must forfeit bonuses awarded in the previous 12 months.

- Restrictions are placed on the type of non-audit work that can be performed for a company by its firm of auditors.

- The senior audit partner working on a client's audit must be changed at least every five years (i.e. audit partner rotation is compulsory).

- An independent five-man board called the Public Company Oversight Board has been established, with responsibilities for enforcing professional standards in accounting and auditing.

- Regulations on the disclosure of off-balance sheet transactions have been tightened up.

- Directors are prohibited from dealing in the shares of their company at 'sensitive times'.

King Report IV

The Institute of Directors in Southern Africa (IoDSA) formally introduced the King Code of Governance Principles and the King Report on Governance (King IV).

King IV was released on 1 November 2016. Previous versions were issued in 1994, 2002 and 2009.

It applies to all entities regardless of the manner and form of incorporation. Principles are drafted on the basis that, if they are adhered to, any entity would have practiced good governance.

King IV provides a new definition of corporate governance as being the achievement of:

1   Ethical culture

2   Good performance

3   Effective control

4   Legitimacy

The Code of governance should be used in conjunction with the Report in which recommendations of best practices are provided.

The Code is divided into five sections which address:

- leadership, ethics and corporate citizenship

- strategy, performance and reporting

- governing structures and delegation

- governance functional areas

- stakeholder relations

King IV has opted for an 'apply and explain' governance framework. This means that an application of the principles is assumed and companies need to explain how they have implemented the practices. This is to facilitate an outcomes-based approach rather than a rules-based approach.

King IV can be seen in full at:

http://www.iodsa.co.za

12 Rules and principles based approaches to corporate governance

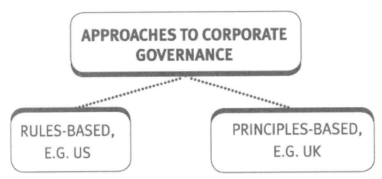

- A rules-based approach instils the code into law with appropriate penalties for transgression.

- A principles-based approach requires the company to adhere to the spirit rather than the letter of the code. The company must either comply with the code or explain why it has not through reports to the appropriate body and its shareholders.

The UK model is principles based and although it requires the company to adhere to the spirit of the code, and therefore best adopt best practice, it is governed by the Stock Exchange Listing Rules.

The listing rules provide statutory authority (via the Financial Service and Markets Act 2000) and require public listed companies to state how they have complied or explain why they have not under the "comply or explain" clause noted above. This provides a basis for comparing Corporate Statements.

There is no such requirement for disclosure of compliance in private company accounts.

The framework recommended by the UK Corporate Governance Code is principles-based and there is no 'one size fits all' solution.

The US model is enshrined into law by virtue of SOX. It is, therefore, a rules-based approach.

Choice of governance regime

The decision as to which approach to use for a country can be governed by many factors:

- dominant ownership structure (bank, family or multiple shareholder)
- legal system and its power/ability
- government structure and policies
- state of the economy
- culture and history
- levels of capital inflow or investment coming into the country
- global economic and political climate.

Comply or explain

A principles-based code requires the company to state that it has complied with the requirements of the code or to explain why it could not do so in its annual report. This will leave shareholders to draw their own conclusions regarding the governance of the company.

Arguments in favour of a rules-based approach (and against a principles-based approach)

Organisation's perspective:

- Clarity in terms of what the company must do – the rules are a legal requirement, clarity should exist and hence no interpretation is required.

- Standardisation for all companies – there is no choice as to complying or explaining and this creates a standardised and possibly fairer approach for all businesses.

- Binding requirements – the criminal nature makes it very clear that the rules must be complied with.

Wider stakeholder perspective:

- Standardisation across all companies – a level playing field is created.

- Sanction – the sanction is criminal and therefore a greater deterrent to transgression.

- Greater confidence in regulatory compliance.

Arguments against a rules-based approach (and in favour of a principles-based approach)

Organisation's perspective:

- Exploitation of loopholes – the exacting nature of the law lends itself to the seeking of loopholes.

- Underlying belief – the belief is that you must only play by the rules set. There is no suggestion that you should want to play by the rules (i.e. no 'buy-in' is required).

- Flexibility is lost – there is no choice in compliance to reflect the nature of the organisation, its size or stage of development.

- Checklist approach – this can arise as companies seek to comply with all aspects of the rules and start 'box-ticking'.

Wider stakeholder perspective:

- 'Regulation overload' – the volume of rules and amount of legislation may give rise to increasing costs for businesses and for the regulators.

- Legal costs – to enact new legislation to close loopholes.

- Limits – there is no room to improve, or go beyond the minimum level set.

- 'Box-ticking' rather than compliance – this does not lead to well governed organisations.

Issues in corporate governance relate to companies, and in particular listed companies whose shares are traded on major stock markets. However, similar issues might apply to smaller companies, and certainly to many large not-for-profit organisations.

	Large listed company	Private company	Not-for-profit organisation
Primary accountability	Shareholders and regulators	Shareholders	Fund providers, regulators, general public, members (where applicable).
Principal stakeholders	Shareholders	Shareholders	Donors, grant providers, regulators, general public, service users, members (if applicable).
Main methods of monitoring performance	Financial statements	Financial statements	Financial statements, other financial and nonfinancial measures.
Governance/ board structure	Executive and NEDs Appointment through formal process in line with governance requirements.	Executive directors Appointment may be the result of shareholding or other recruitment processes.	Volunteer trustees, paid and unpaid management team. Appointments through recruitment, recommendation or word of mouth, or election process.
Openness and transparency	In line with corporate governance requirements.	Limited disclosure requirements.	Limited requirements but large demand due to methods of funding.

- Corporate governance is a matter of great importance for large public companies, where the separation of ownership from management is much wider than for small private companies.

- Public companies raise capital on the stock markets, and institutional investors hold vast portfolios of shares and other investments. Investors need to know that their money is reasonably safe.

- Should there be any doubts about the integrity or intentions of the individuals in charge of a public company, the value of the company's shares will be affected and the company will have difficulty raising any new capital should it wish to do so.

- The scope of corporate governance for private and not-for-profit organisations will be much reduced when compared with a listed company, especially as there are no legal or regulatory requirements to comply with.

- The ownership and control, organisational objectives, risks and therefore focus may be different from a listed company. However, many of the governance principles will still be applicable to other entities.

- The public and not-for-profit sectors have voluntary best practice guidelines for governance which, while appreciating the differences in organisation and objective, cover many of the same topics (composition of governing bodies, accountability, risk management, transparency, etc.) included within the UK Corporate Governance Code.

- In not-for-profit organisations, a key governance focus will be to demonstrate to existing and potential fund providers that money is being spent in an appropriate manner, in line with the organisations' objectives.

Other governance codes

The Charity Governance Code

- **Principle 1: Organisational purpose** – The board is clear about the charity's aims and ensures that these are being delivered effectively and sustainably.

- **Principle 2: Leadership** – Every charity is headed by an effective board that provides strategic leadership in line with the charity's aims and values.

- **Principle 3: Integrity** – The board acts with integrity, adopting values and creating a culture which help achieve the organisation's charitable purposes. The board is aware of the importance of the public's confidence and trust in charities, and trustees undertake their duties accordingly.

- **Principle 4: Decision making, risk and control** – The board makes sure that its decision-making processes are informed, rigorous and timely, and that effective delegation, control and risk-assessment, and management systems are set up and monitored.

- **Principle 5: Board effectiveness** – The board works as an effective team, using the appropriate balance of skills, experience, backgrounds and knowledge to make informed decisions.

- **Principle 6: Equality, diversity and inclusion** – The board approach to diversity supports its effectiveness, leadership and decision-making.

- **Principle 7: Openness and accountability** – The board leads the organisation in being transparent and accountable. The charity is open in its work, unless there is good reason for it not to be.

The Good Governance Standard for Public Services

- Good governance means focusing on the organisation's purpose and on outcomes for citizens and service users.

- Good governance means performing effectively in clearly defined functions and roles.

- Good governance means promoting values for the whole organisation and demonstrating the values of good governance through behaviour.

- Good governance means taking informed, transparent decisions and managing risk.

- Good governance means developing the capacity and capability of the governing body to be effective.

- Good governance means engaging stakeholders and making accountability real.

13 Advantages and disadvantages of a governance code

Reasons for developing a code

- It should reduce instances of fraud and corruption improving shareholder perception and market confidence.

- There is statistical evidence that poor governance equates to poor performance.

- Management consultancy, McKinseys, found that global investors were willing to pay a significant premium for companies that are well governed.

- The existence of good governance is a decision factor for institutional investors.

- Even if it does not add value, it reduces risk and huge potential losses to shareholders.

Practical problems with a governance code

- The process is reactionary rather than proactive, responding to major failures in governance rather than setting the agenda.

- The impact varies depending on the nature of the company and the global viewpoint.

- Directors complain that it restricts or even dilutes individual decision-making power.

- It adds red tape and bureaucracy in the use of committees and disclosure requirements.

- Adherence to governance requirements harms competitiveness and does not add value.

- It cannot stop fraud.

14   Board committees

Importance of committees

Board sub-committees are a generally accepted part of board operations.

Positives that come out of the creation and use of such structures are:

- Reduces board workload and enables them to improve focus on other issues.

- Creates structures that can use inherent expertise to improve decisions in key areas.

- Communicates to shareholders that directors take these issues seriously.

- Increase in shareholder confidence.

- Communicates to stakeholders the importance of remuneration and risk.

- Satisfy requirements of the UK Corporate Governance Code (or other governance requirements).

Audit committee

Audit committees were first required under the Cadbury Code (and are now required by the UK Corporate Governance Code) in response to criticisms of the relationship between the directors and the auditors.

It was felt that the auditors were not sufficiently independent of the board of directors and that, as a result, the auditors were not providing their monitoring and reporting role as they should be.

Particular criticisms of the relationship were about:

- Remuneration of the auditors – decided by the directors.

- Appointment of the auditors – at the discretion of the directors in practice.

- Reports of the auditors – received by the directors.

- The directors had the power to give other lucrative work to auditors.

To address these concerns, audit committees were to be established.

- Audit committees are made up of non-executive directors (at least one of which should have recent relevant financial experience) and have formal terms of reference.

- The audit committee should meet at least three times per year, and also at least once a year have a meeting with the auditors without the presence of any executive directors.

Responsibilities of an audit committee

The responsibilities of the audit committee would typically include:

- Review of the financial statements, and any interim reports produced.

- Review of the company's system of internal financial controls.

- Discussion with the auditors about any significant matters that arose on the audit.

- Review of the internal audit programme and significant findings of the internal auditors.

- Recommendations on the appointment and removal of the auditors.

- The setting of the audit fee in discussion with the auditors.

- Review of the audit report and any management letter provided by the external auditors.

- Review all the company's internal control and risk management systems (unless this is delegated to a separate risk committee).

- Ensure that a system is in place for whistleblowing.

Nominations/Appointments Committee

The need for nominations committee is identified in many codes of best practice.

As an example, the UK Corporate Governance Code requires that **there should be a formal, rigorous and transparent procedure for the appointments of new directors to the board:**

- Creation of a nominations committee.

- This should have a majority of NEDs, the chairman should chair except when considering his or her successor.

- Evaluation of candidate's skills, knowledge and expertise is vital.

- Chairman's other commitments should be noted in the annual report.

- NED terms and conditions available for inspection, other commitments stated.

- Executives should not be members of any other FTSE 100 company board.

- A separate section of the annual report should describe the work of the committee.

Responsibilities of nominations committee

The main responsibilities and duties of the nominations committee are to:

- Review regularly the structure, size and composition of the board and make recommendations to the board.

- Consider the balance between executives and NEDs on the board of directors.

- Ensure appropriate management of diversity to board composition.

- Provide an appropriate balance of power to reduce domination in executive selection by the CEO/chairman.

- Regularly evaluate the balance of skills, knowledge and experience of the board.

- Give full consideration to succession planning for directors.

- Prepare a description of the role and capabilities required for any particular board appointment including that of the chairman.

- Identify and nominate for the approval by the board candidates to fill board vacancies as and when they arise.

- Make recommendations to the board concerning the standing for reappointment of directors.

- Be seen to operate independently for the benefit of shareholders.

Remuneration committee

The role of the remuneration committee

The role of the remuneration committee is to have an appropriate reward policy that attracts, retains and motivates directors to achieve the long-term interests of shareholders.

Objectives of the committee

- The committee is, and is seen to be, independent with access to its own external advice or consultants.

- It has a clear policy on remuneration that is well understood and has the support of shareholders.

- Performance packages produced are aligned with long-term shareholder interests and have challenging targets.

- Reporting is clear, concise and gives the reader of the annual report a bird's-eye view of policy payments and the rationale behind them.

The whole area of executive pay is one where trust must be created or restored through good governance and this is exercised through the use of a remuneration committee.

Responsibilities of the remuneration committee

The overall responsibilities of the remuneration committee are to:

- Determine and regularly review the framework, broad policy and specific terms for the remuneration and terms and conditions of employment of the chairman of the board and of executive directors (including design of targets and any bonus scheme payments).

- Recommend and monitor the level and structure of the remuneration of senior managers.

- Establish pension provision policy for all board members.

- Set detailed remuneration for all executive directors and the chairman, including pension rights and any compensation payments.

- Ensure that the executive directors and key management are fairly rewarded for their individual contribution to the overall performance of the company.

- Demonstrate to shareholders that the remuneration of the executive directors and key management is set by individuals with no personal interest in the outcome of the decisions of the committee.

- Agree any compensation for loss of office of any executive director.

15 The effects of corporate governance on directors' powers and duties

Directors' powers and duties can generally be determined by reference to the company's constitution and shareholder agreement. In addition, they may be derived from individual contracts of service and company law.

A director owes his or her duties to the company itself, that is to the shareholders as a body and those duties are enforceable by the company.

One of the ways in which corporate governance affects a director's duties and powers is by having a board with non-executive directors. Non-executive directors can scrutinise decisions made by executive directors. They can also take responsibility for monitoring the performance of executive management, especially with regard to the progress made towards achieving the determined company strategy and objectives.

The board sub-committees discussed above (nominations/remunerations/audit) can also detach a director from making decisions which in the past would have been within their powers.

The rules and standards which make up corporate governance are aimed at a much wider audience than just shareholders. The rules are intended to benefit stakeholders. It can therefore be argued that the legal duties a director has and the rules and standards which make up corporate governance have different aims. A director could be in breach of his or her legal duty yet still be complying with the principles of corporate governance.

16 Test your understanding questions

Test your understanding 1

List examples of profit-seeking organisations.

Test your understanding 2

What does a code of corporate governance cover?

Test your understanding 3

Which of the following is correct?

A   It is a criminal offence for listed companies to fail to comply with the UK Corporate Governance Code.

B   A listed public company has complied with the UK Corporate Governance Code if it produces a report explaining why it has not implemented its recommendations.

C   The UK Corporate Governance Code has no status and may be ignored by all companies.

D   A public company may be sued for breach of statutory duty if it fails to comply with the UK Corporate Governance Code.

Test your understanding 4

Which of the following apply a rules-based approach to corporate governance?

A   Sarbanes-Oxley

B   UK Corporate Governance Code

C   King IV

D   All of the above

Test your understanding 5

How often should the audit committee meet?

Test your understanding answers

Test your understanding 1

Sole traders

Partnerships

Limited liability companies

Test your understanding 2

A code will tend to cover:

- The role of the board of directors

- The reliability of financial reports and the relationship between the company and its auditors

- The interest of the company's shareholders in the company.

Test your understanding 3

B

The UK Corporate Governance Code is not contained in any statute. The code is effectively a 'comply or explain' code. It follows that a company which explains why it has not taken up the recommendations of the Code would nonetheless be complying with it.

Test your understanding 4

A

Sarbanes-Oxley follows a rules-based approach.

Test your understanding 5

The audit committee should meet at least three times per year, and also at least once a year have a meeting with the auditors without the presence of any executive directors.

Controls

Chapter learning objectives

Upon completion of this chapter you will be able to:

- identify the requirements for external audit and the basic processes undertaken

- explain the meaning of fair presentation

- distinguish between external and internal audit

- explain the purpose and basic procedures of internal audit; the need for financial controls and the purpose of audit checks and audit trails

- explain the role of internal audit in non-financial monitoring and control activities

- illustrate the added value internal audit provides to both the board and management of the corporation

- explain the nature of errors

- explain the nature of fraud

- describe the different methods of fraud prevention and detection.

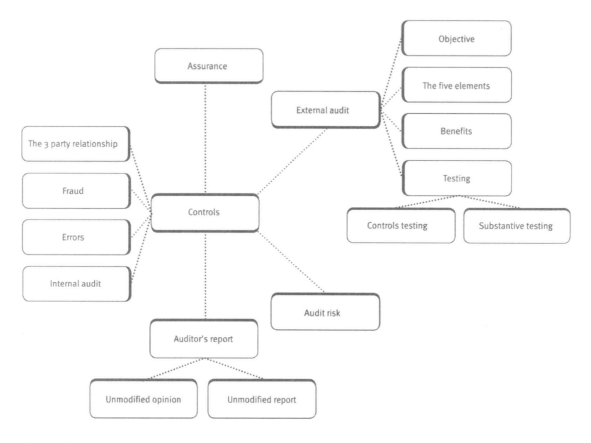

1 Assurance

An assurance engagement is one in which a **practitioner** expresses a conclusion designed to enhance the degree of confidence the **intended users** other than the **responsible party** have about the outcome of the evaluation or measurement of a subject matter against **criteria**.

The 3 party relationship

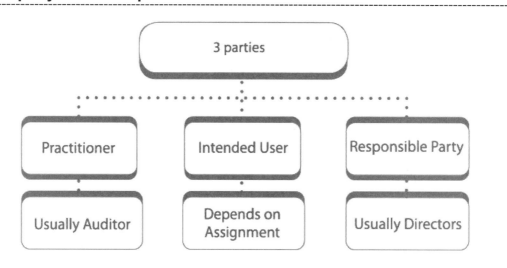

Examples of assurance engagements

- Statutory/external audit
- Fraud investigations
- Due diligence
- Internal controls assessment
- Business plan/projection reviews
- Environmental audits.

The objectives and processes of an external audit engagement will now be considered in more detail.

2 External audit engagement

Objective of an external audit engagement

The objective of an **external audit engagement** is to enable the auditor to express an opinion on whether the financial statements

- Give a fairly presented view (or fairly presented in all material respects).
- Are prepared, in all material respects, in accordance with an applicable financial reporting framework.

The financial reporting framework to be applied will vary from country to country.

The objectives of an **auditor** are to:

- Obtain reasonable assurance about whether the financial statements as a whole are free from material misstatement, whether due to fraud or error.
- Express an opinion on whether the financial statements are prepared, in all material respects, in accordance with an applicable financial reporting framework.
- Report on the financial statements, and communicate in accordance with the auditor's findings.

The purpose of an audit is to enhance the degree of confidence of the intended users in the financial statement. This is not 100% guarantee, but reasonable assurance.

The five elements of an external audit engagement

1   The three parties involved:

  – the preparers – management/directors

  – the users – shareholders

  – the practitioner – the auditors.

2   The subject matter: the financial statements (prepared by management).

3   Sufficient appropriate evidence: obtained by performing audit procedures and reviewing the financial statements.

  – **Sufficiency** relates to the **quantity** of evidence.

  – **Appropriateness** relates to the **quality** or relevance and reliability of evidence.

4   This includes evaluating whether the financial statements are prepared in accordance with a relevant financial reporting framework (i.e. suitable criteria).

5   The audit report: which is presented to the shareholders. This report summarises the auditor's opinion as to whether the financial statements are fairly presented i.e. "true and fair".

An external audit is when an independent expert examines and checks the financial statements. The auditor will then prepare a report to present to the shareholders.

Some organisations are required by law to have their financial statements audited by an independent, qualified accountant. Others choose to have their financial statements audited on a voluntary basis, as the existence of an audit report may be beneficial to them.

The objective of an audit is for the auditor to express an opinion as to whether the financial statements are fairly presented, i.e. that they

• show a true (accurate) and fair (unbiased) view

• have been prepared in accordance with 'specific legislation' (thus will vary internationally).

The purpose of an audit is to give users confidence in the financial statements. This is not 100% guarantee, but reasonable assurance.

Need for external audit

- Shareholders provide the finance for a company and may or may not be involved in the day to day running of the company.

- Directors manage the company on behalf of the shareholders in order to achieve the objectives of that company (normally the maximisation of shareholder wealth).

- The directors must prepare financial statements to provide information on performance and financial position to the shareholders.

- The directors have various incentives to manipulate the financial statements and show a different level of performance.

- Hence the need for an independent review of the financial statements to ensure they give a true and fair view – the external audit.

In most developed countries, publicly quoted companies and large companies are required by law to produce annual financial statements and have them audited by an external auditor.

Companies that are not required to have a statutory audit may choose to have an external audit because the company's shareholders or other influential stakeholders want one and because of the benefits of an audit.

Benefits of an audit

- Improves the quality and reliability of information, giving investors faith in and improving the reputation of the market.

- Independent scrutiny and verification may be valuable to management.

- May reduce the risk of management bias, fraud and error by acting as a deterrent.

- May detect bias, fraud and error.

- Enhances the credibility of the financial statements, e.g. for tax authorities or lenders.

- Deficiencies in the internal control system may be highlighted by the auditor.

Expectations gap

Some users incorrectly believe that an audit provides absolute assurance; that the audit opinion is a guarantee the financial statements are 'correct'. This and other misconceptions about the role of an auditor are referred to as the **'expectations gap'**.

Examples of the expectations gap

- a belief that auditors test **all** transactions and balances; they test on a sample basis.

- a belief that auditors are required to detect **all** fraud; auditors are required to provide reasonable assurance that the financial statements are free from **material** misstatement, which may be caused by fraud.

- a belief that auditors are responsible for **preparing** the financial statements; this is the responsibility of management.

Auditors provide reasonable assurance which is not absolute assurance. The **limitations of an audit** mean that it is not possible to provide a 100% guarantee.

Limitations of an audit

- **F**inancial statements include subjective estimates and other judgemental matters.

- **I**nternal controls may be relied on which have their own inherent limitations.

- **R**epresentations from management may have to be relied upon as the only source of evidence in some areas.

- **E**vidence is often persuasive not conclusive.

- **D**o not test all transactions and balances. Auditors test on a sample basis.

Rights of auditors

In order to carry out their duties, auditors are given certain rights:

- access to accounting records

- access to information and explanations as necessary

- to receive notice of, attend and speak at general meetings of shareholders

- rights relating to their removal, resignation and retirement.

Fair presentation or true and fair

Fair presentation or 'true and fair' means that financial statements prepared for external publication should fairly reflect the financial position of the organisation. They should be free of material misstatements arising from negligence or deliberate manipulation. It may not be economically viable to test every single transaction, or to ensure 100 per cent accuracy, but fair presentation assumes that the financial statements do not contain any significant errors that would affect the actions of those reading them. This is based on the materiality convention discussed below. It is the duty of the registered auditor to test the financial statements for material misstatement and to report on whether they are presented fairly.

The materiality convention and the auditor

The purpose of an audit is to allow the auditor to form an opinion and to report accordingly on whether or not the financial statements fairly present the position and performance of a company.

To achieve this the auditor tests the transactions, accounting balances and disclosures reported in the financial statements. They cannot test everything so they select samples for testing based upon their assessment of where the greatest risk of material misstatement lies.

Following testing the auditor considers the results and conclusions of the tests, evaluating in particular any identified misstatements.

Testing

On the whole auditors perform two broad forms of tests.

The first is known as controls testing, which involves assessing the reliability of accounting systems, procedures and controls. If these appear to be working satisfactorily, the auditors can place a degree of reliance on them and that means that they do not need to test those areas in detail.

If there are areas of doubt, areas of high risk or items of a material nature, the auditors choose to carry out more detailed testing designed to detect material misstatement, known as substantive testing.

Audit risk

- Auditors usually adopt a risk–based approach to auditing.
- Effective risk assessment should:
    - Make the audit more efficient with work directed to likely problem areas.
    - Lead to fewer inappropriate opinions.
    - Result in fewer negligence claims against auditor.

Risk the auditor comes to an incorrect opinion = AUDIT RISK

$$AR = IR \times CR \times DR$$

Inherent risk

The susceptibility of a transaction, account balance or disclosure to material misstatement irrespective of the internal controls in place.

Inherent risk can be considered at the:

- Industry level
    - Affects the whole industry
    - e.g. highly regulated industries such as banking.

- Entity level
    - Affects the whole entity
    - e.g. Company may not be a going concern, management get profit related bonuses.

- Balance level
    - Inherent risk is isolated to one balance
    - e.g. items which are complex or subjective.

Control risk

The risk that a material misstatement would not be prevented, detected or corrected by the accounting and internal control systems.

Detection risk

The risk that the auditor's procedures will not detect a misstatement that exists in an account balance or class of transactions that could be material, either individually or when aggregated with misstatements in other balances or classes.

Example:

Audit risk = Inherent risk × Control risk × Detection risk

$\downarrow$ $\downarrow$

Highly regulated business   Poor controls

HIGH × HIGH × LOW

As the auditor has little or no control over the levels of inherent risk or control risk, this means that the only way to ensure the overall audit risk is acceptable is for the auditor to manipulate the detection risk, by increasing or reducing substantive testing.

In order for the auditor's opinion to be considered trustworthy auditors must come to their conclusions having completed a thorough examination of the books and records of their clients and they must document the procedures performed and evidence obtained, to support the conclusions reached.

As discussed earlier the auditor needs to obtain sufficient appropriate evidence.

Sufficiency relates to the quantity of evidence.

Appropriateness relates to the **quality** or relevance and reliability of evidence.

Sufficient evidence

There needs to be 'enough' evidence to support the auditor's conclusion. This is a matter of professional judgement. When determining whether there is enough evidence the auditor must consider:

- the risk of material misstatement
- the materiality of the item
- the nature of accounting and internal control systems
- the auditor's knowledge and experience of the business
- the results of controls tests
- the size of a population being tested
- the size of the sample selected to test
- the reliability of the evidence obtained.

Appropriate evidence

Appropriateness of evidence breaks down into two important concepts:

*   reliability

*   relevance.

Reliability

Auditors should always attempt to obtain evidence from the most trustworthy and dependable source possible. Evidence is considered more reliable when it is:

*   obtained from an independent external source

*   generated internally but subject to effective control

*   obtained directly by the auditor

*   in documentary form

*   in original form.

Broadly speaking, the more reliable the evidence the less of it the auditor will need. However, if evidence is unreliable it will never be appropriate for the audit, no matter how much is gathered.

Relevance

To be relevant audit evidence has to address the objective/purpose of a procedure. For example, when attending an inventory count, the auditor will:

*   select a sample of items from physical inventory and trace them to inventory records to confirm the **completeness** of accounting records

*   select a sample of items from inventory records and trace them to physical inventories to confirm the **existence** of inventory assets.

Whilst the procedures are perhaps similar in nature their purpose (and relevance) is to test different **assertions** regarding inventory balances.

3 Agency and stewardship

The concepts of agency and stewardship were discussed in the previous chapter. We will now consider how these concepts apply to the role of the auditor.

Agency

The relationship of the company with its auditors is a principal-agent relationship.

*   The audit is seen as a key component of corporate governance, providing an independent review of the financial position of the organisation.

*   Auditors act as agents to principals (shareholders) when performing an audit and this relationship brings similar concerns with regard to trust and confidence as the director-shareholder relationship.

- Like directors, auditors will have their own interests and motives to consider.

- Auditor independence from the board of directors is of great importance to shareholders and is seen as a key factor in helping to deliver audit quality. However, an audit necessitates a close working relationship with the board of directors of a company.

- This close relationship has led (and continues to lead) shareholders to question the perceived and actual independence of auditors so tougher controls and standards have been introduced to protect them.

Stewardship

Auditors can be seen as stewards of a company. They are directly accountable to the shareholders for their period of office and hence owe a duty of care to the company's existing shareholders as a body i.e. to the company as a whole.

The Audit Firm Governance Code (explained in more detail later on in this chapter) requires auditors to engage regularly with the owners of the companies which they audit.

4 The engagement letter

The engagement letter specifies the nature of the **contract** between the audit firm.

Its purpose is to

- minimise the risk of any misunderstanding between the auditor and client
- confirm acceptance of the engagement
- set out the terms and conditions of the engagement.

The letter will be **sent before the audit commences**.

It should be **reviewed every year** to ensure that it is up to date but does not need to be reissued every year unless there are changes to the terms of the engagement. The auditor must issue a **new engagement letter if the scope or context** of the assignment **changes** after initial appointment.

The contents of the engagement letter

The main contents should include:

- the objective and scope of the audit.
- the responsibilities of the auditor.
- the responsibilities of management.
- the identification of an applicable financial reporting framework.
- reference to the expected form and content of any reports to be issued.

In addition the following items will be included:

- Reference to professional standards, regulations and legislation applicable to the audit.

- Limitations of an audit.

- Expectation that management will provide written representations.

- Basis on which the fees are calculated.

- Agreement of management to notify the auditor of subsequent events after the audit report is signed.

- Agreement of management to provide draft financial statements in time to allow the audit to be completed by the deadline.

- Form (and timing) of any other communication during the audit.

Other matters that the engagement letter may cover include:

- Arrangements concerning the involvement of internal auditors and other staff of the entity.

- Limitations to the auditor's liability.

5 Planning an audit

Audits are potentially complex, risky and expensive processes. It is vital that engagements are planned to ensure that the auditor:

- devotes appropriate attention to important areas of the audit

- identifies and resolves potential problems on a timely basis

- organises and manages the audit so that it is performed in an effective and efficient manner

- selects team members with appropriate capabilities and competencies

- directs and supervises the team and reviews their work

- effectively coordinates the work of others, such as experts and internal audit.

Planning ensures that the risk of performing a poor quality audit (and ultimately giving an inappropriate audit opinion) is reduced to an acceptable level.

The planning process

Planning consists of a number of elements. They can be summarised as:

- Preliminary engagement activities:
  - evaluating compliance with ethical requirements
  - establishing the terms of the engagement.
- Planning activities:
  - developing the audit strategy
  - developing an audit plan.

The audit strategy

The audit strategy sets the scope, timing and direction of the audit. It allows the auditor to determine the following:

- the resources to deploy for specific audit areas (e.g. experience level, external experts)

- the amount of resources to allocate (i.e. number of team members)

- when the resources are to be deployed

- how the resources are managed, directed and supervised, including the timings of meetings, debriefs and reviews.

The audit plan

Once the audit strategy has been established, the next stage is to develop a specific, detailed plan to address how the various matters identified in the overall strategy will be applied.

The strategy sets the overall approach to the audit, the plan fills in the operational details of how the strategy is to be achieved.

6 Reporting to those charged with governance

'Those charged with governance' includes the directors of a company and the members of its Audit Committee where one exists.

Matters to be communicated to those charged with governance include

- The responsibilities of the auditor in relation to the financial statements audit

- An overview of the planned scope and timing of the audit

- Significant findings of the audit

- For listed clients, matters that have a bearing on auditor Independence and the safeguards that have been put in place to eliminate them.

Communication shall be in any appropriate form, although the matters that must be communicated with regards to independence for listed clients must be communicated in writing.

Communicating deficiencies in internal control to those charged with governance

This covers reporting deficiencies in internal control that have been identified during the course of the audit. It is a by-product of the audit and may not be a comprehensive list of deficiencies.

This report, traditionally known as a management letter, is usually sent at the end of the audit process.

The report would generally include:

- A covering letter.

- Appendices showing, typically in tabular format, the control deficiencies, implications and recommendations for improvement.

The table in the appendix would normally have 3 sections:

Deficiency	Consequences	Recommendations
Statement of fact – in the exam this is normally given to you so does not need to be repeated	Cost to the business (e.g. losses, adverse impact on cash flow, loss of customer goodwill) Possibility of misstatements in the financial statements	Specific (who/what/when/how) Commercially feasible

When the auditor reports deficiencies, it should be made clear that:

- The report is not a comprehensive list of deficiencies, but only those that have come to light during normal audit procedures.

- The report is for the sole use of the company.

- No disclosure should be made to a third party without the written agreement of the auditor.

- No responsibility is assumed to any other parties.

7 Written representation letter

 A **written representation** is: a written statement by management provided to the auditor to confirm certain matters or to support other audit evidence.

The purpose of obtaining this form of evidence is:

- to obtain evidence that management, and those charged with governance, have fulfilled their responsibility (as agreed and acknowledged in the terms of the audit engagement) for the preparation of the financial statements, including:

  - preparing the financial statements in accordance with an applicable financial reporting framework

  - providing the auditor with all relevant information and access to records

  - recording all transactions and reflecting them in the financial statements.

- to support other audit evidence relevant to the financial statements if determined necessary by the auditor.

A representation to support other audit evidence may be appropriate where more reliable forms of evidence are not available, particularly in relation to matters requiring management judgement or knowledge restricted to management. Examples include:

- plans or intentions that may affect the carrying value of assets or liabilities

- confirmation of values where there is a significant degree of estimation or judgement involved, e.g. provisions and contingent liabilities

- formal confirmation of the directors' judgement on contentious issues, e.g. the value of assets where there is a risk of impairment

- aspects of laws and regulations that may affect the financial statements, including compliance.

A written representation should be in the form of a representation letter addressed to the auditor.

Note that written representations cannot substitute for more reliable evidence that should be available and do not constitute sufficient appropriate evidence on their own, about any of the matters with which they deal.

Written representations should only be sought to support other audit evidence.

In practice, the auditor will often draft the written representations letter but it must be printed on client headed paper and signed by the client.

The letter must be signed by an appropriate senior member of client management, with appropriate responsibilities for the financial statements and knowledge of the matters concerned. This would normally be the chief executive and chief financial officer.

The date of the written representation letter should be the same as the date the financial statements are authorised. It must be obtained (and signed) before the audit report is finalised.

8   Audit report

As discussed above one of the objectives of an auditor is to express an opinion which is executed through a written report.

When the auditor concludes that the financial statements are prepared, in all material respects, in accordance with the applicable financial reporting framework they issue an **unmodified opinion** in the audit report.

If there are no other matters which the auditor wishes to draw to the attention of the users, they will issue an **unmodified report**.

Contents of an unmodified audit report

The other types of audit report are:

- Modified without modifying the opinion – the financial statements show a true and fair view but there is something that needs to be brought to the attention of the user by way of an additional paragraph.

- Modified with a modified opinion – the financial statements don't fully show a true and fair view or the auditor has not obtained sufficient appropriate evidence to make that conclusion.

9   Audit Firm Governance Code

In January 2010 the FRC and Institute of Chartered Accountants in England and Wales (ICAEW) published the Audit Firm Governance Code. The code was revised in July 2016.

The Code is the result of a recommendation in the October 2007 report of the FRC's Market Participants Group that "every firm that audits public interest entities should comply with the provisions of a Combined Code-style best practice corporate governance guide or give a considered explanation".

The Working Group recommended that the code should be applicable to those firms that audit more than 20 listed companies and that it should apply to financial years beginning on or after 1 June 2010.

The Code applies to eight audit firms that together audit about 95% of the companies listed on the Main Market of the London Stock Exchange.

The purpose of the Code is to provide a formal benchmark of good governance practice against which firms which audit listed companies can report for the benefit of the shareholders in such companies.

The full code can be accessed here:

https://www.frc.org.uk/auditors/audit-assurance/audit-firm-governance-code

Contents

The Code is split into five sections. It comprises twenty principles which are supported by thirty-one provisions.

The main principles of each section are outlined below (reference to 'a firm' means 'a firm that audits listed companies'):

Leadership

1　The management of a firm should be accountable to the firm's owners and no individual should have unfettered powers of decision.

2　A firm should have effective management which has responsibility and clear authority for running the firm.

Values

1　A firm should perform quality work by exercising judgement and upholding values of integrity, objectivity, professional competence and due care, confidentiality and professional behaviour in a way that properly takes the public interest into consideration and meets auditing and ethical standards.

2　A firm should publicly commit itself to this Audit Firm Governance Code.

3　A firm should maintain a culture of openness which encourages people to consult and share problems, knowledge and experience in order to achieve quality work in a way that properly takes the public interest into consideration.

Independent Non-Executives

1　A firm should appoint independent non-executives to the governance structure who through their involvement collectively enhance the firm's performance in meeting the purpose of the Code.

2　The independent non-executives' duty of care is to the firm. They should command the respect of the firm's owners and collectively enhance shareholder confidence by virtue of their independence, number, stature, experience and expertise. They should have a balance of relevant skills and experience including of audit and a regulated sector. At least one independent non-executive should have competence in accounting and/or auditing, gained for example from a role on an audit committee, in a company's finance function, as an investor or at an audit firm.

3   Independent non-executives of a firm should have rights consistent with their role including a right of access to relevant information and people to the extent permitted by law or regulation, and a right to report a fundamental disagreement regarding the firm to its owners and, where ultimately this cannot be resolved and the independent non-executive resigns, to report this resignation publicly.

Operations

1   A firm should comply with professional standards and applicable legal and regulatory requirements. Operations should be conducted in a way that promotes audit quality and the reputation of the firm. The independent non-executives should be involved in the oversight of operations.

2   A firm should maintain a sound system of internal control and risk management over the operations of the firm as a whole to safeguard the firm and reassure stakeholders.

3   A firm should apply policies and procedures for managing people across the whole firm that support its commitment to the professionalism, openness and risk management principles of this Audit Firm Governance Code.

4   A firm should establish and apply confidential whistleblowing policies and procedures across the firm which enable people to report, without fear, concerns about the firm's commitment to quality work and professional judgement and values in a way that properly takes the public interest into consideration. The independent non-executives should be satisfied that there is an effective whistleblowing process in place.

Reporting

1   The management of a firm should ensure that members of its governance structures, including owners and independent non-executives, are supplied with information in a timely manner and in a form and of a quality appropriate to enable them to discharge their duties.

2   A firm should publicly report how it has applied in practice each of the principles of the Audit Firm Governance Code and make a statement on its compliance with the Code's provisions or give a considered explanation for any non-compliance.

3   A firm should publish on an annual basis in its transparency report a commentary on the firm's performance, position and prospects.

4   A firm should establish formal and transparent arrangements for monitoring the quality of external reporting and for maintaining an appropriate relationship with the firm's auditors.

5   A firm should publish audited financial statements prepared in accordance with a recognised financial reporting framework such as International Financial Reporting Standards or UK GAAP, and should be clear and concise.

Dialogue

1   A firm should have dialogue with listed company shareholders, as well as listed companies and their audit committees, about matters covered by this Audit Firm Governance Code to enhance mutual communication and understanding and ensure that it keeps in touch with shareholder opinion, issues and concerns.

2   Shareholders should have dialogue with audit firms to enhance mutual communication and understanding.

3   Shareholders should have dialogue with listed companies on the process of recommending the appointment and re-appointment of auditors and should make considered use of votes in relation to such recommendations.

Current issues and developments affecting the audit profession

Despite the rules and regulations detailed above, audit failures such as Carillion and Wirecard (covered in Chapter 3) continue to happen. As a result, several investigations have been performed and reports issued which propose major reforms to the auditing profession.

The UK government ordered a review of the UK regulator, the Financial Reporting Council (FRC), by Sir John Kingman.

Kingman Report findings

- The FRC is not fit for purpose, outdated and in need of being rebuilt from the ground up. A new regulatory body is required to change the culture and increase effectiveness.

- Appointments of key staff are often made without open advertising or the use of external consultants. Recruitment processes therefore require overhauling.

- The FRC is funded partially by a levy on audit firms and is too close to those it is supposed to regulate which reduces its independence and effectiveness. The Audit, Reporting and Governance Authority (ARGA), the proposed new regulator should have statutory recognition and funding to overcome this conflict. The FRC is currently in transition to ARGA, with the transition expecting to be completed in 2023.

- Auditors should have a duty to report viability or other serious concerns to try and prevent corporate failures, similar to the system in France.

- ARGA should be given the power to make recommendations to a company's shareholders that they take action in serious cases which require intervention, such as dismissing senior staff or cutting dividends.

- ARGA must be more proactive in taking action against firms who fail to uphold the reputation of the profession.

In addition to the Kingman Report, an independent review of the quality and effectiveness of audit has been carried out by Sir Donald Brydon.

Brydon Report findings

The Brydon Report contains a range of proposals for audit reform including:

- Redefining audits and requiring auditors to provide decision useful information to users of the auditor's report.

- A statement to be provided by the auditor that they are acting in the public interest and have regard to the interests of users other than shareholders.

- The auditing profession should be independent of, rather than an extension to, the accounting profession. ARGA should be the statutory regulator of the auditing profession.

- Professional suspicion should be introduced in addition to professional scepticism and professional judgement.

- Providing the shareholders with a formal opportunity to influence the scope of the audit and hold the audit committee and auditor to account.

- Replacing the true and fair wording with the term 'present fairly in all material respects'.

- Introducing new reporting requirements for directors in the form of a Corporate Audit and Assurance Policy, a Resilience Statement and a Public Interest Statement on which the auditor would be required to provide assurance.

- Similar requirements to those of Sarbanes Oxley Act in respect of CEO and CFO attestation of the internal controls of the company.

- Increased responsibilities in relation to fraud detection and prevention.

- Greater disclosure by the auditor of the profitability of the audit work, the remuneration of the audit engagement partner, the hours spent on each audit by grade, clear reasons for resignation, dismissal or decision not to retender.

- ARGA should work with auditors to increase the use of technology and data analytics to promote increased audit quality.

10   Internal audit

Function and importance of internal audit

- Internal audit is a management control. The department reviews the effectiveness of other controls within a company.

- It is part of the control systems of a company, with the aim of ensuring that other controls are working correctly.

- In some regimes, it is a statutory requirement to have internal audit. In others, codes of corporate governance strongly suggest that an internal audit department is necessary.

- The work of internal audit is varied – from reviewing financial controls through to checking compliance with legislation.

- The department is normally under the control of a chief internal auditor who reports to the audit committee.

Roles of internal audit

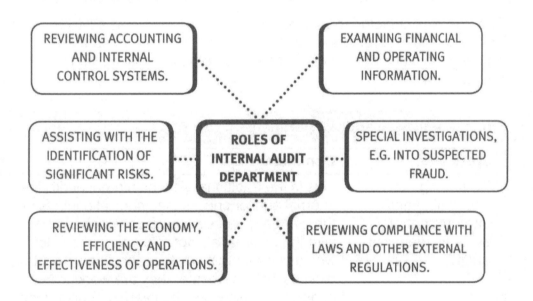

Companies must create a strong system of internal control in order to fulfil their responsibilities.

However, it is not sufficient to simply have mechanisms in place to manage a business; their effectiveness must be regularly evaluated. All systems need some form of monitoring and feedback. This is the role of internal audit.

Having an internal audit department is generally considered to be 'best practice,' but is not required by law. This allows flexibility in the way internal audit is established to suit the needs of a business.

In small, or owner managed businesses there is unlikely to be a need for internal audit because the owners are able to exercise more direct control over operations, and are accountable to fewer stakeholders.

The need for internal audit, therefore will depend on:

- Scale and diversity of activities. In a larger, diversified organisation there is a risk that controls don't work as effectively because of the delegation of responsibility down the organisation. Internal audit can report back to the audit committee if controls are not as effective as they should be.

- Complexity of operations. The more complex the organisation is, the more benefit can be obtained from having an internal audit function to evaluate as there is greater risk of things going wrong. With a larger organisation the consequences of poor controls/risk management/corporate governance practices are likely to be greater.

- Number of employees. The greater the number of employees the greater the risk of fraud.

- Cost/benefit considerations. It will only be worth establishing an internal audit function if the benefits outweigh the costs. For example a company might be losing money as a result of fraud, not using the most cost effective or reliable suppliers, incurring fines for noncompliance with laws and regulations. If these costs outweigh the cost of employing an internal audit function it will be beneficial to the company to establish a department.

- The desire of senior management to have assurance and advice on risk and control. The directors may wish to have the comfort that there is ongoing monitoring of the organisation to help them discharge their responsibilities.

Roles of internal audit department

Work area	Comment
Reviewing accounting and internal control systems (financial audit)	This is the traditional view of internal audit. The internal auditor checks the financial controls in the company, possibly assisting or sharing work with the external auditor. The internal auditor would comment on whether appropriate controls exist as well as whether they are working correctly. In this work, the internal auditor does not manage risk, but simply reports on controls.
Assisting with the identification of significant risks	In this function, the internal auditor does start to work on risks. The auditor may be asked to investigate areas of risk management, with specific reference on how the company identifies, assesses and controls significant risks from both internal and external sources.
Reviewing the economy, efficiency and effectiveness of operations (operational audit)	This is also called a value for money (VFM) audit. The auditor checks whether a particular activity is cost effective (economical), uses the minimum inputs for a given output (efficient) and meets its stated objectives (effective).

Examining financial and operating information	Internal auditors ensure that reporting of financial information is made on a timely basis and that the information in the reports is factually accurate.
Special investigations	Investigations into other areas of the company's business, e.g. checking the cost estimates for a new factory.
Reviewing compliance with laws and other external regulations	This objective is particularly relevant regarding SOX where the internal auditor will be carrying out detailed work to ensure that internal control systems and financial reports meet stock exchange requirements.

Types of audit work

The internal audit department will carry out many different types of audit, as highlighted by the department's varied roles.

Examples of audit types are:

- financial audit

- operational audit

- project audit

- value for money audit

- social and environmental audit

- management audit.

Types of audit

Financial audit

Financial auditing is traditionally the main area of work for the internal audit department. It embraces:

- the conventional tasks of examining records and evidence to support financial and management reporting in order to detect errors and prevent fraud

- analysing information, identifying trends and potentially significant variations from the norm.

Operational auditing covers:

- examination and review of a business operation

- the effectiveness of controls

- identification of areas for improvement in efficiency and performance including improving operational economy, efficiency and effectiveness – the three Es of value for money auditing.

There are four main areas where such an approach is commonly used

- procurement

- marketing

- treasury

- human resources.

Project auditing

Best value and IT assignments are really about looking at processes within the organisation and asking:

- were things done well?

- did the organisation achieve value for money?

Project auditing is about looking at a specific project:

- commissioning a new factory

- implementing new IT systems

and asking whether these were done well. So the focus is different and has more to do with:

- were the objectives achieved?

- was the project implemented efficiently.

- what lessons can be learned from any mistakes made?

A number of projects when taken together can become a programme.

Value for money audit

An area that internal auditors have been getting increasingly involved in is the value for money audits. These have been replaced in terminology more recently by "best value" audits, but many of the principles remain the same.

In a value for money audit the auditor assesses three main areas.

- Economy

  The economy of a business is assessed by looking at the inputs to the business (or process), and deciding whether these are the most economical that are available at an acceptable quality level. For example, if assessing the economy of a commercial company the inputs would be capital (plant and machinery, buildings, etc.), raw materials, the workforce and any administrative function required to run the business.

- Efficiency

  The efficiency of an operation is assessed by considering how well the operation converts inputs to outputs. In a manufacturing company this might involve looking at wastage in production or quality control failures for example.

- Effectiveness

  The effectiveness of an organisation is assessed by examining whether the organisation is achieving its objectives. To assess effectiveness there must be clear objectives for the organisation that can be examined. In some organisations, particularly not for profit and public service organisations, deciding suitable objectives can be one of the most difficult parts of the value for money exercise.

Social and environment audit

An environment audit is defined as:

> 'A management tool comprising a systematic, documented, periodic, and objective evaluation of how well organisations, management, and equipment are performing, with the aim of contributing to safeguarding the environment by facilitating management control of environmental practices, and assessing compliance with company policies, which would include meeting regulatory requirements and standards applicable.'

The social audit would look at the company's contribution to society and the community. The contributions made could be through:

- Donations.

- Sponsorship.

- Employment practices.

- Education.

- Health and safety.

- Ethical investments, etc.

A social audit could either confirm statements made by the directors, or make recommendations for social policies that the company should perform.

Management audit

A management audit is defined as 'an objective and independent appraisal of the effectiveness of managers and the corporate structure in the achievement of the entities' objectives and policies. Its aim is to identify existing and potential management weaknesses and recommend ways to rectify them.'

Limitations of internal audit

- Internal auditors may be employees of the company they are reporting on and therefore may not wish to raise issues in case they lose their job.

- In smaller organisations in particular, internal audit may be managed as part of the finance function. They will therefore have to report upon the effectiveness of financial systems that they form a part of and may be reluctant to say their department (and manager) has deficiencies.

- If the internal audit staff have worked in the organisation for a long time, possibly in different departments, there may be a familiarity threat as they will be audited the work of long standing colleagues and friends.

It is therefore difficult for internal audit to remain truly objective. However, acceptable levels of independence can be achieved through one, or more, of the following strategies:

- Reporting channels separate from the management of the main financial reporting function.

- Reviews of internal audit work by managers independent of the function under scrutiny.

- Outsourcing the internal audit function to a professional third party.

Qualities of an effective internal audit function

If the internal audit department is to be effective in providing assurance it needs to be:

- Sufficiently resourced, both financially and in terms of qualified, experienced staff.

- Well organised, so that it has well developed work practices.

- Independent and objective.

- Chief internal auditor appointed by the audit committee to reduce management bias.

- No operational responsibilities.

- Work plan agreed by the audit committee.

- No limitation on the scope of their work i.e. full access to every part of the organisation.

Outsourcing the internal audit function

In common with other areas of a company's operations, the directors may consider that outsourcing the internal audit function represents better value than an in-house provision.

Outsourcing is where the company uses an external company to perform its internal audit service instead of employing its own staff.

Advantages

- Greater focus on cost and efficiency of the internal audit function.
- Staff may be drawn from a broader range of expertise.
- Risk of staff turnover is passed to the outsourcing firm.
- Specialist skills may be more readily available.
- Costs of employing permanent staff are avoided.
- May improve independence.
- Access to new market place technologies, e.g. audit methodology software without associated costs.
- Reduced management time in administering an in-house department.

Disadvantages

- Possible conflict of interest if provided by the external auditors (In some jurisdictions – e.g. the UK, ethics rules specifically prohibit the external auditors from providing internal audit services where significant reliance will be placed on the work of the internal auditor).
- Pressure on the independence of the outsourced function due to, e.g. threat by management not to renew contract.
- Risk of lack of knowledge and understanding of the organisation's objectives, culture or business.
- The decision may be based on cost with the effectiveness of the function being reduced.
- Flexibility and availability may not be as high as with an in-house function.
- Lack of control over standard of service.
- Risk of blurring of roles between internal and external audit, losing credibility for both.

Reporting

Unlike an external audit report, the internal audit report does not have a formal reporting structure. It is likely that the format is agreed with the audit committee or board of directors prior to commencing the assignment.

These reports will generally be for internal use only. The external auditors may inspect them if they are intending on placing reliance on the work of internal audit.

A typical report will include:

- Terms of reference – the requirements of the assignment.

- Executive summary – the key risks and recommendations that are described more fully in the body of the report.

- Body of the report – a detailed description of the work performed and the results of that work.

- Appendix – containing any additional information that doesn't belong in the body of the report but which is relevant to the assignment.

11   Distinction between external and internal audit

Distinction between external and internal audit

	External audit	Internal audit
Objective	Express an opinion on the truth and fairness of the financial statements in a written report.	Improve the company's operations by reviewing the efficiency and effectiveness of internal controls.
Reporting	Reports to shareholders.	Reports to management or those charged with governance.
Availability of report	Publicly available.	Not publicly available.
		Usually only seen by management or those charged with governance.
Scope of work	Verifying the truth and fairness of the financial statements.	Wide in scope and dependent on management's requirements.
Appointment and removal	By the shareholders of the company.	By the audit committee or board of directors.
Relationship with company	Must be independent of the company.	May be employees (which limits independence) or an outsourced function (which enhances independence).

12 Errors

No bookkeeping system can be guaranteed to be entirely free of errors. Human beings are fallible, and even automated and computerised systems are less than perfect. For example, a computer cannot possibly know that a supplier has sent you an invoice that never arrived.

The following are types of errors:

- Errors of omission, where a transaction has been completely omitted from the ledger account.

- Errors of commission, where one side of the transaction has been entered in the wrong account (but of a similar type to the correct account, for example, entered in the wrong receivable's account, or in the wrong expense account). An error of commission would not affect the calculation of profit, or the position shown by the statement of financial position.

- Errors of principle, where the correct and incorrect accounts are of different types, for example, entered in the purchases account instead of a non-current asset account. This type of error would affect the calculation of profit, and the position shown by the statement of financial position.

Preventing errors

There are a number of ways in which errors can be prevented, or at least limited in their number and effect. Many of these also prevent deliberate fraud.

Authorisation procedures

Transactions should be authorised at an appropriate level. For example,

- the purchase of major non-current assets should be justified/agreed by senior management and recorded in the minutes of meetings

- cheques for large amounts should require two signatures

- new receivable and payable accounts should be authorised by a senior person

- all purchase orders should be authorised by a responsible officer

- all payments made should be approved. In particular

    - payments to suppliers should be checked against goods received, invoices and credit notes

    - refunds to customers should be authorised

    - payrolls should be checked and authorised prior to making payment.

Documentation

Documentation should be used to give evidence of transactions, and should be properly filed and referenced. This helps to provide an 'audit trail' of transactions through the system. As an example, consider the ordering of goods for resale, and the documentation involved.

- Raising of the order. On official order forms, properly authorised, after obtaining several quotations.

- Receipt of goods. Checked on arrival, checked with order, shortages and breakages recorded.

- Receipt of invoice. Checked with order and receipt of goods; prices, discounts and calculations checked.

- Payment of invoice. Only after all credit notes have been received, and checked with purchase ledger account prior to payment.

Organisation of staff

Staff should be properly recruited, trained and supervised. No one person should have complete control over any section of the bookkeeping system. Duties should be shared out between different members of staff. This is known as **segregation of duties**.

This can be illustrated by considering the procedures arising from selling goods on credit. In summary the tasks involved are:

- issuing sales invoices

- issuing credit notes

- credit control

- banking receipts from customers.

If one person were to be solely responsible for all (or even more than one) of these tasks, it would be easy for money to be diverted and the corresponding paperwork destroyed or falsified. Staff should also rotate their duties from time to time.

Safeguarding assets

Assets should be properly maintained, insured, utilised, valued and recorded.

Detecting errors

Some errors may come to light purely by chance, and some are never found at all. For example, if you receive a cheque from a customer who has no outstanding balance on their account, it is possible that an invoice has been omitted from the books. If you never receive the cheque, the error might never come to light.

It would be extremely unwise to trust to chance, and therefore there are several checks that can be incorporated to help detect errors.

Spot checks

These are particularly useful in detecting fraud. For example, spot checks on petty cash balances may uncover 'teeming and lading' activities, whereby an employee borrows money from the petty cash on a regular basis, but puts it back when the imprest is being checked, only to remove it again afterwards.

Spot checks are also commonly carried out on bank balances, ledger accounts and inventories.

13 Fraud

 What is fraud?

Fraud is an intentional act involving the use of deception to obtain an unjust or illegal advantage – essentially 'theft by deception'.

 Fraud or error

Fraud is a crime, but does not have a precise legal definition. The term 'fraud' refers to an intentional act by one or more individuals among management, those charged with governance, employees or third parties, involving the use of deception to obtain an unjust or illegal advantage. (International Standard of Auditing 240 *The Auditor's Responsibility to Consider Fraud in an Audit of Financial Statements*).

A distinction is made between:

- fraud, which is deliberate falsification, and

- errors, which are unintentional mistakes.

Note that fraud may be carried out by management, employees or third parties. For example:

- Managers may deliberately select inappropriate accounting policies.

- Employees may steal the proceeds of cash sales and omit to enter the sale into the accounting records.

- Third parties may send bogus invoices to the company, hoping that they will be paid in error.

Findings about Fraud

The CIMA publication "Fraud risk management: a guide to good practice" mentions that various surveys have highlighted the following facts about fraud:

- organisations may be losing as much as 7% of their annual turnover as a result of fraud

- corruption is estimated to cost the global economy about $1.5 trillion each year

- only a small percentage of losses from fraud are recovered by organisations

- a high percentage of frauds are committed by senior management and executives

- greed is one of the main motivators for committing fraud

- fraudsters often work in the finance function

- fraud losses are not restricted to a particular sector or country

- the prevalence of fraud is increasing in emerging markets.

Different types of fraud

Examples of fraud include:

- the theft of cash or other assets

- false accounting: this includes concealing or falsifying accounting records with a view to personal gain or providing false information that is misleading or deceptive

- crimes against consumers or clients, e.g. misrepresenting the quality of goods; pyramid trading schemes; selling counterfeit goods

- employee fraud against employers, e.g. payroll fraud; falsifying expense claims; theft of cash

- crimes against investors, consumers and employees, e.g. financial statement fraud

- crimes against financial institutions, e.g. using lost and stolen credit cards; fraudulent insurance claims

- crimes against government, e.g. social security benefit claims fraud; tax evasion

- crimes by professional criminals, e.g. money laundering; advance fee fraud

- e-crime by people using computers, e.g. spamming; copyright crimes; hacking.

Pyramid schemes

Pyramid schemes are also known as multi-level plans and network marketing plans. Although the law on these schemes varies between countries, as a general rule some pyramid schemes are legitimate and some are illegal.

The nature of a pyramid scheme is for the originator of the scheme to offer other people the opportunity to become a distributor for a product or service, which could range in size and value from vitamins to car leases. The distributor is given the opportunity to sell the product or service from home, in return for a commission.

In addition, a person who becomes a distributor is encouraged to sign up other people as distributors, and in return receives a commission for each new distributor they persuade to join the scheme.

The concept of the pyramid is that the originator of the scheme signs up a few distributors, who then sign up new distributors themselves. These new distributors in turn sign up more distributors, who then sign up more distributors.

Each new distributor signing up to the scheme is asked to make a payment, for an initial amount of products to sell, or for marketing material. Sometimes, new distributors might be persuaded to pay to go on a training course in the product or service.

If a pyramid scheme is intended primarily to sell the product or service to outside customers, it could well be legal. In the UK, for example, these schemes are legal provided they comply with certain regulations.

However, **these schemes are illegal** if their primary purpose is to sign up new distributors rather than to sell products or services to external customers.

When distributors earn money mainly by signing up more distributors, the pyramid selling scheme is illegal (in many countries) because there is a limit to the number of new distributors. At some stage, there will be no more distributors willing to sign up to the scheme. The distributors at the bottom of the pyramid will have spent money buying inventory and/or marketing material, with very little prospect of getting any money back. The scheme is then likely to be wound up, possibly with many commissions still unpaid, having made a large amount of money for its originator.

Fraud prevention

The aim of preventative controls is to reduce opportunity and remove temptation from potential offenders. Prevention techniques include the introduction of policies, procedures and controls, and activities such as training and fraud awareness to stop fraud from occurring.

The existence of a fraud strategy is itself a deterrent. This can be achieved through:

- An anti-fraud culture

  Where minor unethical practices are overlooked, for example, expenses or time recording, this may lead to a culture in which larger frauds occur. High ethical standards bring long term benefits as customers, suppliers, employees and the community realise they are dealing with a trustworthy organisation.

- Risk awareness

  Fraud should never be discounted, and there should be awareness among all staff that there is always the possibility that fraud is taking place. It is important to raise awareness through training programmes. Particular attention should be given to training and awareness among those people involved in receiving cash, purchasing and paying suppliers.

  Publicity can also be given to fraud that has been exposed. This serves as a reminder to those who may be tempted to commit fraud and a warning to those responsible for the management of controls.

- Whistleblowing

  Fraud may be suspected by those who are not personally involved. People must be encouraged to raise the alarm about fraud.

- Sound internal control systems

  Sound systems of internal control should monitor fraud by identifying risks and then putting into place procedures to monitor and report on those risks.

Fraud detection

A common misbelieve is that external auditors find fraud. This is actually rarely the case. Their letters of engagement typically state that it is not their responsibility to look for fraud.

Most frauds are discovered accidentally, or as a result of information received (whistleblowing).

Some methods of discovering fraud are:

- Performing regular checks

  For example stocktaking and cash counts.

- Warning signals

  For example:

  - Failures in internal control procedures.
  - Lack of information provided to auditors.
  - Unusual behaviour by individual staff members.
  - Accounting difficulties.
  - Whistleblowers.

Fraud response

- The fraud response plan sets out the arrangements for dealing with suspected cases of fraud, theft or corruption.

- It provides procedures for evidence-gathering that will enable decision-making and that will subsequently be admissible in any legal action.

- The fraud response plan also has a deterrent value and can help to restrict damage and minimise losses to the organisation.

The organisation's response to fraud may include:

- Internal disciplinary action, in accordance with personnel policies.

- Civil litigation for the recovery of loss.

- Criminal prosecution through the police.

Responsibilities

Within the response plan responsibilities should be allocated to:

- **Managers**, who should take responsibility for detecting fraud in their area.

- **Finance Director**, who has overall responsibility for the organisational response to fraud including the investigation. This role may be delegated to a **fraud officer** or internal security officer.

- **Personnel** (Human Resources Department), who will have responsibility for disciplinary procedures and issues of employment law and practice.

- **Audit committee**, who should review the details of all frauds and receive reports of any significant events.

- **Internal auditors**, who will most likely have the task of investigating the fraud.

- **External auditors**, to obtain expertise.

- **Legal advisors**, in relation to internal disciplinary, civil or criminal responses.

- **Public relations**, if the fraud is so significantly large that it will come to public attention.

- **Police**, where it is policy to prosecute all those suspected of fraud.

- **Insurers**, where there is likely to be a claim.

14 Test your understanding questions

Test your understanding 1

Which of the following is not an objective of an auditor?

A   To confirm that no fraud has occurred

B   Obtain reasonable assurance that the financial statements are free from material misstatement

C   Express an opinion whether the financial statements are prepared in accordance with an applicable financial reporting framework

D   Report on the financial statements

Test your understanding 2

In relation to assurance who are the three parties?

Test your understanding 3

Who are the users in an external audit engagement?

Test your understanding 4

Explain the difference between an unmodified audit report and a modified audit report.

Test your understanding 5

Which of the following statements regarding internal audit is incorrect?

A   It should improve the company's operations

B   The reports are publicly available

C   The staff are appointed by the audit committee or board of directors

D   They report to management

Test your understanding answers

Test your understanding 1

A

This is not an objective of an auditor. It is management's responsibility to detect fraud.

Test your understanding 2

The 3 parties are:

- Practitioner
- Intended user
- Responsible party

Test your understanding 3

Shareholders

Test your understanding 4

An unmodified report is where there are no other matters which the auditor wishes to draw to the attention of the users.

A modified report can either be:

- modified without modifying the opinion – the financial statements show a true and fair view but there is something that needs to be brought to the attention of the user by way of an additional paragraph; or

- modified with a modified opinion – the financial statements don't fully show a true and fair view or the auditor has not obtained sufficient appropriate evidence to make that conclusion.

Test your understanding 5

B

The reports are not publicly available. They are usually only seen by management or those charged with governance.

Corporate Social Responsibility

Chapter learning objectives

Upon completion of this chapter you will be able to:

- describe the OECD general policies

- explain the role of national and international laws and regulations

- describe conflicting demands of stakeholders

- identify issues with CSR and the supply chain

- describe the guidelines of reporting CSR within annual reports

- identify synergies and tensions with CSR and brand management.

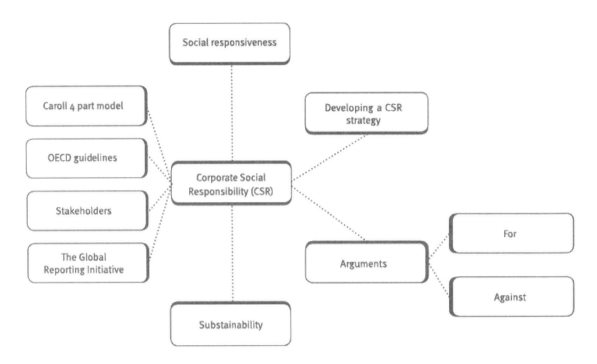

1 Corporate social responsibility (CSR)

A corporation:

- Is an artificial person in law. It has the same rights and responsibilities as human beings.

- Is notionally owned by shareholders but exists independently of them. The shareholder has a right to vote and be paid a dividend but the company owns its assets.

- Managers have a fiduciary right to protect shareholder investment.

Milton Friedman argued that, in relation to this definition, a corporation has no responsibility outside of making profit for shareholders:

- Only human beings have moral responsibility for their actions.

- It is the managers' duty to act solely in the interest of shareholders:
  - this is a point of law. Any other action is shareholder betrayal.
- Social issues are the province of the state and not corporations.

The argument against this viewpoint needs to provide the organisation with an alternative view that leads to the same outcome of profit.

Enlightened self-interest

- Corporations perceived as ethically sound are rewarded with extra customers.
- Corporations which are ethically unsound are boycotted.
- Employees are more attracted to work for, and are more committed to, socially responsible companies.
- Voluntarily committing to social actions and programmes may forestall legislation and promote independence from government.
- Positive contribution to society may be a long-term investment in a safer, better educated and more equitable community creating a more stable context in which to do business.

What is CSR?

A formal definition of CSR has been proposed by the World Business Council for Sustainable Development (WBCSD):

'CSR is the continuous commitment by business to behave ethically and contribute to economic development while improving the quality of life of the workforce and their families as well as the local community and society at large'.

WBSCD Vision 2050

In 2010 WBSCD set out their Vision 2050, where they envisage a world where more than nine billion people can live well within planetary boundaries. They provide a framework for action that is designed to help companies drive change in their sustainability planning and business strategies.

https://timetotransform.biz/wp-content/uploads/2021/03/WBCSD_Vision_2050_Time-To-Transform.pdf

Carroll's 4 Part Model

Economic

Economic responsibilities must be satisfied by organisations. Responsibilities relate to the ability of the organisation to stay in business and therefore provide for its stakeholders. For example:

- shareholders requiring a return on their investments

- employees to be provided with safe and fairly paid jobs

- customers to be able to obtain good quality products at a fair price.

The responsibilities are connected with why the organisation was established. The economic responsibility must be achieved in order to attain higher level responsibilities.

Legal

Legal responsibility implies that an organisation will follow the laws of the jurisdiction in which it is based as well as any internal moral views or objectives that the organisation has set. As with economic responsibility it is assumed that the organisation must act within the law to show that it is socially responsible.

Not complying with the law results in lack of social responsibility. For example:

- anti-competitive behaviour focusing on maximising market share and profits may be seen as lacking in social responsibility by limiting competition and charging excessively high prices (e.g. antitrust actions against Microsoft)

- price fixing by collusion (operation of cartels – always thought to be the case in the oil industry).

Legal responsibilities may therefore limit economic responsibilities by providing some social stance to organisations.

Ethical

Ethical responsibilities relate to what is expected by society from organisations compared with what those organisations have to do from an economic or legal viewpoint. Ethical responsibilities therefore relate to doing what is seen to be right compared with doing what is simply legal. For example:

- a company may decide to limit carbon emissions from its factory to a level below the legal maximum because this is seen to be acting in the interests of society

- Shell disposed of an oil platform on land rather than sinking it at sea (as it legally could have done) due to concern about the environmental consequences of this action.

Ethical responsibilities are therefore higher than both economic and legal responsibilities.

Philanthropic

Philanthropic responsibilities generally concern actions desired of organisations rather than those required by organisations. For example, organisations may:

- make donations to charities

- provide sports facilities for employees

- sponsor the arts (e.g. Tate & Lyle sponsoring the Tate Gallery in London).

These activities are carried out more because the organisation believes it is the correct thing to do rather than because it must. The term 'philanthropic' derives from the Greek 'love of society', so there is no obligation to act.

It has been argued that philanthropic responsibilities are less important than the other three levels because they are simply desired, not required, of organisations.

The meaning of CSR

Marks and Spencer

Marks and Spencer promotes itself as a responsible business that takes the challenge of CSR seriously. It aims to listen and respond to the needs of its shareholders and build up good relationships with its employees, suppliers and society at large.

Marks and Spencer approach CSR by following three basic principles:

- products – throughout the three stages of each product's life (production, selling and usage), the aim is to encourage ethically and environmentally responsible behaviour

- people – everyone who works at the company is entitled to a mix of benefits. This approach is also encouraged amongst the company's suppliers, franchisees and other business partners

- places – the company recognises its obligations to the communities in which it trades. Successful retailing requires economically healthy and sustainable communities.

Social responsiveness

This refers to the capacity of the corporation to respond to social pressure, and the manner in which it does so.

Carroll suggests four possible strategies: reaction, defence, accommodation and proaction.

Reaction

The corporation denies any responsibility for social issues.

Defence

The corporation admits responsibility but fights it, doing the very least that seems to be required.

Accommodation

The corporation accepts responsibility and does what is demanded of it by relevant groups.

Proaction

The corporation seeks to go beyond industry norms.

Developing a CSR strategy

Strategic CSR

Organisations are now, more than ever before, under the watchful eye of their stakeholders.

By taking a strategic approach to CSR organisations can determine what activities they have the resources to devote to being socially responsible and therefore choose those that will strengthen their competitive advantage.

Including CSR as part of an organisation's strategic planning process can ensure that the pursuit of profit does not sideline or overshadow the need to behave ethically to their stakeholders.

In summary, strategic CSR provides companies with the structure for:

- Identifying and responding to threats and opportunities facing their stakeholders.

- Determining how to manage their stakeholder relationships.

- Development of sustainable business practices.

- Balancing the creation of economic value with societal value.

- Determining the organisations capacity for philanthropic activities.

The details on stakeholders will be covered in the following section.

Developing a CSR strategy in more detail

"What gets planned gets done." – Peter Drucker

Business leaders understand that to achieve their company's goals, they need strategies to ensure that everyone in the organisation is headed in the right direction at the right time and that resources are available to support these goals when and where required.

For example, Hewlett-Packard's (HP) 2006 strategy to "Establish HP as the world's leading information technology company" was both clear and at the same time inspirational to the company's employees. The three subsidiary strategies established to achieve this goal were similarly very clear i.e. targeted growth, capital strategy, and efficiency.

HP personnel knew that if you contribute to one or more of these three strategies, you are helping the company achieve its greater goal of information technology supremacy. Therefore as an employee, you know that every year, your performance will be measured on your success in contributing to one or more of these strategies.

Unfortunately, few CSR strategies are as clear and compelling largely because the actual goals for most CSR efforts aren't in support of typical corporate functions such as marketing, manufacturing, sales, etc. so many companies are not exactly certain of what goals to set for them, or what strategies to pursue. This often results in unrelated strategies acting against rather than toward achieving corporate goals.

A suggested approach to develop a CSR strategy:

- The board make a firm published commitment to CSR, e.g. Marks and Spencer Plan A.

Senior executives must commit to and engage in CSR. A clear vision of CSR needs to be embedded within and reflect the core values of the firm, and be linked to the mission, vision and values of the organisation – recognizing that it creates not only social or environmental value, but that it creates business value as well. CSR should be managed as a core business strategy like for example marketing or research and development. CSR should report to a top-level executive in the company.

For example, innovative companies like Timberland have board committees overseeing corporate responsibility, and Gap takes board members on factory tours in China so they can see the value of supplier codes of conduct and audits. Generally the higher up CSR reports in the company, the more closely linked to providing value it is as a strategy.

- Determine the critical business objectives and priorities of the company, and develop a CSR strategy that will contribute to the achievement of those objectives.

To develop a CSR strategy, the company's leaders must first determine what specific business objectives this strategy must support. Defining business objectives is not as easy as it might appear and you're likely to get different answers from each business leader you ask.

For example, CSR can be used as a talent attraction and retention strategy if it is communicated clearly to potential and current employees, and they can engage in its principles. Similarly CSR can be used as a strategy to open up new markets for energy efficient products, penetrating new customer segments or grabbing market share from competitors whose customers care about environmentally friendly product lines.

- Align CSR strategy with the firm's core competencies.

CSR can be implemented in many businesses is typically executed in a non-integrated fashion. CSR initiatives originate from all parts of an organisation, and are often not directly linked to what the firm actually knows, does, or is expert in. Firms should, however, seek causes and social/ environmental strategies for which they own part of the solution. This requires focus and discipline and sticking true to that you know despite the myriad worthy causes and issues in our world.

For example, Ford Motor Company Foundation's support for breast cancer research which is approximately $100,000 each year.

There is no argument that this is a worthy cause with significant need, but there is no strategic link between the company's support for breast cancer research and the building of cars and trucks. Automotive companies know cars, transportation engineering, and design. It makes far more sense for an automobile manufacturer like Ford to support research in alternatively-fuelled vehicles or to address the global and environmental challenges around gasoline dependency because these initiatives fit the firm's core competencies and business objectives of selling more cars while potentially creating new products and revenue streams.

- Integrate CSR into the culture, governance and strategy development of the company.

CSR can be both a risk mitigation strategy and an opportunity-seeking strategy providing an intersection between business and social/environmental returns.

- Develop key performance indicators to measure the impact of their CSR strategies.

CSR performance metrics should be both internal – such as reputation improvements, gains in market share, brand perception, increased sales, decreased operational expenditures, and employee satisfaction – as well as external ones focused on society and the environment.

CSR will not be fully embraced and executed with as much precision as are the more commonly measured functions such as sales and staff management until it is built into the recognition and performance appraisal system for a company's employees For example, Johnson and Johnson measures its employees on both their functional performance as well as their performance against their well respected ethical stance. Walmart in the supplier selection process measure them against price, quality, stock availability and sustainability.

Arguments against CSR

It can be argued that companies should not pursue corporate social responsibility. Milton Friedman argues that:

'The business of business is business.'

This means that the primary purpose of a business is to try and earn a profit. In a company, for instance, the managers have been employed in order to earn the owners of the business a return on their investment.

As such, it is a manager's duty to act in a way that maximises shareholder wealth, while conforming to all relevant laws and customs. If a manager does anything that is not directly related to wealth maximisation, he or she is failing in their responsibilities to the owners and therefore acting unethically.

For example, it can be argued that it is not right for a manager to donate any company funds to charity. The manager should instead work to maximise the return to the owner. If the owner wishes to make donations to charity, he or she can do so out of their own earnings from the business.

In addition, it can be argued that maximising the wealth of business owners is, in itself, socially responsible. This is because:

- Increased returns will lead to increased tax payments made to the state. These can then be passed on to 'worthy causes'.

- A high proportion of company shares are owned by pension funds. This means that any gains will go to help provide pensions to individuals who may well be disadvantaged.

Don't forget that there may also be practical reasons why a business chooses not to pursue CSR. These can include:

- Increased cost of sourcing materials from ethical sources (e.g. Fairtrade products or free-range eggs).

- Having to turn away business from customers considered to be unethical (e.g. an 'ethical' bank may choose not to invest in a company that manufactures weapons).

- The management time that can be taken up by CSR planning and implementation.

Arguments for CSR

Not everyone agrees with Friedman's statements. There are a number of reasons why many businesses feel that CSR is a vital part of their strategy. These include:

- A key part of running a successful business is the ability to offer customers and consumers what they need. One of those needs is often a requirement for socially responsible behaviour from the organisation.

  Basically, **having good CSR can attract customers!** This can be because good CSR tends to enhance a company's reputation and therefore its brand. It can also be used a basis for differentiation in the market place – given the choice, many customers will prefer to trade with a company they feel is ethical.

- Good CSR is likely to involve good working conditions for employees, allowing the business to **attract a higher calibre of staff**.

- Avoiding discrimination against workers is likely to give the company **access to a wider human resource base**.

- Avoiding pollution will tend to save companies in the long run – many governments are now **fining or increasing taxes of more polluting businesses**.

- Sponsorship and charitable donations are tax deductible, improve staff morale and can be seen as a **form of advertising**.

Sustainability

One aspect of CSR that is also becoming increasingly important is sustainability.

Sustainability is the use of resources in such a way that they do not compromise the needs of future generations. It also involves not polluting the environment at a rate faster than they can be absorbed.

There are many examples of this. For example, some logging companies plant a tree for every one they fell.

Other companies try to make their products easy to recycle, helping to ensure that materials are reused rather than wasted. The computer manufacturer Apple has used this as part of its marketing approach for some years.

The reason that sustainability is so important for many businesses is that acting in a sustainable manner not only helps look after the environment and the wider community, but it strengthens the business and helps ensure its long-term survival.

It is worth noting that sustainability is increasingly being seen as important within the public sector. Ensuring that goods and services procured by the public sector are sustainable can help meet environmental goals across government, save considerable amounts of public money; and help support innovation and economic growth. This will involve taking account of a wide range of costs, such as pollution impacts, carbon emissions and waste disposal.

The difficulty for many businesses is that many companies focus on short term gains, rather than the long-term sustainability of the business and its environment. This is often evident in businesses that offer senior managers bonuses based on short-term or annual performance.

However, it should be noted that sustainability can lead to cost savings for an organisation in the short term. For example, an organisation that reduces packaging on its products may have a positive impact on the environment by generating less waste, but it will also reduce its costs, thereby improving profits.

Incorporating ethics and CSR into strategy

CIMA itself has been heavily involved in identifying and discussing the implications of sustainability for the business. To this end, in 2010 they published a research article discussing this.

http://www.cimaglobal.com/Documents/Professional%20ethics%20docs/Incorporatingethicsintostrategyweb 1.pdf

The article came to six key conclusions:

- Strong ethical principles that go beyond upholding the law can add great value to a brand, whereas failure to do the right thing can cause social, economic and environmental damage, undermining a company's long–term prospects in the process.

- Once they have adopted an ethical approach, companies will often find there are bottom-line benefits from demonstrating high ethical standards.

- The ethical tone comes from the top.

- High-quality management information on social, environmental and ethical performance is vital for monitoring the environmental and social impacts of a company and for compiling connected reports showing how effective its governance arrangements are.

- Corporate communications and reporting on sustainability need to do more than just pay lip service to the green agenda. They need to provide hard evidence of the positive impact on society, the environment and the strategic returns for the business, and how any negative effects are being addressed.

- Management accountants have a particular ethical responsibility to promote an ethics-based culture that doesn't permit practises such as bribery.

Championing sustainability

Rather than taking a reactive, passive approach to sustainability, finance professionals should take the initiative in raising awareness of social responsibility and the need to consider the impact of decisions and actions on sustainability. However, they need to remain objective while doing this.

This will involve promoting sustainable practices through the organisation in relation to the following:

Products and services

- Does making the product use inputs/materials/ingredients from renewable sources only?

- Does the firm source raw materials in ways that support their replenishment, safeguard natural habitats and ensure good animal welfare standards?

- What is the expected life of the product?

- How much of the product (including packaging) can be recycled?

- Is the level of packaging excessive?

Customers

- Does the firm have a recycling programme?

- What incentives are given to customers to encourage them to recycle?

- Does the firm encourage/help customers reduce their carbon footprint?

The supply chain

- Does the firm incorporate environmental considerations when selecting suppliers? For example, would it use a supplier with a poor record on pollution?

- Does the firm use suppliers who are geographically close to reduce the impact of transportation in terms of fuel used and exhaust emissions?

- Does the firm pay fair prices to suppliers or does it use its buying powers to drive prices down to very low levels?

- Does the firm encourage/help suppliers reduce their carbon footprint?

- Does the firm help suppliers reduce waste sent to landfill?

The workplace

- Does the firm have measurable targets for energy/water usage?

- Is the building energy efficient?

Employees

- Does the firm look after its employees in terms of working conditions, employment rights, job security, etc. or are staff 'hired and fired' when necessary?

- Does the firm contribute to community projects?

Other business functions and processes

- Does the firm take into account environmental impacts of activities when making decisions?

- Does the firm measure the impact of social initiatives?

5 key strategies to embed sustainability leadership

This article looks at the ways in which businesses can take steps to ensure that sustainability thinking is spread throughout the organisation.

Today's consumers are increasingly demanding sustainably produced products — and they're willing to pay more for such products. Members of Generation Z, in particular, choose brands that are both people- and planet-friendly. Of the consumers from 28 countries surveyed by US-based National Retail Federation last year, 57% were willing to change their purchasing habits to reduce the negative impact on the environment.

Apart from such demand from consumers, organisations have internal reasons to set sustainability goals. The main reasons come down to achieving excellence in environmental, social, and governance (ESG) performance as a means to increase investor confidence, manage business risks, and fulfil an obligation to contribute to the global environmental agenda. Organisations are inclined to set sustainability goals, alongside business goals, to support causes such as mitigating climate change.

But achieving sustainability goals through a set of sustainability professionals is old-school thinking. The new paradigm is to think and do "sustainability" in everything. How organisations can make that happen so that the business is sustainable, consistently and reliably, is something that must be explored.

Critical questions to ask

First, we need to question fundamentals of the business, some of which relate to the organisation's purpose and how the purpose is achieved:

1. Does the organisation's purpose fundamentally drill down to shareholder value and wealth creation, or is the purpose bigger and broader?

2. Are the organisation's business KPIs separate from other sustainability performance targets, or are they integrated towards a common goal?

3. Do sustainability professionals operate in a separate business function to drive sustainability goals, or do business and operations drive sustainability-integrated business KPIs?

If the answers to these questions appear to find fault with your organisation's current approach, it is an indication that the integration of sustainability into your organisation's functions needs further work.

Who are sustainability leaders?

The US-based Sustainability Leadership Institute defines sustainability leaders as "individuals who are compelled to make a difference by deepening their awareness of themselves in relation to the world around them. In doing so, they adopt new ways of seeing, thinking, and interacting that result in innovative, sustainable solutions."

In other words, they are employees who are capable of envisioning long-range sustainability outcomes and are able to strategise and deliver them. They operate with the traits of a business leader, yet they look at the world through an added sustainability lens and drive action towards achieving those goals.

The key strategies explained

Here are five factors to explore in order to harness sustainability leadership in organisations and make sure that capability is sourced, developed, enhanced, and retained.

1. **Recruitment**

   The initial step of acquiring organisational talent can be pivotal to assuring that the key ingredients of sustainability leadership are given due attention during hiring.

   Looking for attributes of sustainability leadership during candidate assessment could increase the likelihood of recruiting the right leaders to drive the business agenda and to ensure that nurturing sustainability skills is a possibility.

What are some of the basic aspects to look for in a sustainability leader? Russell Reynolds Associates, a recruitment firm, suggests a few aspects that can be assessed through open-ended questions and situational responses in candidate screening.

- Sustainability mindset, which is about the candidate's ability to think with a broader purpose and maintain a continuous drive related to the purpose.

- Systems thinking, which is the intellectual ability to see the bigger picture.

- Relationship building, which is about the understanding of and the ability to relate to a diverse environment.

The human resources function could also incorporate the organisation's specific sustainability awareness, as well as the organisation's values, practices, and expectations, into the onboarding process once a candidate is hired.

2   Training

It is important to understand that sustainability leadership is an attribute that needs to be present in all organisational and business leaders, not just those in sustainability functions. A continual process of cross-skilling, upskilling, and re-skilling is needed to get everyone thinking and working toward the sustainability goals. This is an investment organisations need to be willing to make to keep the skill levels up to date and ready to be applied in practice.

Ensuring that individual learning and development plans capture the skills gaps is a formal way to ensure that skills development can be organised through training, exchanges, secondments, or continuing professional development (CPD) schemes. While plans could be put in place to acquire those skills, assessing the effectiveness of these trainings is also crucial. This can be done as a part of annual performance reviews of employees.

3   Integration

Integrating sustainability into daily business practice is the true value of sustainability leadership, but this is also the biggest challenge.

Business functions will need to modify their business as usual to include a sustainability aspect, and this has to begin from strategy. Setting long-term plans, goals, and targets to achieve improved business performance, while moving to another level with sustainability performance, is not only necessary but also crucial. One of the common examples among businesses is to have a set of operational improvements or projects to reduce carbon emissions. Other sustainability practices are substituting raw materials, factoring inputs for production with ethically sourced material, and replacing traditional raw material with recycled or recovered content, while assuring product quality standards and adopting product packaging designed to be regenerative after use.

Developing expertise to carry out these strategic changes could be daunting for businesses. This specialised expertise can be sourced externally at first, but the long-term goal should be to build a knowledge and a skill base within the organisation. This is achieved through making domain/functional expertise and specialised sustainability skills transferrable across business units and projects. Setting new career paths and professional development goals that encourage multi-skilling and cross-skilling is a critical aspect to consider in pursuing this.

4   Appraisal

The motivation for action of the general workforce is closely linked to what a performance management system says in a typical organisation.

Having a clear statement on what performance means by elaborating requirements that capture sustainability elements would spotlight its importance to the organisation. This means stating what actions are preferred and what behaviours are encouraged, and clearly communicating these expectations. As an example, a procurement professional should still be rewarded during his or her performance review for choosing an ethically sourced product, even though procurement cost could be affected, and a construction project manager who chooses to use a recycled material and reduces material cost could be rewarded for initiative, innovation, and cost reduction.

The performance criteria could be action-driven, outcome-driven, or impact-driven, based on the seniority of positions. Performing the right actions could make a difference for frontline staff in their performance review, while the strategic-level managers can claim rewards for the visible impact they created.

Conversations about career progression need to involve discussion of how leadership attributes should involve different levels of responsibility to drive sustainability principles.

5   Incentives

Integration will not be complete without appraising those who do well in their specific decisions, actions, and behaviours that promote the sustainability agenda of the organisation.

Organisations can reward employees who attempt to incorporate sustainability into business decisions. An example of this is a procurement approach referred to as "procurement for innovation", where the organisational objective to encourage innovation is incentivised through suppliers, by having sustainability thinking incorporated in the supplier selection criteria. This approach is practised widely in the UK for encouraging sustainable procurement by public organisations.

Welcoming initiatives and projects towards sustainability and rewarding and incentivising them through career advancement, recognition, or monetary rewards would be another desirable aspect. Encouraging employee-initiated innovation, especially from nonsustainability-oriented functions and rewarding such innovative ideas would be a great way to go.

How to know whether you are there yet

During this progressive path to integrate sustainability aspects, the idea is to embed sustainability into the business in a way that no one feels they are doing something out of their job scope. In such an organisation, innovation that achieves sustainability outcomes is encouraged, appreciated, and rewarded. This is an intermediate landing that organisations should aim to achieve.

A mark of success is to have a highly skilled and enterprising set of organisational professionals who are able to envision sustainability outcomes. This can only be achieved by building employees' capacity and empowering them to act as leaders to drive sustainability in the long run.

This article appeared in Financial Management, September 2021.

Further CIMA information on sustainability

In December 2010, CIMA collaborated with the American Institute of Certified Public Accountants and the Canadian Institute of Chartered Accountants in a report entitled 'Evolution of corporate sustainability practices'.

Some key issues that this report raised include:

General

Business sustainability is about ensuring that organisations implement strategies that contribute to long–term success. Organisations that act in a sustainable manner not only help to maintain the well–being of the planet and people, they also create businesses that will survive and thrive in the long run.

The accounting profession can play an important role in this. Accountants can serve as leading agents for change by applying their skills and competencies to develop sustainability strategies, facilitate effective implementation, accurate measurement and credible business reporting.

Why do businesses have sustainability plans?

According to research conducted by CIMA, the key reasons include:

- **Compliance** – the need to comply with laws and regulations.

- **Reputational risk** – companies are concerned with how stakeholders will view them if they fail to act in a sustainable manner.

- **Cost-cutting and efficiency** – acting in a sustainable manner (for example becoming more energy-efficient) can help to reduce business expenditure. This is especially valuable for smaller companies.

Ten elements of organisational sustainability

The following areas are considered crucial to the successful embedding of sustainability within an organisation. It is worth noting that the accounting function will be useful in a number of these areas.

Strategy and oversight

- Board and senior management commitment.

- Understanding and analysing the key sustainability drivers for the organisation.

- Integrating the key sustainability drivers into the organisation's strategy.

Execution and alignment

- Ensuring that sustainability is the responsibility of everyone within the organisation (not just a specific department).

- Breaking down the sustainability targets and objectives for the organisation as a whole into targets and objectives which are meaningful for individual subsidiaries, divisions and departments.

- Processes that enable sustainability issues to be taken into account clearly and consistently in day-to-day decision-making.

- Extensive and effective sustainability training.

Performance and reporting

- Including sustainability targets and objectives in performance appraisal.

- Champions to promote sustainability and celebrate success.

- Monitoring and reporting sustainability performance.

Corporate social responsibility is seen as vital for many organisations. One company that is often hailed as a leader in this area is Ben & Jerry's – a US based manufacturer of ice-cream, frozen yoghurt and sorbet. The company has stated that 'business has a responsibility to the community and the environment'.

Ben & Jerry's CSR has included the following:

- Fair Trade ingredients – this ensures that suppliers of many of the company's raw materials enjoy safe working conditions, reasonable work hours and are paid fairly.

- Ethically sourced supplies – as well as a commitment to Fair Trade, the company also ensures, where possible, that it sources ingredients from suppliers who share its values. For example, Ben & Jerry's has historically sourced free-range eggs and sustainably produced dairy for its products.

- Community work – the company has engaged with communities to improve sustainability. Ben & Jerry's Vermont Dairy Farm Sustainability Project was launched in 1999 and sought to develop practical methods for dairy farms to reduce nitrogen and phosphorous run-off in order to prove water quality and overall sustainability.

- Corporate philanthropy – the company donates a portion of its pre-tax profits to corporate philanthropy via, in part, the Ben & Jerry's Foundation.

How sustainability impacts operations management

Operations management might contribute to achieving an organisation's sustainability targets in a number of ways:

Process design

The process should be designed to minimise waste, reduce energy use and reduce carbon emissions.

Product design

The product design should consider factors such as:

- Use of recycled inputs.

- Use of sustainable inputs.

- Ability to recycle product or dispose of it safely.

- Minimising wastage, e.g. unnecessary packaging.

Quality management

Higher quality should help to improve efficiency and reduce waste.

Supply chain management

Supply chain management is an important part of a company's CSR policy. It is common place to have policies in place to prevent slavery in the supply chain, lower carbon footprint and promote sustainable sourcing. Companies are expected to be able to track the carbon footprint not only of their own manufacturing activities but also their transportation, distribution and procurement activities.

The following are examples of practices adopted:

- **Purchasing:** Only products from a sustainable and ethical source should be purchased, e.g. a furniture manufacturer may purchase timber from sustainable forests only.

- **Supplier selection:** One of the key criteria to use when choosing between suppliers should be their adoption of sustainable development policies.

- **Location:** The distance between the supplier and the company should be minimised.

Brand image

A strong brand is what differentiates a company and/or its products in a competitive industry. A company can link unique characteristics and images to its brand name and passing its message to consumers, so that their distinct feelings about the brand are positively affected. As a result, brand image management is a key point in marketing strategy.

In recent times CSR has become a key element in the promotion of brand images. Customers have expectations that companies are implementing CSR policies. When CSR policies are communicated, it becomes a strategic branding tool. CSR initiatives can therefore strengthen a company's brand image and is therefore becoming a strategic necessity.

Danger of poor supply chain management

Companies doing business in China have had difficulties maintaining quality throughout the supply chain, as illustrated by recent food and product recalls. For example, in 2008 there was a melamine-tainted baby milk scandal, which caused the death of at least six infants. Inherent problems in manufacturing processes and supply chains led to a breakdown of quality assurance. The scandal severely damaged China's dairy industry and shattered consumer confidence.

Managing Responsible Business 2015 Edition

This CGMA report draws on insight from nearly 2,500 Chartered Global Management Accountant designation holders and CIMA students working in both private and public sectors to review how the ethical landscape has changed since 2012.

The following is an extract from the report:

Four in five organisations view ethical issues concerning the supply chain as relevant to their business. In the last few years, regulation and legislation, media attention and public demand for greater transparency have all grown significantly. Today, this means that companies need to consider carefully not only their own business strategies and activities, but also those of the organisations who work with them and even those whom they supply.

2 The Global Reporting Initiative (GRI)

Purpose

GRI is an international independent organisation that helps businesses, governments and other organisations understand and communicate the impact of business on critical sustainability issues such as climate change, human rights, corruption and many others.

Their vision is "to create a future where sustainability is integral to every organisation's decision making process."

GRI Standards

The most accepted framework for reporting sustainability is the Global Reporting Initiative's Sustainability Reporting Standards (GRI Standards). The latest version of these was issued in June 2018.

The GRI Standards provide universal guidance for reporting on sustainability performance. They are applicable to all entities including SMEs and not-for-profit entities worldwide.

Background to and objectives of the GRI Standards

Preface to the GRI Standards

The following quote from the preface to the GRI Standards explains the background to them:

"Sustainability reporting is an organization's practice of reporting publicly on its economic, environmental, and social impacts.

The GRI Standards represent global best practice in sustainability reporting. They are designed to be used as a set by any organization that wants to report about its impacts, and how it contributes towards sustainable development.

The GRI Standards are also a trusted reference for policy makers and regulators worldwide; they encourage and enable credible non-financial reporting by the companies under their jurisdictions."

Materiality considerations

Materiality is placed at the centre of the GRI Standards.

GRI focuses heavily on the issues that are material to the organisation and important for stakeholders.

CEOs worldwide have identified the need to build public trust as a crucial part of improving operational effectiveness and engaging with customers following the 2008 financial crisis.

Sustainability reporting, says the GRI, plays a key role in this, with non-financial reporting being singled out as a particularly effective means of communicating long-term commitment to sustainability.

Organisations must identify those sustainability issues most material to their stakeholders and activities, and then explain their impact, both positive and negative, in these areas.

Reporting Principles of the GRI Standards

GRI 101 – Foundation provides the Reporting Principles of report content and report quality. These help organisations decide which topics are material and should be included in their sustainability report, and how to ensure the quality of the information disclosed.

Reporting Principles – report content

When deciding which topics to include in their sustainability report, organisations should consider the following:

Stakeholder inclusiveness

The reporting entity should identify its stakeholders and explain in the report how it has responded to their expectations and interests.

Sustainability context

The report should present the entity's performance in the wider context of sustainability. This often includes environmental issues but could also include information on social or economic topics such as wage levels and the poverty levels of employees.

Materiality

Organisations are faced with a wide range of topics on which they could report. Relevant topics are those that may reasonably be considered important for reflecting the organisation's economic, environmental and social impacts, or influencing the decisions of stakeholders, and, therefore, potentially merit inclusion in the report. Materiality is the threshold at which issues or topics become sufficiently important that they should be reported. This may be due to a combination or internal and external factors.

Completeness

Coverage of all the material topics and indicators should be enough to reflect significant environmental, economic and social impacts and allow stakeholders to assess the reporting entity's performance.

Reporting Principles – report quality

As well as the principles for defining report content identified above, GRI Standard 101 provides the following principles for defining report quality:

Accuracy

The reported information should be sufficiently accurate and detailed for stakeholders to assess the entity's performance.

Balance

The report should reflect both positive and negative aspects of an entity's performance to enable a reasoned overall assessment.

Clarity

Information should be understandable and accessible to stakeholders.

> ### Comparability
>
> Issues and information should be reported consistently. Reported information should be presented in a way which allows stakeholders to assess trends over time and compare the entity to other organisations.
>
> ### Reliability
>
> The entity should gather, record, compile, analyse and disclose information and processes used in the preparation of a report in a way that they can be subject to examination and that establishes the quality and materiality of the information.
>
> ### Timeliness
>
> Reporting should occur regularly and in time for stakeholders to make informed decisions.

Disclosures required by the GRI Standards

The disclosures required for GRI are divided into two parts; Universal Standards (providing contextual details of the business and management approach) and Topic Specific Standards (disclosing the specific performance of the entity on specific material areas within economic, environmental and social categories).

GRI 102: General Disclosures

This requires an organisation to disclose details of its business to provide context to the other disclosures. These include items such as the organisation's location, ownership structure, size, supply chain, strategy, key risks and opportunities, ethical policies, governance details, stakeholder engagement and reporting policies.

GRI 103: Management approach

The final Universal Standard requires organisations to explain which topics it believes to be material, why they are deemed to be material, where the impact occurs, the extent to the organisation's involvement with the impact and how management approach and manage the issue. This Standard is used in conjunction with the Topic Specific Standards below.

Topic Specific Standards

These Standards give information on the economic, environmental and social performance of an entity related to its material topics. Disclosures have to be made in each of these three categories (economic, environmental and social).

- **Economic (200 Series Standards)**

  The **economic** dimension of sustainability concerns the entity's impacts on the economic conditions of its stakeholders, and on economic systems at local, national, and global levels.

- **Environmental (300 Series Standards)**

  The **environmental** dimension of sustainability concerns the entity's impact on living and non-living natural systems, including land, air, water and ecosystems.

- **Social (400 Series Standards)**

  The **social** dimension of sustainability concerns the impacts the entity has on the social systems within which it operates. This includes labour practices, human rights, product responsibility and wider social impacts.

Examples of disclosures

Based on the above guidance, examples of disclosures that entities might make to comply with the GRI Standards are shown below.

For more examples and a full list of Topic Specific Standards, see the GRI's website (www.globalreporting.org).

Economic

Key aspect	Example of disclosures
Economic performance	Revenues/costs, levels of pension contributions, taxes paid and subsidies received
Market presence (i.e. the economic impact on the local area)	Comparison of wage rates to other firms locally, proportion of senior managers hired from the local community
Indirect economic impacts	Extent of investment in infrastructure projects
Procurement practices	Proportion of spending with local suppliers

Environmental

Key aspect	Example of disclosures
Materials	Materials used by weight or volume, and the proportion of materials used in production that are recycled
Energy	Total fuel consumption, reductions in the energy requirements of sold products and services
Biodiversity	The nature of significant impacts on biodiversity e.g. species affected and duration of impact
Emissions	Total emissions of greenhouse gases and ozone depleting substances, emissions reductions achieved as a direct result of initiatives to reduce emissions
Supplier Environmental Assessment	The percentage of new suppliers that were screened using environmental criteria

Social

Key aspect	Example of disclosures
Employment	Rate of staff turnover, number of new staff appointed, benefits provided to staff (e.g. life insurance, parental leave)
Training and education	Average hours of training provided per employee
Diversity and equal opportunity	Analysis of employees (and members of the entity's governance bodies) by age, gender, ethnic background, disability etc.
Human rights assessment	The number/percentage of the entity's investments and contracts that underwent human rights screening
Freedom of association and collective bargaining	Measures taken to support rights to exercise freedom of association (e.g. joining a trade union) and collective bargaining
Local communities	Operations with local community engagement and those with significant actual/potential negative impacts on local communities
Public policy	Financial donations to political parties analysed by country and by recipient
Anti-competitive behaviour	Number of legal actions faced by the entity relating to anti-competitive behaviour and violations of monopoly legislation
Customer health and safety	A summary of breaches of health and safety legislation reported by customers, and a summary of the results of any investigations
Customer privacy	The number of complaints received regarding customer privacy issues (for example leaks, thefts or losses of customer data)

3 Stakeholders

A stakeholder is a group or individual, who has an interest in what the organisation does, or an expectation of the organisation.

Types of stakeholder

Stakeholders can be broadly categorised into three categories; internal, connected and external.

Internal stakeholders

Internal stakeholders are intimately connected to the organisation, and their objectives are likely to have a strong influence on how it is run. Internal stakeholders include:

Stakeholder	Need/expectation
Employees managers/directors	pay, working conditions and job security status, pay, bonus, job security

Connected stakeholders

Connected stakeholders either invest in or have dealings with the firm. They include:

Stakeholder	Need/expectation
shareholders	dividends and capital growth and the continuation of the business
customers	value-for-money products and services
suppliers	paid promptly
finance providers	repayment of finance

External stakeholders

These stakeholders tend to not have a direct link to the organisation but can influence or be influenced by its activities.

Stakeholder	Need/expectation
community at large	will not want their lives to be negatively impacted by business decisions
environmental pressure groups	the organisation does not harm the external environment
government	provision of taxes and jobs and compliance with legislation
trade unions	to take an active part in the decision making process

Stakeholder needs analysis

Stakeholder needs analysis involves an organisation undertaking research to determine:

- Who its key stakeholders are, and

- What their needs are.

Each company must sit down with a blank sheet of paper and identify the stakeholders of their business.

For example, if a company has $1m in the bank earning modest interest, then the bank is probably not a key stakeholder. In another company with a $100m debt to the bank and large interest payments, the bank is clearly an extremely important stakeholder.

Once the organisation has identified its stakeholders, it needs to understand what their needs and wants are. There is no better way of accomplishing this than asking them directly. Possible methods include:

- questionnaires

- focus groups

- direct interviews or interviews with representatives.

Stakeholders needs analysis

Car manufacturers

As well as being sensitive to the requirements of customers with respect to factors such as price and performance, a car manufacturer should also consider the following:

- public attitudes to pollution

- government policies on road tax and fuel tax.

As a result it may choose to develop more environmentally-friendly vehicles as part of its long term strategy even if current demand is for larger cars, say.

To some stakeholders, the company owes obligations arising from the law (e.g. to pay employees their salary each month, or to compensate them if they are made redundant). However, other obligations arise voluntarily due to the company's commitment to CSR (e.g. to discuss their plans with interested pressure groups before a particular plan is adopted).

Responsibilities of business to stakeholders

888.com

888.com is an internet gambling site that is listed on the London Stock Exchange. It is headquartered in Gibraltar and operates under a licence granted by the Government of Gibraltar. It has responsibilities to the following stakeholders:

- Shareholders – since it is listed on the London Stock Exchange it must comply with the rules of that exchange, including adopting the Corporate Governance Code.

- Employees – to be a good employer to all its members of staff.

- Customers – to offer a fair, regulated and secure environment in which to gamble.

- Government – to comply with the terms of its licence granted in Gibraltar.

- The public – the company chooses to sponsor several sports teams as part of strengthening its brand. The company also tries to address public concerns about the negative aspects of gambling, e.g. by identifying compulsive gamblers on their site and taking appropriate action.

4   CSR initiatives

In 2009 the OECD published an Overview of Selected Initiatives and Instruments Relevant to Corporate Social Responsibility.

The report "provides an overview of the unique status and characteristics of the OECD Guidelines for Multinational Enterprises, the ILO Tripartite Declaration of Principles Concerning Multinational Enterprises and Social Policy and the UN Global Compact".

The following is an extract from the report:

The Universal Declaration of Human Rights states that "every individual and organ of society" has the responsibility to strive "to promote respect for these rights and freedoms" and "by progressive measures, national and international, to secure their universal and effective recognition and observance". As important "organs" of society, businesses have a responsibility to promote worldwide respect for human rights.

The ILO Conventions establish norms covering all aspects of working conditions and industrial relations. Some of the most important cover core labour standards (i.e. basic human rights in the workplace). These include the right to freedom of association, the right to organise and to collective bargaining, and freedom from forced labour. ILO conventions are binding on all countries that have ratified them.

The ILO Tripartite Declaration of Principles Concerning Multinational Enterprises and Social Policy is a global instrument designed to provide guidance to government, employer and worker organisations in areas of employment, training, conditions of work and industrial relations. All core labour standards are covered. Although it is a non-binding instrument, its implementation is nevertheless the object of regular reviews.

The ILO Declaration on Fundamental Principles and Rights at Work is based on the core labour standards outline in the ILO Conventions. The Declaration is not binding but applies to all ILO member states. As part of a strategy to help countries to have well-functioning labour markets, it provides for a mechanism for annual review of the efforts made by member states that have not yet ratified the core labour standards. The Declaration also reinforces the application of core labour standards in private voluntary instruments.

The 1992 Rio Declaration sets out 27 principles defining the rights and responsibilities of states in relation to human development and well-being. The Agenda 21 agreement provides guidance for governments, business and individuals on how to contribute to efforts to make development socially, economically and environmentally sustainable. Its Chapter 30 recognises the value of promoting "responsible entrepreneurship". The Millennium Development Goals identify a series of government-agreed targets and timetables in relation to issues such as poverty reduction, improvement of child health care and education, and the promotion of gender equality.

The Johannesburg Declaration on Sustainable Development (2002) states that the private sector has "a duty to contribute to the evolution of equitable and sustainable communities and societies", and that "there is a need for private sector corporations to enforce corporate accountability". Its Plan of Implementation notes the need to "enhance corporate environmental and social responsibility and accountability". The UN Framework Convention on Climate Change and Convention on Biodiversity were also signed by a majority of governments.

The 2005 World Summit Outcome reiterated the importance of full respect for existing labour, human rights and environmental commitments and encouraged "responsible business practices, such as those promoted by the Global Compact".

Under the 2003 UN Convention Against Corruption, ratifying countries undertook to: criminalise an array of corrupt practices; develop national institutions to prevent corrupt practices and to prosecute offenders; cooperate with other governments to recover stolen assets; and help each other to fight corruption.

ILO Tripartite Declaration of Principles Concerning Multinational Enterprises and Social Policy.

The main areas covered by the Declaration are:

- General policies (obey national laws and respect international standards).
- Employment (employment promotion; equality of opportunity and treatment; security of employment).
- Training (policy development for vocational training, skills formation).
- Conditions of Work and Life (wages, benefits, conditions of work; minimum age; safety and health).
- Industrial Relations (freedom of association and right to organise; collective bargaining; consultation; grievances; settlement of disputes).

UN Global Compact

The UN Global Compact invites companies to embrace, support and enact, within their sphere of influence, the following ten principles:

Human Rights

Principle 1: Businesses should support and respect the protection of internationally proclaimed human rights; and

Principle 2: Make sure that they are not complicit in human rights abuses.

Labour Standards

Principle 3: Businesses should uphold the freedom of association and the effective recognition of the right to collective bargaining

Principle 4: The elimination of all forms of forced and compulsory labour

Principle 5: The effective abolition of child labour; and

Principle 6: The elimination of discrimination in respect of employment and occupation.

Environment

Principle 7: Businesses should support a precautionary approach to environmental challenges

Principle 8: Undertake initiatives to promote greater environmental responsibility; and

Principle 9: Encourage the development and diffusion of environmentally friendly technologies.

Anti-Corruption

Principle 10: Businesses should work against corruption in all its forms, including extortion and bribery.

5   OECD Guidelines

The OECD Guidelines for Multinational Enterprises (referred to here as the OECD Guidelines), were adopted in 1976, at a time when there was growing concern about the negative impact of corporate practices, particularly on developing countries.

The OECD Guidelines are non-binding recommendations addressed by governments to multinational enterprises operating in or from adhering countries. They provide voluntary principles and standards for responsible business conduct in areas such as:

- Information disclosure
- Respect for labour standards
- Contribution to sustainable development
- Respect for human rights
- Supply chain responsibility
- Consumer interests
- Science and technology
- Competition
- Taxation
- Environment
- Bribery and corruption
- Whistleblower protection.

This is set out in the ten "chapters" of the OECD Guidelines. The OECD Guidelines have application to all sectors of business and cover companies operating in or from OECD member states worldwide and addresses their supply chain responsibilities.

The full set of guidelines can be accessed here:

http://mneguidelines.oecd.org/text/

General policies

Enterprises should take fully into account established policies in the countries in which they operate, and consider the views of other stakeholders. In this regard:

Enterprises should:

1   Contribute to economic, environmental and social progress with a view to achieving sustainable development.

2   Respect the internationally recognised human rights of those affected by their activities.

3   Encourage local capacity building through close co-operation with the local community, including business interests, as well as developing the enterprise's activities in domestic and foreign markets, consistent with the need for sound commercial practice.

4   Encourage human capital formation, in particular by creating employment opportunities and facilitating training opportunities for employees.

5   Refrain from seeking or accepting exemptions not contemplated in the statutory or regulatory framework related to human rights, environmental, health, safety, labour, taxation, financial incentives, or other issues.

6   Support and uphold good corporate governance principles and develop and apply good corporate governance practices, including throughout enterprise groups.

7   Develop and apply effective self-regulatory practices and management systems that foster a relationship of confidence and mutual trust between enterprises and the societies in which they operate.

8   Promote awareness of and compliance by workers employed by multinational enterprises with respect to company policies through appropriate dissemination of these policies, including through training programmes.

9   Refrain from discriminatory or disciplinary action against workers who make bona fide reports to management or, as appropriate, to the competent public authorities, on practices that contravene the law, the Guidelines or the enterprise's policies.

10 Carry out risk-based due diligence, for example by incorporating it into their enterprise risk management systems, to identify, prevent and mitigate actual and potential adverse impacts as described in paragraphs 11 and 12, and account for how these impacts are addressed. The nature and extent of due diligence depend on the circumstances of a particular situation.

11 Avoid causing or contributing to adverse impacts on matters covered by the Guidelines, through their own activities, and address such impacts when they occur.

12 Seek to prevent or mitigate an adverse impact where they have not contributed to that impact, when the impact is nevertheless directly linked to their operations, products or services by a business relationship. This is not intended to shift responsibility from the entity causing an adverse impact to the enterprise with which it has a business relationship.

13 In addition to addressing adverse impacts in relation to matters covered by the Guidelines, encourage, where practicable, business partners, including suppliers and sub-contractors, to apply principles of responsible business conduct compatible with the Guidelines.

14 Engage with relevant stakeholders in order to provide meaningful opportunities for their views to be taken into account in relation to planning and decision making for projects or other activities that may significantly impact local communities.

15 Abstain from any improper involvement in local political activities.

Enterprises are encouraged to:

1 Support, as appropriate to their circumstances, cooperative efforts in the appropriate fora to promote Internet Freedom through respect of freedom of expression, assembly and association online.

2 Engage in or support, where appropriate, private or multi-stakeholder initiatives and social dialogue on responsible supply chain management while ensuring that these initiatives take due account of their social and economic effects on developing countries and of existing internationally recognised standards.

6 Test your understanding questions

Test your understanding 1

List the stakeholders which organisations would consider as part of their CSR strategy.

Test your understanding 2

Explain the elements of Carroll's four-part model.

Test your understanding 3

What are the steps of developing a CSR strategy?

Test your understanding 4

Which of the following is the responsiveness strategy where the corporation denies any responsibility for social issues?

A   Reaction

B   Defence

C   Accommodation

D   Proaction

Test your understanding 5

Which of the following category would a shareholder be classified as?

A   Internal stakeholder

B   External stakeholder

C   Connected stakeholder

D   None of the above

Test your understanding answers

Test your understanding 1

Environment

Employees

Shareholders

Suppliers

Customers

Local community

Test your understanding 2

Carroll's four-part model is made up of:

- Economic responsibility

- Legal responsibility

- Ethical responsibility

- Philanthropic responsibility

Test your understanding 3

1   Identify stakeholders

2   Classify stakeholders

3   Establish stakeholders' claims

4   Assess importance of stakeholders

5   Decide upon response to social pressure

Test your understanding 4

A

Test your understanding 5

C

The Law of Contract

Chapter learning objectives

Upon completion of this chapter you will be able to:

- identify the essential elements of a valid contract and situations where the law requires the contract to be in a particular form

- explain how the law determines whether negotiating parties have reached agreement and the role of consideration in making that agreement enforceable

- explain when the parties will be regarded as intending the agreement to be legally binding and how an agreement may be avoided because of misrepresentations

- explain how the terms of a contract are established and their status determined

- explain the ability of a company to contract.

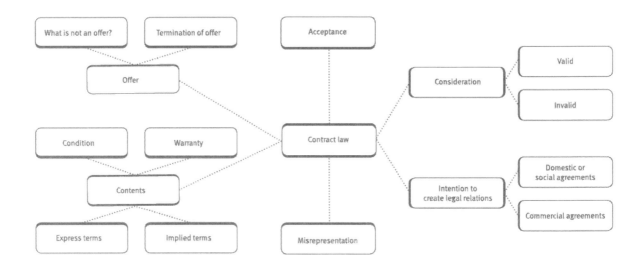

1 Introduction

This is the first chapter which deals with the business law part of the syllabus. The primary focus of this chapter is on general principles of contract law. The following two chapters look at general principles of employment law and company law.

Law in itself is quite a big topic and can vary from country to country. CIMA would like its students to have a general understanding of key legal principles without learning the details of any particular legal system.

Throughout this chapter and the following two chapters there will be some illustrations used to demonstrate legal principles in action. These are based on English case law, however, it must be noted that there is no requirement to learn these cases. They are included to help students understand how the law is applied.

2 Definition of law

 The Oxford Dictionary defines law as "The system of rules which a particular country or community recognizes as regulating the actions of its members and which it may enforce by the imposition of penalties."

3 Definition of a contract

A contract is a legally binding agreement between two or more parties.

Contract law is of vital importance in business life, and forms the basis of most commercial transactions such as dealings in land and goods, credit, insurance, carriage of goods, the formation and sale of business organisations, and employment.

For example, all of the following everyday transactions are contracts: purchasing a newspaper, buying a bus or rail ticket, purchasing a sandwich and a drink at lunchtime, buying a book or a CD, going to the cinema, the theatre or a football game.

Form of a contract

There is a general misconception that for there to be a valid contract it must be in writing. A contract can be in any form. It may be written, or oral or inferred from the conduct of the parties. However, in some situations the law may stipulate that in order for the contract to be enforceable it must be in a particular form e.g. in England any agreements for the transfer of land must be in writing.

Subject to contract

Where the words 'subject to contract' are used this means the parties to an agreement are not legally bound until a contract has been executed. Even though the parties have agreed terms, the matter effectively remains in a state of negotiation. Furthermore, either party can withdraw from the transaction without liability.

Standard form contracts

In many instances, rather than individually negotiating contracts, it is now common business practice for a customer to be presented with a written contract, the terms of which have already been set down in print. In these cases all that remains is for the customer to accept the terms by signing the contract. Examples of the use of such standard form contracts include contracts for gas and electricity services, telephone services, television packages, credit agreements and insurance etc.   Although such contracts are beneficial in that they save time and set down the terms of the agreement, they may be open to abuse by some unscrupulous businesses who seek to include terms of particular benefit to the business and to the detriment of the consumer. Thus although these contracts are subject to all the following principles regarding the essential elements of a valid contract, many jurisdictions have introduced additional consumer protection such as requiring terms in such contracts to be "fair" or allowing the consumer a "cooling – off" period after the initial acceptance during which it can be cancelled.

4   The essential elements of a valid contract

In most jurisdictions, the law provides that a contract cannot come into existence without the following:

An offer

- A definite and unequivocal statement of willingness to be bound on specified terms without further negotiation.

An acceptance

The unqualified and unconditional assent to all the terms of the offer.

Consideration

- Each party must provide something of value.

Intention to be legally bound

- Both parties must intend to enter into a legal relationship.

Each of these essential elements will be considered below.

 ## What is an offer?

An offer is a definite promise to be bound on specific terms made by the offeror to the offeree.

The offer can be made in any form but must be communicated to the offeree.

The offeree can be a particular person, a class of persons or even the whole world.

 English case law example

CARLILL v CARBOLIC SMOKE BALL 1893

Facts:

The manufacturers of a medicinal 'smoke ball' advertised in a newspaper that anyone who bought and used the ball as directed and still contracted influenza would be paid a £100 reward. Mrs. Carlill used the ball in accordance with the instructions and still caught flu. The manufacturers said there was no contract with Mrs. Carlill because an offer could not be made to the whole world.

Held:

An offer could be made to the whole world, the wording of the advert amounted to such an offer and Mrs Carlill had accepted it by using the ball correctly.

A legally binding offer includes:

- clearly stated terms
- an intention to enter into a contract
- communication of that intention.

What is not an offer?

Some countries may have rules on what is not an offer. The following are some general examples.

An invitation to treat

- An "invitation to treat" is an indication by one party that he or she is prepared to receive an offer from another party with a view to entering into a binding contract; it is not an offer.

Examples of invitations to treat

- most adverts (Carlill v Carbolic Smoke Ball is an exception to this)
- shop window displays
- goods on shop shelves
- company prospectus
- circulation of a price list or displays on a website
- tenders (a person asking for tenders is making an invitation to treat, the person submitting the tender is making the offer).

Jane offered to sell one of her paintings to John for £50. She also advertised some of her paintings in the local newspaper and put one on display in the window of her shop with a price tag attached to it. Jane has made an offer to John, but the advert in the local paper and the shop window display would not be offers but invitations to treat.

A supply of information or a statement of intention

A statement made early in the negotiations is unlikely to be held to be a valid offer and a statement of an intention to sell is not an offer.

Vague statements

A statement cannot constitute an offer if it is not sufficiently specific. For example, an offer to sell someone a car for £5,000 is valid, but a statement that a person will sell '...one of my cars for about £5,000' is not an offer: it is vague and uncertain.

Termination of the offer

In many jurisdictions, once an offer has been terminated it cannot be accepted and can only be revived by the person who originally made the offer.

An offer can be terminated in the following ways:

- Rejection and counter offer
- Revocation
- Lapse of time
- Failure of a pre-condition.

Rejection

An offer can be terminated by a rejection, either outright, by the offeree stating that they will not accept it, or by a counter offer.

A counter offer is an offer made in response to an offer. The most obvious example of this is where the offeree tries to negotiate the price downwards. For example where X offers his car to Y for £5,000 and Y responds by saying "I'll give you £4,500 for it." Y has made a counter offer and the effect at law is to terminate the original offer. A less obvious example perhaps, would be if Y in the above example had said "I accept and I'll pay you over the next 3 months." Even though Y has used the word "accept" this is also a counter offer, as Y has not unconditionally accepted X's offer but has added other conditions ("I'll pay you over the next 3 months").

English case law example

HYDE v WRENCH 1840

Facts: Wrench offered to sell Hyde a farm for £1,000. Hyde made a counter offer by offering £900.

Wrench rejected this counter offer. Later, Hyde came back to Wrench and said that he now accepted the offer at £1,000.

Held: Hyde could no longer accept the original offer as it no longer existed and was not capable of acceptance. Hyde's statement that he would pay the original £1,000 was a new offer, which Wrench did not accept.

A request for more information is not a rejection of an offer.

Request for information about an offer

Jack offered to sell some goods to Jill for £4,000 and some machinery to Bill for £6,000. Jill asked Jack if she could take half of the goods now and the remainder in one month's time. Jack didn't reply so Jill accepted his original offer. Bill replied by offering Jack £5,500 for the machinery. Jack didn't reply so Bill accepted Jack's original offer.

Jill has not made a counter offer. Had she done so then her attempt to accept the original offer would have been ineffective. She had simply requested more details of the terms of the offer and her subsequent acceptance was valid.

Bill's reply amounted to a counter offer which had the effect of terminating Jack's original offer. Bill was unable to accept the original offer which no longer existed. Bill's offer of £5,500 was a new offer made to Jack which he was free to accept or reject.

Revocation

An offer will be terminated if it is revoked (withdrawn) by the offeror. It can be revoked by the offeror or a person authorised to act on their behalf at any time before it has been accepted by the offeree.

The revocation may be by express words or it may be implied from the offeror's conduct. It must be communicated to the offeree by the offeror or by a reliable third party.

Revocation of an offer

Fred offered to sell his car to Emma and agreed to keep his offer open for two days. However, Fred changed his mind and, before the two days had expired, sold his car to Lucy, and informed Emma of the sale. Emma attempted to accept Fred's original offer arguing that he had given her two days to accept. However, Fred was not obliged to keep the offer open for two days as an offeror may revoke an offer at any time before it is accepted.

If however the offeree pays the offeror to keep the offer open, this creates a collateral contract and whilst the offeror can still revoke the original offer this would be a breach of that collateral contract. The offeree could claim damages (the most usual remedy for a breach of contract) for the loss of the opportunity to accept the original offer.

It may not be possible to revoke an offer where there is a unilateral contract. A unilateral contract arises where an offer has been made to the whole world that performing a particular act will result in a certain benefit. For example where a notice is published offering a reward for the return of a lost dog (or for using a carbolic smoke ball). In such cases it is impossible to notify everyone who may have seen the offer that it has been revoked (withdrawn). Also if an offeree had started to carry out the required act it is thought that it would be unjust to simply allow the offeror to withdraw the offer at that stage. It follows that a revocation is ineffective where an offeree is in the process of completing the required act.

Lapse of time

An offer ceases to exist if not accepted within a specified time limit and, if no time limit is specified, then it will lapse after a reasonable time. What is reasonable may depend on the subject matter of the contract. The time for an offer to purchase perishable goods is likely to be shorter than for non perishable goods.

An offer will also lapse on the death of the offeree or of the offeror unless the offeree accepts in ignorance of the death.

Failure of a pre-condition

A 'conditional' offer is one which is dependent on a specified event or change in circumstances. A conditional offer may not be accepted unless and until the condition or change of circumstances is met.

5   Acceptance

 Acceptance is the unequivocal and unconditional assent to all the terms of the offer.

Acceptance can be oral, in writing or by conduct

The acceptance can be express or implied by the conduct of the offeree (Carlill case). If an offeror stipulates the type of acceptance then that form of acceptance must be used.

Acceptance must be communicated

As a general rule acceptance must always be communicated to the offeror.

If a fax or telephone message is received during normal business hours then it is communicated when received. A fax or voicemail received outside of normal business hours is communicated once the business opens.

The law is unclear as to when a communication by email is received but there seems little reason to distinguish between this form and other types of instantaneous communication such as fax or telephone calls. It appears therefore, that the contract will be formed when the acceptance is received by the offeror's email system during business hours. If received outside business hours then it is communicated when the business reopens.

Acceptance must involve some act on the part of the offeree

An offeror cannot impose silence as the means of acceptance. There must be some words or action by the offeree to indicate acceptance.

An offeror cannot impose silence as the means of acceptance

> Rosie wrote to Jim that she was interested in buying his boat. She stated that she would assume the boat was hers for £1,000 if she did not hear from Jim. Jim didn't reply. Can Jim's silence amount to acceptance? The answer is "no". Rosie was unable to impose a contract on Jim by stating that his silence amounted to acceptance.

The Postal Rule

In some jurisdictions there is an exception to the rule that acceptance must always be communicated and this is known as the "Postal Rule". The postal rule states that acceptance is complete as soon as the letter is posted.

The rule only applies where the letter is properly stamped and addressed and if it would not be unreasonable to use the post (it would be unreasonable, for example, during a postal strike).

The postal rule applies even if the letter is never received by the offeror but not if the offeror states he or she must actually receive acceptance.

Carrying out an act in ignorance of an offer

A person must know of an offer before it can be accepted. For example, where a reward is offered, acceptance will only be effective where the offeree is aware of the offer.

Acceptance of a reward

Tilly offers a reward to anyone who finds and returns her cat. Tom, unaware of this offer, finds and returns her cat.

Did Tom accept Tilly's offer?

Tom cannot have "accepted" her offer since he was unaware of it and he is therefore not entitled to the reward.

6   Consideration

The third essential element of a valid contract is consideration.

In most jurisdictions a valid contract requires consideration. There may be some exceptions to this for example in English law a contract made by deed does not require consideration unless its terms require it.

 Consideration is the price by which one party bought the other party's act or promise.

Valid consideration

Executed consideration

- means that the consideration is in the form of an act carried out at the time the contract was made, such as payment for goods at the time the goods are delivered.

  For example handing over payment and receiving coffee. Both the payment and the handing over of the coffee are executed at the time of the contract.

Executory consideration

- means that there is an exchange of promises to do something in the future such as a promise to pay for goods to be delivered and paid for at a later date.

  For example when a person agrees to pay for some goods 'cash on delivery'. Both the payment and the delivery are 'executory', i.e. to be completed at a later date.

  If a buyer pays now for the seller to deliver in the future, then the buyer's consideration is executed and the seller's executory.

Sufficient consideration

- the consideration must have some monetary value; but

- there is no need for each party's consideration to be equal in value.

    The parties have freedom to contract under any terms they wish and a court will not attempt to make a contract a fair bargain as long as there is some identifiable value.

 Adequacy of consideration

> If John agrees to rent out his house for £1 a year to Janet there would be sufficient (and therefore valid) consideration even though the nominal figure of £1 would hardly be considered adequate.

Invalid consideration

Past consideration

Consideration is past if it involved something which had already been done at the time the promise is made.

 English case law example

> **RE MCARDLE 1951**
>
> **Facts:**
>
> A husband and wife carried out improvements to a house. At a later date a promise was made to reimburse the couple.
>
> **Held:**
>
> The works had been carried out before the promise to pay had been made. Past consideration is no consideration.

If a person requests a service and no price is mentioned, then there is an implied promise to pay a reasonable sum. In practice this usually means the market rate for the goods or services.

Existing statutory duty

Generally, performance of an existing statutory duty i.e. legal duty is not good consideration.

However, if it can be shown that some extra service over and above that statutory duty is required this will constitute good consideration.

Existing contractual duty

The same principle as above applies. If there is only performance of an agreed contractual duty then this will not be considered good consideration.

However, if the original contractor asks for more than the original work required by the contract, then carrying out that additional work amounts to consideration.

Existing contractual duty

The following two English case law examples demonstrate the difference between what will not constitute sufficient consideration and what will.

STILK v MYRICK 1809

Facts:

A captain promised to share the wages of deserting seamen with the rest of the crew if they completed the voyage.

Held:

The promise was not binding as there was no extra consideration from the seamen who, by completing the voyage, were doing no more than they were contractually bound to do.

HARTLEY v PONSONBY 1857

Facts:

A large number of seamen deserted from a ship making the ship undermanned and hence unseaworthy. The captain offered extra pay to the remaining seamen if they would complete the voyage.

Held:

The promise of more money was recoverable by the seamen as they were involved in a dangerous situation and were doing more than they had originally contracted to do.

Illegal acts

An illegal act cannot amount to consideration.

7 Intention that the agreement should be legally binding

The final essential element in a valid contract is the intention to create legal relations.

If a contract is to be created both parties must intend to enter into a legal relationship. If it is not clear from the contract that the parties intended legal consequences then the law presumes the intention of the parties based on the type of agreement.

Domestic or social agreements

It is presumed there is no intention to be legally bound in a social or domestic arrangement.

This presumption can be rebutted or overturned by showing that there was clear evidence that the parties did intend to create legal relations.

English case law examples

BALFOUR v BALFOUR 1919

Facts:

Mr B, who was about to go abroad, promised to pay his wife £30 per month in consideration of her agreeing to support herself without calling on him for any further maintenance. The wife said the husband was contractually bound by the promise.

Held:

There was no legally binding contract between the parties. It was a domestic arrangement and it was presumed the parties did not intend to be legally bound.

But compare this case with the following where the parties were not living together happily.

MERRITT v MERRITT 1970

Facts:

A husband who was separated from his wife promised to transfer the house into her name if she paid off the outstanding mortgage debt.
The wife paid off the debt but the husband refused to transfer the house.

Held:

In this case, the husband's promise was enforceable, the agreement having been made when the parties were not living together amicably.

Commercial agreements

It is presumed that there is an intention to be legally bound, unless it can be shown otherwise.

This is a strong presumption that can only be rebutted by clear evidence to the contrary.

Transactions binding in honour only

If the parties state that an agreement is 'binding in honour only', this amounts to an express denial of the intention to create a legal relationship.

8   Misrepresentation

During the negotiations preceding a contract, statements are often made with a view to inducing the other party to enter into a contract. If any such statement is false, the party thereby misled is not agreeing to what is the true state of affairs and the contract may be voidable for misrepresentation.

Misrepresentation, therefore, may be defined as a false statement of fact or law (but not a mere expression of opinion), made by one party to the other before the contract, and made with a view to inducing the other party to enter into it.

The statement must have been intended:

* to be acted upon, and

* it must actually have deceived the other party and induced them to make the agreement.

As a **general rule**, silence cannot amount to misrepresentation. However, there are exceptions to this general rule and a party can be liable for what they did not say. For example, if a party (the representor) makes a representation during the course of negotiations that is true but which becomes false before the making of the contract is concluded, they are under a duty to disclose this fact to the other party (the representee). If they do not, the original statement has become a misrepresentation. In contracts of utmost good faith where one party only is in possession of vital information, it must be communicated to the other party so that they can assess whether to enter into a contractual relationship. Insurance contracts are an example of contracts of utmost good faith. If a person takes out buildings insurance and they know of any defects in the house they must make full disclosure to the insurer so that they can decided whether to enter into a contractual relationship and accept the risk.

Once it has been established that a false statement has been made it is then necessary for the representee to demonstrate that the false statement induced them to enter the contract. There can be no inducement or reliance if the representee was unaware of the false statement.

A contract entered into on the basis of a misrepresentation is said to be voidable on the part of the innocent party. "Voidable" means that the contract is valid and will continue until the innocent party takes steps to cancel the contract. Voidable must be distinguished from "void". If a contract is declared void that effectively means that it never existed.

The contract may be ended by the innocent party and the parties restored to their pre-contract positions. For example any money paid should be handed back and any goods recovered.

The right to be restored to the pre-contract position will be lost if the innocent party waits too long or it is not possible to recover property, as where for example, it has been destroyed.

9   The contents of the contract

In many jurisdictions the terms of the contract will be both express and implied terms.

Express terms

These can be written, oral or a combination of the two.

Such terms are specifically inserted into the contract by either or both parties.

They must be clear for them to be enforceable.

Implied terms

These are terms which are not expressly included but are still part of the contract. They can be implied by:

- the nature of the contract

  The courts can imply terms that are required by the contractual relationship. These terms may be implied into all similar contractual relationships, unless excluded or inconsistent with the express terms.

  The courts may imply a term where the parties have failed to provide for a particular matter which, unless remedied, would make the contract unworkable. Such implied terms are based on the presumed but unexpressed intention of the parties.

- custom and usage

  Any contract may be deemed to incorporate any relevant custom of the market, trade or locality in which it is made, unless the custom is inconsistent with the express terms or the nature of the contract.

  A term may be implied on the basis of what the particular parties have done in the past – this is called usage.

- legislation

  Many countries will have legislation which implies terms into contracts. This can happen for many reasons, for example implying terms into contracts for the sale of goods and services to provide better consumer protection, and implying terms into employment contracts to ensure greater health and safety protection.

Conditions and warranties

If there is a breach of contract and the innocent party seeks a remedy, it may be important to determine whether the breached term is considered to be a condition or a warranty.

Condition

A condition is a vital term of the contract, breach of which may be treated as a substantial failure to perform a basic element of the agreement.

The innocent party has the choice of cancelling the contract and claiming damages or continuing with the contract and claiming damages. "Damages" refers to monetary compensation for any loss or injury.

Warranty

A warranty is a less important term which is incidental to the main purpose of the contract.

The remedy for a breach of warranty is a claim for damages only.

It may not be obvious from the contract whether the parties intend a particular term to be a condition or warranty. In this situation the courts will classify the term according to the consequences of a breach of the term. If the breach would cause the parties to be deprived of the main benefit of the contract then the clause is a condition, if only minor loss was caused the term is a warranty.

The difference between a condition and a warranty

Compare the following two English cases:

POUSSARD v SPIERS 1876

Facts:

Madame Poussard agreed to sing in a series of operas for Spiers. She failed to appear on the opening night and Spiers refused her services for subsequent nights.

Held:

The obligation to appear on the opening night was a condition. Since Madame Poussard was in breach of this condition. Spiers was entitled to treat the contract as at an end and was therefore not himself in breach by refusing her services for the remaining nights.

> ## BETTINI v GYE 1876
>
> ### Facts:
>
> Bettini, who agreed to sing in a series of concerts and to attend six days of rehearsals beforehand failed to appear for the first four rehearsal days. Gye in consequence refused Bettini's services for the balance of the rehearsals and performances.
>
> ### Held:
>
> The obligation to appear for rehearsals was a warranty and therefore Bettini's breach did not entitle Gye to treat the contract as at an end. Gye was accordingly in breach of contract when he refused Bettini's services for the remainder of the contract.

10 The ability of a company to contract

The legal concept of a company will be discussed in chapter 8. For the purposes of contract law, a company can enter into contracts in its own company name when it comes into existence. Nowadays companies can contract for any business purpose. If a company wishes to restrict its ability to enter into particular contracts then it will restrict the directors from doing so by internal arrangements.

If a company has restricted the ability of its directors to contract on its behalf and the directors ignore the restriction the consequences are as follows:

- If the directors are about to take the company into a contract in excess of their authority, shareholders may be able to apply to court for an injunction to stop them

- If the directors enter into the contract in excess of their authority then it is usually still enforceable by both parties but the directors may be sued for breach of their duty.

11 Test your understanding questions

Test your understanding 1

List the essential elements necessary for the formation of a contract.

Test your understanding 2

What effect will a counter offer have on an offer?

Test your understanding 3

Dennis wrote to Mark, offering to sell him a Renoir painting for £100,000. One week later, Mark wrote back saying he would pay that amount but not for another 2 months. Dennis did not respond and Mark, who decided that he wanted the painting, then heard that Dennis had sold the painting to Tom. Was there a contract between Dennis and Mark?

A   Yes. Dennis has made a valid offer which Mark has accepted

B   Yes. Mark's response was a request for further information and he was able to accept the offer afterwards

C   No. Mark's response constitutes a counter-offer which effectively destroyed Dennis's original offer

D   No. Dennis's letter to Mark constituted an invitation to treat, not an offer

Test your understanding 4

In contract law, once an offer has been terminated it cannot be accepted.

Which of the following does not terminate an offer?

A   A request for further information

B   Revocation by the offeror

C   Lapse of reasonable time

D   Rejection by the offeree

Test your understanding 5

Which of the following is incorrect?

A   A term may be implied into a contract by legislation

B   A term may be implied into a contract by a court on the ground that the term is customary in the parties' trade

C   A term may be implied into a contract by a court on the ground that it would make the contract more fair

D   A term may be implied into a contract due to the nature of the contract

Test your understanding 6

Which of the following is incorrect?

A   A condition is a term which the parties intend to be of vital importance

B   A warranty is a term which the parties do not intend to be of vital importance

C   If a condition is breached, then the contract must be cancelled

D   If a warranty is breached, then the injured party cannot terminate the contract

Test your understanding 7

Beryl enters a shop to purchase a new dress. She tells the shop assistant that she would like to buy the blue dress which is displayed in the shop window and priced at £100. The assistant removes the dress from the window for Beryl, but when she tries to pay for it at the till, the manager informs her that it is not for sale. He tells her that the dress is for display purposes only.

Required:

Delete as appropriate and complete the following sentences:

Beryl **is/is not** entitled to the dress because the display of the dress in the shop window constitutes an .... (3 words) and not an....(1 word). It follows that Beryl **does not have/has** a contract with the shop owners who **have/have not** acted in breach of contract.

Test your understanding answers

Test your understanding 1

The essential elements necessary for the formation of a contract are:

- offer
- acceptance
- consideration
- the intention to be legally bound.

Test your understanding 2

A counter offer has the effect of terminating the original offer. The counter offer itself constitutes a new offer which can either be rejected or accepted.

Test your understanding 3

C

C is the correct answer, because Mark is trying to impose his own terms, and thus is making a counter offer which is capable in turn of acceptance, and which destroys Dennis's original offer.

Test your understanding 4

A

A request for further information does not terminate an offer.

Test your understanding 5

C

A, B and D are all ways in which a term can be implied into a contract.

Test your understanding 6

C

C is the correct answer because whilst a breach of condition can result in the contract being terminated, it is wrong to say the contract must be terminated.

Test your understanding 7

Beryl **is not** entitled to the dress because the display of the dress in the shop window with a price tag constitutes an **invitation to treat** and not an **offer**. It follows that Beryl **does not have** a contract with the shop owners, who **have not** acted in breach of contract.

The Law of Employment

Chapter learning objectives

Upon completion of this chapter you will be able to:

- explain how the contents of a contract of employment are established
- explain what policies and procedures may be present in the workplace
- explain the distinction between unfair and wrongful dismissal and the consequences.

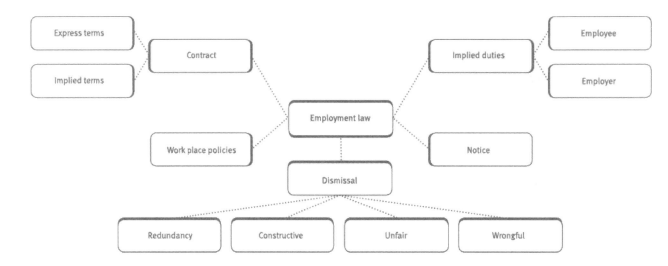

1 The contract of employment

An employment contract is like any other contractual relationship. The basic rules of contract will apply.

To be valid there must be agreement (offer and acceptance), consideration and intention to create legal relations. Therefore, in a contract of employment, the following applies:

- The employer offers employment.

- The employee accepts the offer of employment.

- Consideration is present in the form of the remuneration package provided by the employer in return for the work of the employee.

- Clearly this is a business agreement (as opposed to a social or domestic arrangement) and the parties are presumed to intend legal relations.

An employment contract is usually made in writing although it can be created orally. It is likely to contain a mixture of express and implied terms.

Express terms

Express terms are those agreed by the parties themselves. Their agreement may be written or oral.

A change in terms generally requires the consent of both parties, unless it is introduced by new legislation.

Sometimes an express term will give the employer the right to vary the terms of employment. For example, a mobility clause allows the employer to change the location of the employment. Such changes must, however, be reasonable.

Implied terms

Terms can be implied into a contract of employment from any of the following sources:

Sources of terms

- The courts

  A court may imply terms into an employment contract. Examples of terms implied in the past include a duty of good faith on the part of the employee, a duty of mutual co-operation on the part of the employer and employee and other duties noted below.

- Legislation

  For example terms in relation to the right to equal pay; the right not to be discriminated against; the right to be paid a minimum wage.

- Custom and practice

  Relevant business practices either nationally or locally can be implied into a contract of employment. Such practices must be reasonable, certain and not unlawful. This source of terms has diminished with the increased formalisation of employment contracts and if there is any conflict then, of course, the contract prevails.

- Collective agreements between employers and trade unions or staff associations

  The terms of an agreement between union and employer may expressly or impliedly form part of a contract of employment.

It should be noted that works and staff rules e.g. in an employee handbook or on staff notice boards may not be implied as terms of the employment contract, but a failure to obey them could be treated as evidence of a failure to obey reasonable orders. It may be more beneficial to the employer for these rules not to have the status of a contractual term since they can then be varied or introduced as the employer sees fit without the consent of the employee which would otherwise be necessary if they were contractual terms.

Different jurisdictions will imply different rights and duties on the employer and employee but many common ones are set out below.

Implied duties of the employee

- Duty to give honest and faithful service (fidelity)

  The duty of fidelity is of fundamental importance. It is breached if, for example, an employee works for a competitor in their spare time.

- Duty to obey lawful and reasonable orders.

English case law example

PEPPER v WEBB 1968

Facts: A gardener refused to plant the plants where instructed by the employer.

Held: He was in breach of the duty to obey lawful and reasonable orders and this, coupled with the fact that he was rude and surly, justified his dismissal.

- Duty to exercise reasonable care and skill

  The employee must act with reasonable care in performing his or her duties. A single act of negligence will not usually justify dismissal, unless it is gross negligence.

  An extension of this duty of care is a duty to indemnify the employer for any damages incurred as a result of the employee's negligence.

English case law example

LISTER v ROMFORD ICE & COLD STORAGE LTD 1972

Facts: An employee negligently ran over another employee with a fork-lift truck.

Held: He was liable in damages to his employer for breach of contract.

- Duty not to misuse confidential information

  An employee must not disclose trade secrets to a third party nor misuse confidential information he or she has acquired in the course of his or her employment. This duty can continue even after the employment has ended.

- Duty to give personal service

  The employee must carry out his or her duties personally unless he or she has express or implied permission to delegate.

- Duty of mutual cooperation

  This is a mutual obligation imposed on both parties and is based on respect and consideration for each other.

Implied duties of the employer

- To pay reasonable remuneration.

- To indemnify employees for properly incurred expenses.

- To take reasonable care for the safety of their employees e.g. safe plant and machinery, safe system of work and reasonably competent fellow employees.

- To give reasonable notice of termination of employment.

- To maintain mutual co-operation, trust and confidence.

Note that there is generally no duty to:

- provide work. However, such a duty may be implied where payment is by commission or piece work, or where the employee is skilled and needs practice to maintain those skills, there may be an obligation to provide a reasonable amount of work.

- provide a reference. However, if a reference is provided it must be truthful.

Zero hour contracts

In 2015 zero hour contracts were introduced into employment legislation in England and Wales. Since then they have been the source of much controversy.

A zero hours contract is a contract of employment where the undertaking to work is conditional on work being offered and there is no certainty that work will be offered.

From an employer's perspective it gives access to a flexible workforce. However, critics will argue that it allows labour to be exploited. In some instances, employers are penalising workers on a zero hours contract for not being available when requested or cancelling pre-arranged work at short notice.

2   Notice and dismissal

Notice

Many contracts of employment will expressly state how much notice is to be given by either party in order to terminate the contract. Some jurisdictions have legislation which lays down certain minimum periods. These are usually based on the employee's length of continuous service with the employer.

Dismissal

Breach of a term of the contract, if it is serious enough, may entitle the innocent party to treat the contract as at an end and bring a claim for breach of contract. Breach by an employer may give the employee the right to bring a claim for wrongful and/or unfair dismissal.

Employment law varies across different jurisdictions and not all terms have the same meaning. What follows is a general description of some common concepts but individual legal advice should always be sought in each jurisdiction.

Wrongful dismissal

This is the term often used where the employer terminates the contract:

- without giving proper notice, or

- during its fixed term.

Dismissal without notice is known as summary dismissal.

Summary dismissal is usually wrongful dismissal unless the employee:

- waives their rights or accepts payment in lieu of notice

- repudiates the contract themselves or is in fundamental breach (e.g. wilful refusal to obey lawful orders; failure to show professional skill; serious negligence; breach of duty of good faith).

Remedies

An individual who believes he or she has been wrongfully dismissed would sue for compensation in the form of damages (a monetary sum linked to the period of notice he or she failed to receive).

> ## Wrongful dismissal
>
> Bill employed Ben and Jack. Their contracts of employment provided that Bill must give a minimum of one week's notice to his employees. (This was also the minimum implied by legislation). Ben was a conscientious employee but Bill dismissed Ben with only one day's notice. Ben would have a claim for wrongful dismissal as he had not received the proper notice. Jack was not a conscientious employee and had been found by Bill committing a serious assault on his work colleagues in the staff canteen. Bill dismissed Jack on the spot. Jack's dismissal was a summary dismissal. It is however unlikely to be a wrongful dismissal as Jack was in very serious breach of his contract due to his gross misconduct.

Unfair dismissal

This is the term often used to describe the situation where an employer terminates an employee's contract of employment without justification.

A claim for unfair dismissal is usually governed by legislation and often requires the employee to have had a minimum length of service. The law usually provides that the employee must prove that he or she was dismissed. Dismissal for these purposes can be shown where the employer terminated the contract with or without notice, terminated before the expiry of a fixed term or terminated by constructive dismissal. Constructive dismissal occurs where an employee terminates the contract, with or without notice, by reason of the employer's conduct. The employer's conduct must be sufficiently serious for the employee to leave at once. If he or she continues for any length of time without leaving, he or she may be regarded as having affirmed the contract. Affirmation results in himself or herself losing the right to treat himself or herself as discharged.

Once the employee has proved that he or she was dismissed the onus is placed upon the employer to prove that the dismissal was fair and that he or she acted reasonably in dismissing the employee.

Legislation often provides that some reasons for dismissal are "automatically" unfair (for example in England dismissal for pregnancy is automatically unfair) whereas other reasons may be "potentially fair".

When analysing whether dismissal is fair or a breach of contract, a number of issues are relevant:

- **Conduct** – a well documented and fair disciplinary procedure should be in place.

- **Capability** – the employer must demonstrate that the employee failed to meet the required standard and should detail formal/informal warnings given and any remedial actions attempted, for example the offer of extra training or transfer to another (more suitable) role.

- **Breach of statutory duty**– dismissal would be considered fair if continuing employment would breach statutory duty, e.g. health and safety legislation.

- **Some other suitable reason** – e.g. dishonesty, refusal to transfer within the organisation.

- **Redundancy** – see below.

Constructive dismissal

Even if the employer can prove that the reason for dismissal was fair they must also prove that they acted reasonably in dismissing the employee for that reason.

Unfair dismissal
The following examples might not be considered reasonable: - If an employee was dismissed without warning (except in the most flagrant cases). - If the dismissal was on the grounds of capability or qualifications and the employer did not allow time for improvement, training and consultation to discuss areas of difficulty. - If the employer is relying on the grounds of ill health and there is insufficient medical evidence to support that ground. - In the case of misconduct where the employer did not fully investigate the complaint and did not listen to what the employee had to say by way of explanation or mitigation. - If the employer is relying on redundancy and the employee was selected purely because of his or her trade union activities.

Remedies

If the employee is found to have been unfairly dismissed the legislation may provide a variety of remedies including the possible reinstatement or re-engagement of the employee or, more likely, some monetary compensation.

- Reinstatement

    This is an order that the employee may return to the same job without any break in continuity. It will only be ordered where requested by the applicant and practically achievable.

- Re-engagement

    This is an order that the employee must be re-engaged upon comparable employment.

Redundancy

In many jurisdictions, a dismissal on the grounds of redundancy may be justified on any of the following grounds:

- cessation of business

- cessation of business in the place where the employee was employed

- cessation of the type of work for which the employee was employed.

The place where a person is employed means in this context, the place where he or she is habitually employed and any place where, under the contract, he or she can be required to work. There will not, therefore, usually be a redundancy situation where the transfer of location is reasonable or where the contract gives the employer the right to move the employee in question from one place to another.

Redundancy should be fair and in some countries it is a requirement that consultation must take place, e.g. with employees and trade unions.

3 Workplace policies

There are many issues and many laws applying to matters that occur within the workplace. Some organisations may have specific policies which go beyond what is legally required as they have their own set of core values. A number of examples of workplace policies are included at the end of this chapter in order to illustrate how the policies may be worded. **Please note that you will not be examined on the wording of these examples.**

Diversity and discrimination (equal opportunities policy)

Many jurisdictions have legislation providing that an employee has the right not to be discriminated against in relation to their gender or sexual orientation, race, age, disabilities, or religion and beliefs.

There are two types of discrimination that an equal opportunities policy will attempt to prevent:

- **Direct discrimination** – this occurs when an employer treats an employee less favourably than another, due to their gender, race etc. For example, if a driving job was only open to male applicants.

  This may be allowed by law in certain, tightly defined circumstances.

- **Indirect discrimination** – this occurs when a working condition or rule disadvantages one group of people more than another. For example, a requirement for male employees to be clean-shaven would put some religious groups at a disadvantage.

  Indirect discrimination is often illegal, unless it is necessary for the working of the business and there is no way of avoiding it.

Diversity is about valuing and embracing the differences in people and reaping the benefits of a varied workforce that makes the best of people's talents whatever their backgrounds. Diversity encompasses visible and non-visible individual differences. It can be seen in the makeup of the workforce in terms of gender, ethnic minorities, and people with disabilities by looking at access to management positions, job opportunities and general terms and conditions in the workplace.

Disciplinary procedures

It is common practice for a company to have written disciplinary rules and procedures to deal with employee performance and conduct. Staff should be notified about these rules and procedures.

The rules should state what is acceptable and unacceptable behaviour in the workplace and what action will be taken if the rules are broken.

The rules should also clearly say when someone might face disciplinary action and what that action could be. Employees should also be provided with the name of someone they should appeal to if they are unhappy about a disciplinary decision.

The disciplinary rules should give examples of what will be treated as gross misconduct. This is misconduct judged so serious that it is likely to lead to dismissal without notice, e.g. fraud and theft.

Corruption and bribery

Corruption is now recognized to be one of the world's greatest challenges.

Kofi Annan, former Secretary General of the UN made the following statement:

"Corruption .. undermines democracy and the rule of law, leads to violations of human rights, distorts markets, erodes the quality of life and allows organised crime, terrorism and other threats to human security to flourish .. corruption hurts the poor disproportionately by diverting funds intended for development, undermining a government's ability to provide basic services, feeding inequality and injustice and discouraging foreign aid investment".

In 2013 The World Bank stated that "bribery has become a $1 trillion industry".

What is corruption?

Generally corruption is described as an abuse of trust in order to gain an unfair advantage.

Examples include but are not limited to:

- Bribery

  The giving or receiving of something of value (e.g. gift/loan/fee/reward or other advantage) to influence a transaction.

  Note: firms are allowed to provide hospitality, promotional or other business expenditure. For example, to provide tickets to sporting events, take clients to dinner, offer gifts to clients as a reflection of good relations, or pay for reasonable travel expenses in order to demonstrate goods or services to clients if that is reasonable and proportionate for the business.

  However where hospitality is really a cover for bribing someone, the authorities would look at such things as the level of hospitality offered, the way in which it was provided and the level of influence the person receiving it had on the business decision in question.

- Facilitation payments

  Facilitation payments are additional payments made to induce officials to perform routine functions that they are not otherwise obliged to perform. For example, additional payments to customs officials so they prioritise processing the import of particular goods.

  Some countries may perceive these facilitation payments as bribes if the sums involved are excessive.

- Conflict of interest

  This is where an employee has a duty to act on behalf of an employer and has an economic or personal interest in a transaction.

English Bribery Act 2010

The bribery offences are as follows:

- bribing a person to induce or reward them to perform a relevant function improperly

- requesting, accepting or receiving a bribe as a reward for performing a relevant function improperly

- using a bribe to influence a foreign official to gain a business advantage

- corporate liability for failing to prevent bribery on behalf of a commercial organisation.

Evaluating anti-bribery and corruption procedures

Some countries have a requirement that firms have to ensure that they have adequate procedures and controls to prevent bribery and corruption.

What counts as adequate will depend on the bribery risks the organisation faces and the nature, size and complexity of the business.

Whistleblowing

Whistleblowing means disclosing information that a worker believes is evidence of illegality, gross waste, gross mismanagement, abuse of power, or substantial and specific danger to the public health and safety. The person who exposes the information is known as the whistleblower (from the sporting analogy of a referee blowing the whistle to indicate a foul). The information is often about the employer but it may be about a fellow worker. He or she may disclose as a matter of conscience or ethics or because he or she is following internal rules or procedures.

Sometimes whistleblowers are targeted in the workplace because they have disclosed information. Repercussions for the whistleblower could include termination/suspension/demotion/wage reduction and/or harsh treatment by fellow workers.

In some countries there are laws which protect a whistleblower.

Generally, in order to be protected by law the whistleblower must:

- Reveal information of the right type: a 'qualifying disclosure'

- Reveal information to the right person and in the right way: this makes it a 'protected disclosure'.

Qualifying disclosures

To be protected the whistleblower needs to reasonably believe that malpractice is happening, has happened, or will happen. The malpractice can take the form of:

- a criminal offence, e.g. fraud

- someone's health and safety is in danger

- risk or actual damage to the environment

- a miscarriage of justice

- the company is breaking the law e.g. does not have the right insurance

- a belief that someone is covering up wrongdoing.

Protected disclosure

For a disclosure to a person to be protected the whistleblower must:

- Make the disclosure in good faith i.e. not acting out of revenge or spite or some other ulterior personal motive.

- Reasonably believe that the information is substantially true.

- Reasonably believe that he or she is making the disclosure to the right person.

Most legislation encourages disclosure to be made internally in the first instance but also provides for external disclosure in certain circumstances to others such as:

- To a legal adviser

- To a government minister if the individual is a public sector worker

- To a professional body or in extreme circumstances the media (but in this case stricter rules apply).

Money Laundering

Money laundering is the process by which criminally obtained money or other assets (criminal property) are exchanged for 'clean' money or other assets with no obvious link to their criminal origins. It also covers money, however come by, which is used to fund terrorism.

There are three acknowledged phases to money laundering:

1 Placement

   The illegitimate funds generated from crime are placed in the financial system, for example cash paid into a bank account. This is the point when proceeds of crime are most apparent and at risk of detection.

2 Layering

   Once proceeds of crime are in the financial system, layering obscures their origins by passing the money through complex transactions. These often involve different entities like companies and trusts and can take place in multiple jurisdictions.

3 Integration

   Once the origin of the funds has been obscured, the criminal is able to make the funds reappear as legitimate funds or assets. They will invest funds in legitimate businesses or other forms of investment such as property.

Most financial institutions globally, and many non-financial institutions, are required to identify and report transactions of a suspicious nature to the financial intelligence unit in their country.

English Law

Under English law an employee in a firm of accountants would be required to report to the firm's Money Laundering Reporting Officer (MLRO) if he or she knew or had reasonable grounds for suspecting that a person was engaged in, or attempting , money laundering. The MLRO and the firm would then report the matter to the National Crime Agency.

Data protection

Data protection laws exist to strike a balance between the rights of living individuals to privacy and the ability of an organisation to use data for the purposes of their business.

Some countries will have laws which give individuals the right to know what information is held about them. The law can provide a framework to ensure that personal information is handled properly.

The purpose of any such legislation is to:

- Give rules and principles concerning the use of data.

- Provide individuals with important rights concerning data held about them.

Data protection principles

Subject to certain exemptions, in general, anyone who processes personal information must ensure that the data is:

- processed fairly and lawfully.

- obtained only for specified and lawful purposes.

- adequate, relevant and not excessive.

- accurate and, where necessary, kept up to date.

- kept no longer than is necessary; and

- kept secure.

Laws may provide individuals with important rights such as the right to find out what personal information is held on computer and most paper records, on payment of a reasonable fee.

Much of this legislation has impacted on the way in which organisations conduct business in terms of who can be contacted for marketing purposes, not only by telephone and direct mail but also by electronic means and this has led to the development of permission based marketing strategies.

Social Media

The impact of social media on the workplace is increasing. Social media is the broad term for internet-based tools used on PCs, laptops, tablets and smart phones to help people make contact, keep in touch and interact.

This trend can affect communications among managers, employees and job applicants, how organisations promote and control their reputation, and how colleagues treat one another. It can also distort what boundaries there are between home and work.

An organisation should ensure that it has a social media policy in place. Employers should include what is and what is not acceptable for general behaviour in the use at work of the internet, emails, smart phones and social media, such as networking websites, blogs and tweets. The employer needs to consider whether to use social media to evaluate applicants and whether to impose limits on use by employees due to loss of work time.

Health and Safety

The law typically puts the responsibility for health and safety on both the employer and the employee.

Generally speaking, the employer has a duty, amongst other things, to:

* provide a safe working environment

* provide adequate information, instruction, training and supervision to enable individuals to be safe

* prevent risks to health

* ensure that plant and machinery are safe to use and that safe working practices are set up and followed

* inform staff of any potential hazards

* provide adequate first aid facilities

* check that the right equipment is used and that it is regularly maintained

* set up emergency plans.

If employers fail to provide a safe and healthy working environment they may be liable to a claim from an employee or, even, the State.

Generally an employee has, amongst other things, a duty to:

* take reasonable care of their own health and safety

* take reasonable care not to put other people at risk

* cooperate with their employer to ensure they have adequate training and are familiar with their employer's health and safety policies

* report any injuries suffered as a result of performing their job

* inform their employer if anything affects their ability to work safely.

Examples of workplace policies

As mentioned earlier you will not be examined on the wording of these examples.

Examples of money laundering policy

The company is required under money laundering legislation to put in place appropriate systems and controls to prevent money laundering.

This policy contains the procedures that we have developed in order to comply with these obligations.

Money laundering is the process through which proceeds of crime and their true origin and ownership are changed so that the proceeds appear legitimate.

How do I know if my matter involves money laundering?

You do not have to behave like a police officer but you do have to remain alert to the warning signs of money laundering and make the sort of enquiries that a reasonable person (with the same qualifications, knowledge and experience as you) would make.

Typical signs of money laundering

- obstructive or secretive clients

- instructions outside our usual range of expertise, i.e. why is the client using us?

- clients based a long way from us with no apparent reason for using

- cases or instructions that change unexpectedly or for no logical reason, especially where:

  - the client has deposited funds with us; and

  - the source of funds changes at the last moment

  - you are asked to return funds or send funds to a third party

  - loss-making transactions where the loss is avoidable

- complex or unusually large transactions

- transactions with no apparent logical, economic or legal purpose

- large amounts of cash being used

- money transfers where there is a variation between the account holder and signatory

- payments to or from third parties where there is no logical connection to the client

- movement of funds between accounts, institutions or jurisdictions without reason

- large payment on account of fees with instructions terminated shortly after and the client requesting the funds are redirected.

Reporting suspicions

You have a strict duty to keep the affairs of our clients confidential. The circumstances in which you can disclose information about our clients are very limited.

However, legislation imposes obligations to report knowledge or suspicion of money laundering by way of a Suspicious Activity Report (SAR). These obligations can override your duty of confidentiality.

Any member of staff can submit a SAR form to the Nominated Officer.

What are knowledge and suspicion?

Knowledge means actual knowledge rather than wilfully shutting one's eyes to the truth.

Suspicion is a possibility which is more than fanciful. A vague feeling of unease will not suffice.

There is no requirement for the suspicion to be clear or firmly grounded on specific facts, but there must be a belief which is beyond mere speculation.

The test for whether you hold a suspicion is generally subjective. However, there is an objective element to the test i.e. would the reasonable solicitor, with the same knowledge, experience and information, have formed a suspicion.

The suspicion held must be that another person is engaged in money laundering and not simply that there is something 'fishy' about the client or the transaction.

If you have formed knowledge or suspicion that another person is engaged in money laundering you must complete the SAR form and send it to the Nominated Officer.

If you are suspicious but are not sure why, for instance there is something that just does not feel right about the client or the matter, you must discuss your concerns with the Nominated Officer, who may instruct you to complete the SAR form if he is satisfied that there are reasonable grounds to suspect money laundering or terrorist financing. You should keep a note of that discussion.

How do I make a report?

If you know or suspect that your matter involves money laundering, you must complete the SAR form.

What happens after I make a SAR?

On receiving your SAR form, the MLRO will consider the reasons for suspicion reported to him or her. He or she may ask you for more information.

The MLRO will then decide whether an external SAR is required. This decision rests only with the Nominated Officer.

You have discharged your reporting obligations under legislation by making the internal SAR.

What can I tell my client?

You must not tell the client that you have submitted a SAR. If you do you will be committing the offence of tipping-off and could be exposed to a criminal record.

There is very little, if anything, that you can tell the client after you have submitted a SAR. Always speak with the MLRO if you are in any doubt.

Example of data protection policy

The company is committed to the highest standards of document and information management and security and treat confidentiality and data security extremely seriously.

We take seriously our obligations under all relevant regulation and legislation.

Purpose

The purpose of this policy is to:

- protect against the potential breaches of confidentiality and failures of integrity or availability of information

- ensure all our information assets and IT facilities are protected against damage, loss or misuse

- increase awareness and understanding in the company of the requirements of information security and the responsibility of staff to protect the confidentiality and integrity of the information that they themselves handle.

Responsibility

Every member of staff is responsible for ensuring that information held is accurate and kept confidential and that the terms of this policy are adhered to.

In the event of a data security breach, the relevant person must be informed immediately.

Our obligations under data protection legislation include that:

- we only hold data with consent
- we keep that data confidential
- we use it only for authorised purpose(s)
- any data we hold is:
  - adequate
  - relevant
  - not excessive
  - accurate, and
  - up-to-date
  - we do not hold it for longer than is necessary.

Our Procedures

Information Management

- Records and information are owned by the company and not by any individual or team.
- Keeping accurate and up-to-date records is an integral part of all business activities.
- Complete and accurate records must be securely stored in the appropriate locations and be easily identifiable and accessible to those who need to see them. This means that:
  - files must be kept in accordance with our normal file management protocols and must be kept organised and up-to-date
  - substantive matter related emails must be placed on file and must not be stored solely in personal mailboxes
  - files must not be removed from the office except as permitted under this policy.

Access to Offices and Files

- All office access doors must be kept secure at all times and clients and visitors must not be given keys or pass-codes.
- Clients and visitors should never be left alone in areas where they could have access to confidential information.

Computers and IT

- Computers must be password protected. Passwords should not be written down or given to others.

- Computers and other devices should be locked when not in use to minimise the risk of accidental data loss or disclosure.

Backup of Data

- All electronic data must be securely backed up at the end of each working day.

- Backup media must be encrypted.

- Backup media that is retained on site prior to being sent for storage off site and must be stored securely in a locked safe and at a sufficient distance away from the original data to ensure both the original and backup copies are not compromised.

IT System Management and Development

- Our IT systems are managed by the IT manager who is responsible for overseeing day-to-day operation and to ensure continued security and integrity.

- Access controls will be maintained at appropriate levels for all systems by ongoing and proactive management. Any changes to permissions must be approved by the IT manager.

- New IT systems, or upgrades to existing systems, must be authorised by the IT manager and the authorisation process must take account of security requirements. The information assets associated with any proposed new or updated systems must be identified and a risk assessment undertaken.

- Any new equipment must have appropriate levels of resilience and fault tolerance and must be correctly maintained.

- Software and applications must be managed to ensure their smooth day-to-day running and to preserve data security and integrity. The purchase or installation of new or upgraded software must be planned and managed and any information security risks must be mitigated. Specifications for new software or upgrades of existing software must specify the required information security controls.

Reporting Breaches

All members of staff have an obligation to report actual or potential data protection compliance failures. This allows us to:

- investigate the failure and take remedial steps if necessary

- maintain a register of compliance failures.

The Company requires good standards of conduct from its employees, together with satisfactory standards of work. The purpose of the disciplinary procedure is to ensure that any concerns over employees' conduct or performance are handled in a fair, consistent and timely manner, with the intention of bringing about an improvement, and to protect the proper operation of the Company's business and the health and safety of its employees.

Purpose and scope

Although line managers are encouraged to address conduct issues through coaching and other informal routes, a more formal approach is sometimes necessary. This would usually be the case where coaching has failed to result in the required improvements, or the issue is serious enough to warrant invoking the formal procedure in the first instance, for example a serious breach of your contract of employment.

Disciplinary offences

Matters that the Company views as amounting to disciplinary offences include (but are not limited to):

- persistent bad timekeeping, unauthorised absence or poor attendance

- minor damage to Company property

- failure to observe Company procedures

- abusive or disruptive behaviour

- unreasonable refusal to follow an instruction issued by a manager or supervisor

- smoking in non-designated areas of the Company's premises

- bribery offences

- and any breach of the Company's policies and procedures.

The Company reserves the right to implement the procedure at any stage as set out below taking into account the alleged misconduct of an employee.

Procedure for conducting formal disciplinary hearings

Depending on the offence, issues will normally be dealt with informally in the first instance. If it is felt that the issues cannot be dealt with informally, the employee will be invited to a disciplinary hearing. No formal disciplinary action will be taken against an employee until the issues have been investigated and in all cases the discipline and dismissal procedure will be adhered to. This procedure is as outlined below:

Step 1: The employee will be invited to attend a disciplinary hearing. The invite letter will set out the purpose of the hearing, when and where it is to take place, who will be in attendance and include details of the alleged misconduct, including any relevant supporting documentation (e.g.: investigation findings).

Step 2: A meeting will be held where the alleged misconduct will be discussed in detail.

Step 3: An outcome will be delivered at the end of the meeting or as soon as possible afterwards; this will either be a disciplinary sanction or a decision will be made to take no further action. This will be confirmed in writing.

In some cases further investigation may need to be carried out. In this case the meeting will be adjourned for investigating purposes. An outcome of the disciplinary hearing will be given at a later date. If further information is gathered, the employee will be allowed a reasonable period of time, to consider the new information prior to the reconvening of the disciplinary proceedings.

Step 4: Once received, the employee can appeal against the outcome of the meeting. Details of how to do so will be included in the outcome letter.

At any formal meeting, employees have the right to be accompanied by a colleague or Union Representative (if applicable). The employee must take all reasonable steps to attend the meeting.

At the hearing

Attendance

Where the employee is unable to attend a disciplinary hearing and provides a good reason for failing to attend, the hearing will be adjourned to another day. Except in exceptional circumstances, if the employee is unable to attend the rearranged hearing, the rearranged hearing will take place in the employee's absence. The employee's fellow worker or trade union official may attend in such circumstances and will be allowed the opportunity to present the employee's case. The employee will also be allowed to make written submissions in such a situation.

Witnesses

Employees must give advance warning if they wish to call his/her own relevant witnesses to the hearing to support their case, however, the Company will not allow the calling of witnesses for the purposes of cross-examination. Instead, where witnesses have provided evidence for an investigation, you will have an opportunity to respond to that evidence during the hearing.

Role of a companion

The employee's chosen companion has the right to address the hearing to put the employee's case, sum up the case and respond on the employee's behalf to any view expressed at the hearing. The companion may also confer with the employee during the hearing. However, there is no requirement for the employer to permit the companion to answer questions on behalf of the employee, or to address the hearing where the employee indicates that he/she does not wish this.

Gross misconduct and summary dismissal

Gross misconduct is misconduct of such a serious and fundamental nature that it breaches the contractual relationship between the employee and the Company. In the event that an employee commits an act of gross misconduct, the Company will be entitled to terminate summarily the employee's contract of employment without notice or pay in lieu of notice.

Matters that the Company views as amounting to gross misconduct include (but are not limited to):

- theft, fraud, deliberate falsification of records

- other offences of dishonesty

- absence without leave and unauthorised leave

- falsification of a qualification that is a stated requirement of the employee's employment or results in financial gain to the employee

- sexual misconduct at work

- fighting with or physical assault on members of staff or the public

- deliberate and/or damage to or misuse of the organisation's property

- serious incapability through alcohol or being under the influence of illegal drugs

- possession, custody or control of illegal drugs on the organisation's premises

- serious breach of the organisation's rules, including, but not restricted to, health and safety rules and rules on computer and social media use

- gross negligence

- imprisonment

- conduct that brings the Company's name into disrepute; and

- bullying, harassment and discrimination.

Appeal

An employee who wishes to appeal against a disciplinary decision must do so in writing within 7 calendar days. A relevant manager or a member of the Human Resources team will hold the appeal meeting and their decision is final. Wherever possible a manager of seniority to be capable of over-riding an original decision (if necessary) will hold the appeal meeting and their decision is final. At the appeal meeting, any disciplinary sanction that has been imposed will be reviewed.

When lodging an appeal, the employee should state:

(a) the grounds of the appeal; and

(b) whether he/she is appealing against the finding that he/she has committed that alleged act or acts of misconduct, or against the level of disciplinary sanction imposed.

Appeal hearings will normally take place within 14 days of receipt of the employee's written notice of appeal.

Extract from an equity, diversity and inclusion policy

Our core values define the Company's culture and provide the framework for what we deliver to our customers and employees each day. We are fully committed to providing services which embrace diversity and promote equality and inclusion. As an employer we celebrate and value equality, diversity and inclusion within our workforce. Our vision is to ensure that these commitments, reinforced by our values, are embedded in our day-to-day working practices with all our learners, colleagues and partners.

The Company expects all its managers and employees to be fully committed to the elimination of unlawful and unfair discrimination and to actively embrace the principles of equality, diversity and inclusion (EDI).

Purpose and scope

The Company is fully committed to providing a good and harmonious working environment where everyone is treated equally and with respect and dignity. Our aim is that remuneration, recruitment, promotion, and retention will not be affected by irrelevant considerations and stereotyping.

The Company is proudly committed to being an equal opportunities employer. Therefore, it is our policy that there will be no discrimination against or harassment of any employee, job applicant or supplier contractor either directly, indirectly or by association or perception, on the basis of any of the following:

- Race (including nationality and ethnicity)
- Sex
- Disability
- Gender reassignment
- Sexual orientation
- Religion or philosophical belief
- Age
- Marital or civil partnership status
- Pregnancy and maternity.

This policy has been developed to:

- Ensure the company fulfils its legal obligations
- Prevent and/or minimise the risk of any discrimination or unfair treatment to employees and job applicants
- Increase awareness of minimum acceptable standards amongst employees and workers
- Promote positive attitudes and behaviours with regard to EDI for the health, well-being and benefit of employees, learners, employers and other stakeholders
- Share good and best practice which leads to continuous improvement through embedding EDI into all the policies, strategies and procedures.

Example of whistleblowing policy

Our core values define the Company's culture, and as part of promoting that culture it is important to the Company that any fraud, misconduct or wrongdoing by workers is reported and dealt with properly.

Purpose and scope

This policy sets out the way in which individuals may raise any concerns they have about business malpractice and how those concerns will be dealt with.

Disclosure

Legislation provides protection for workers who raise legitimate concerns about a specified matter. These are called 'qualifying disclosures'. Legislation only covers qualifying disclosures that are made in the public interest under six categories; criminal offence, miscarriage of justice, endangerment of health and safety, damage to the environment, breach of any other legal obligation and any cover-up of these issues.

To obtain protection employees must first disclose the information to the employer using the internal procedures available.

A worker who makes such a protected disclosure has the right not to be dismissed, or subjected to victimisation, because they have made the disclosure.

This procedure should be used to disclose a concern that, in your honest, reasonable belief, wrongdoing has been committed, is being committed or is likely to be committed.

What is covered

Wrongdoing includes (but is not limited to):

- Serious breach of the Company's Code of Conduct
- An unlawful or criminal offence (e.g. fraud, corruption or theft)
- A breach of a legal obligation
- A miscarriage of justice
- A disregard of legislation governing health and safety at work
- Action that has led to or could lead to damage to the environment
- Breach of the Company's Anti-bribery and Corruption Policy
- The deliberate covering up of information in relation to any of the above.

Reporting a concern

A worker who reasonably believes that inappropriate business conduct has occurred, is occurring or is likely to occur should in the first instance raise the issue with member of the Senior Leadership Team or a Human Resources Manager. Alternatively, the conduct or activity may be reported anonymously by calling the Company's Ethics Hotline.

Every effort will be made to ensure confidentiality and if requested all reasonable steps will be taken to protect the anonymity of the whistleblower. However, under certain circumstances to assist with the investigation the individual's identity may become known or need to be revealed.

Investigation

Once an individual has raised a concern, the matter will be investigated by either the person to whom the matter was raised or, where more appropriate, the Company will appoint an alternative manager. It is not the responsibility of the individual raising the concern to investigate the wrongdoing in order to gather evidence.

The format of the investigation may vary depending upon the circumstances. However, the individual who raised the concern may be required to attend an investigation meeting.

Once the investigation is complete, the individual who raised the concern will be informed of the outcome and further steps that are to be taken.

If the individual who raised the concern is dissatisfied with the investigation or outcome they should raise the matter with a more senior member of the management team or HR.

Safeguards

The Company will not tolerate any negative behaviour towards an employee who has reported a possible wrongdoing. Victimisation of a worker for raising a concern may constitute a disciplinary offence.

No action will be taken against anyone who makes an allegation, reasonably believing it to be true, even if the allegation is not subsequently confirmed by the investigation. However, maliciously making a false allegation or misuse of the whistleblowing procedure is a disciplinary offence.

Purpose and scope

This policy sets out how social media usage is managed in line with Company policy and guidelines, as well as legal obligations.

It is important all employees understand their obligations in line with ensuring appropriate use of social media whilst an employee of the Company.

Definition of social media

For the purposes of this policy, social media is a type of interactive online media that allows parties to communicate instantly with each other or to share data in a public forum. Social Media includes, but is not limited to, online social forums, blogs, wiki's, communities and sites such as Twitter, Facebook and LinkedIn, video- and image-sharing websites such as YouTube, Pinterest and Flickr, and any other web-based or virtual communities in which people may share and exchange information.

Employees should be aware that there are many more examples of social media than can be listed here and this is a constantly changing area. Employees should follow these guidelines in relation to any social media that they use.

Things you should know about your public information

Employees should be aware that many of the communications and information they post on social networking sites is neither private nor temporary. Employees should also be aware that when they choose to publish their opinions through a blog, social networking site or other openly accessible medium, they are legally responsible for those opinions. Ultimately, it is the responsibility of the employee to keep information private if desired.

Use of social media in your personal life and at work

The organisation encourages employees to make reasonable and appropriate use of social media websites as part of their work, as and when required. The Company recognises that when used in an appropriate capacity, social media allows our employees to share insight and add value for our customers. In addition, the organisation recognises that many employees may also make use of social media in a personal capacity.

Employees must be aware at all times that, if recognisable as a Company employee, or when contributing to the organisation's social media activities, they are representing the organisation. The Company recognises that employees may wish to state the Company as their employer on social media, however the employee's online profile (for example, the name of a blog or a Twitter name) must not contain the organisation's name, except in the case of LinkedIn or similar social media sites that are specifically designed for this purpose.

If employees do discuss their work on social media sites, other than via official Company channels, (for example, giving opinions on their specialism or the sector in which the organisation operates), they must include on their profile a statement along the following lines: "The views I express here are mine alone and do not necessarily reflect the views of my employer."

Employees may contribute to the organisation's social media activities, for example by writing for our blogs/managing a Facebook account/running an official Twitter account on behalf of the organisation, however only when authorised to do so within their role. Employees should use the same safeguards as they would with any other form of communication about the organisation in the public sphere.

Any communications that employees make in a professional or personal capacity through social media must not:

- bring the organisation into disrepute, for example by: – criticising or arguing with customers, colleagues or rivals

  - making defamatory comments about individuals or other organisations or groups; or

  - posting images that are inappropriate or links to inappropriate content

- breach confidentiality, for example by:

  - revealing trade secrets or information owned by the organisation

  - giving away confidential information about an individual (such as a colleague or customer contact) or organisation (such as a rival business); or

  - discussing the organisation's internal workings (such as deals that it is doing with a customer/client or its future business plans that have not been communicated to the public)

- breach copyright, for example by:

  - using someone else's images or written content without permission; or

  - failing to give acknowledgement where permission has been given to reproduce something; or

- do anything that could be considered discriminatory against, or bullying or harassment of, any individual, for example by:

  - making (or condoning others to make) offensive or derogatory comments relating to sex, gender reassignment, race (including nationality), disability, sexual orientation, religion or belief or age

- using social media to bully another individual (such as an employee of the organisation); or

- posting images that are discriminatory or offensive (or links to such content).

- make any false or misleading statements or claims about the Company's products or services.

- confirm, deny or make comment on issues that the employee is not authorised to handle, or for which the employee is not considered an expert.

Please note that this list is indicative and is not exhaustive. Be thoughtful and as considerate when communicating online as you would be in person. Any communication online that does not adhere to the Company's core values or internal policies may be determined to be inappropriate.

Excessive use of social media at work

Employees should not spend an excessive amount of time using social media websites while at work, even if they claim to be doing so as part of their work. This is likely to have a detrimental effect on employees' productivity. They should ensure that use of social media does not interfere with their other duties whilst at work and personal use of social media, whether on company equipment or on an employee's own equipment, should be limited to lunch hours, outside of normal working hours and very limited other occasions.

Consequences for breach of this policy

Employees should note that any breaches of this policy may lead to disciplinary action in line with the Company's Disciplinary Policy, and/or legal action if required. Serious breaches of this policy, for example incidents of bullying of colleagues or social media activity causing serious damage to the organisation, may constitute gross misconduct and lead to summary dismissal.

Monitoring use of social media during work time

The organisation reserves the right to monitor employees' internet usage in line with our IT Acceptable Use policy. The organisation considers that valid reasons for checking an employee's internet usage include suspicions that the employee has:

- been spending an excessive amount of time using social media websites for non-work-related activity; or

- acted in a way that is in breach of the rules set out in this policy; or

- breached any other policy or explicit contractual terms.

Access to particular social media websites may be withdrawn or prohibited, in any case of misuse.

Example of health and safety policy statement

This safety policy statement demonstrates the Company's absolute commitment and responsibility as an employer and educator for providing a safe and healthy environment within the work place, for all staff, contractors and visitors in accordance with the health and safety legislation and our responsibility to reduce our impact on the environment.

The company views managing health, safety, fire issues and the associated responsibilities as the highest priority.

Our statement of general policy is:

- to provide adequate control of the health and safety risks arising from our work activities

- to consult with our employees on matters affecting their health and safety

- to provide and maintain safe plant and equipment

- to ensure safe handling and use of substances

- to provide information, instruction and supervision for employees

- to ensure all employees are competent to do their tasks, and to give them adequate training

- to prevent accidents and cases of work-related ill health

- to maintain safe and healthy working conditions; and to review and revise this policy as necessary at regular intervals.

All employees have to:

- co-operate with supervisors and managers on health and safety matters

- not interfere with anything provided to safeguard their health and safety

- take reasonable care of their own health and safety; and

- report all health and safety concerns to an appropriate person.

4 Test your understanding questions

Test your understanding 1

An employer has an implied duty:

A   To provide facilities for smokers

B   To give employees who leave a reference

C   To provide work

D   To pay reasonable remuneration

Test your understanding 2

Which of the following does not constitute an implied term of an employment contract?

A   A decision of the court

B   Legislation

C   Custom and practice

D   Employee handbook

Test your understanding 3

Which of the following is not an implied duty owed by an employee towards the employer?

A   A duty not to misuse confidential information

B   A duty to provide faithful service

C   A duty to maintain trust and confidence

D   A duty to obey all orders given by his employer

Test your understanding 4

What is the remedy available to an employee who has been wrongfully dismissed?

Test your understanding 5

A summary dismissal occurs when:

A   The parties agree to end the contract immediately

B   The employer terminates the contract with notice but no investigation

C   The employer terminates the contract without notice

D   The employee resigns

Test your understanding 6

What is constructive dismissal?

Test your understanding 7

In the context of whistleblowing what is a 'qualifying disclosure'?

A   Revealing information of the right type

B   Revealing information within the appropriate time frame

C   Revealing information to the right person

D   Revealing information in the right way

Test your understanding 8

Which of the following is not a phase of money laundering?

A   Integration

B   Placement

C   Adjustment

D   Layering

Test your understanding answers

Test your understanding 1

D

This is an implied duty of an employer.

Test your understanding 2

D

The rules in a handbook would not be treated as implied terms, but a failure to obey them could be treated as evidence of a failure to obey reasonable orders.

Test your understanding 3

D

An employee is only under an obligation to obey orders which are lawful and reasonable.

Test your understanding 4

The remedy available would be compensation in the form of damages.

Test your understanding 5

C

Summary dismissal is dismissal without notice.

Test your understanding 6

Constructive dismissal is when an employee terminates the contract, with or without notice, by reason of the employer's conduct.

Test your understanding 7

A

A qualifying disclosure is revealing information of the right type.

Test your understanding 8

C

Placement, layering and integration are phases to money laundering.

Company Administration

Chapter learning objectives

Upon completion of this chapter you will be able to:

- describe the essential characteristics of the different forms of business organisations and the implications of corporate personality

- explain the differences between public and private companies

- explain the purpose and legal status of the articles of association

- explain the main advantages and disadvantages of carrying on business through the medium of a company limited by shares.

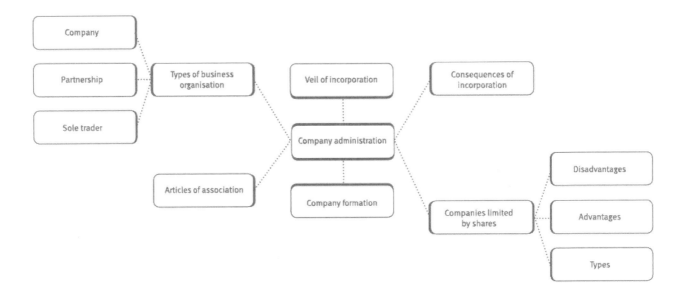

1 Introduction

Business may be carried on by many different forms of organisation. Each jurisdiction will have specific laws governing these organisations and such matters as their creation, their liability, their ownership. In this chapter we are seeking to introduce you to some common forms of business organisations and the general rules that may apply to them.

2 Types of business organisation

Essential characteristics

Sole trader

- The owner 'is' the business – owns the assets and is liable for all the debts.

- Generally no legal formalities are required to set up a sole trader business.

- This form of business is inappropriate for large businesses or those involving a degree of risk.

Partnership

- The relationship which subsists between persons carrying on a business in common with a view of profit.

- A partnership can be an informal arrangement or be formalised and regulated by a written agreement. This agreement is private to the partners.

- In many jurisdictions a partnership is not recognised as a separate legal entity so the partners as individuals are jointly and severally liable for the debts of the partnership. These are often known as ordinary or general partnerships.

- Some jurisdictions however allow the creation of a partnership where one or more partners has limited liability. These partnerships are often created by formal registration under statute and the partnership is recognised as a separate legal entity (e.g. in England the Limited Liability Partnerships Act 2000 allows the creation of limited liability partnerships which must have "LLP" at the end of their name so that a third party can distinguish it from an ordinary partnership).

- In some jurisdictions an LLP is an artificial legal entity with 'perpetual succession'. It can hold property in its own right, enter into contracts in its own name, sue and be sued.

- In some jurisdictions the liability of the members of a limited liability partnership (LLP) is limited to the amount of capital they have agreed to contribute. Requirements similar to that of a company.

Company

- A company is an artificial legal person created by registration with a written constitution (see below).

3 Companies

The doctrine of veil of incorporation

The term 'veil of incorporation' refers to the fact that a company is a separate legal entity (i.e. separate from its members, the owners and its directors, the managers). This separates the legal identity of the company from that of its members, and also its liability from that of the members.

English case law example

SALOMON v SALOMON & CO Ltd 1897

Facts:

S transferred his business to a limited company. He was the director and majority shareholder and a secured creditor. The company went into liquidation and the other creditors tried to obtain repayment from S personally.

Held:

S as shareholder and director had no personal liability to creditors, and he could be repaid in priority as a secured creditor. This enshrined the concepts of separate legal personality and limited liability in the law.

Consequences of incorporation for a company limited by shares

There are a number of consequences of being a separate legal entity:

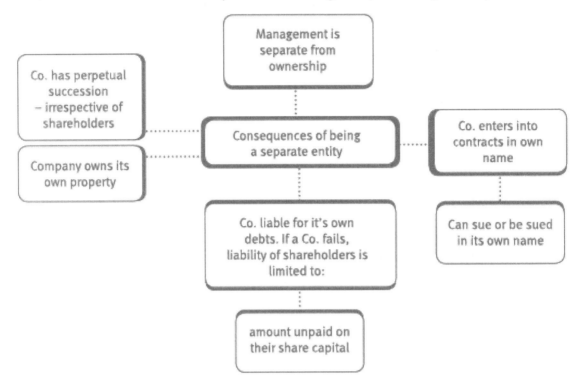

- Management is separate from ownership
- Co. has perpetual succession – irrespective of shareholders
- Company owns its own property
- **Consequences of being a separate entity**
- Co. enters into contracts in own name
- Co. liable for it's own debts. If a Co. fails, liability of shareholders is limited to:
- Can sue or be sued in its own name
- amount unpaid on their share capital

English case law example

MACAURA v NORTHERN LIFE ASSURANCE 1925

Facts:

M owned a forest. He formed a company in which he beneficially owned all the shares and sold his forest to it. He, however, continued to maintain an insurance policy on the forest in his own name. The forest was destroyed by fire.

Held:

He could not claim on the policy since the property damaged belonged to the company, not him, and as shareholder he had no insurable interest in the forest.

Lifting the veil of incorporation

'Lifting the veil of incorporation' means that in certain circumstances the courts can look through the company to the identity of the shareholders. This is intended to prevent inequitable results and expose the commercial reality of the situation.

The usual result of lifting the veil is that the members or directors become personally liable for the company's debts.

English case law example

GILFORD MOTOR CO Ltd v HORNE 1933

Facts:

An employee had a covenant in his contract of employment which stated that he would not solicit his former employer's customers. After he left their employment he formed a company to solicit those customers and claimed it was the company approaching the customers and not him.

Held:

The court held that the company could be restrained from competition, as the previous employee had set it up to evade his own legal obligations. An injunction was granted against him and the company.

There may also be instances where statute will intervene to lift the veil, usually in order to confer a personal liability on those who run a company for breach of their obligations e.g. in England if a director participates in the management of a company in contravention of an order made under the Company Directors Disqualification Act 1986 he or she may be jointly or severally liable along with the company for the company's debts.

4   Companies limited by shares

Introduction

There are many different types of company but by far the most common are companies limited by shares. The company's capital is divided into "shares". Each member holds one or more share. Initially the shares are issued by the company in return for payment by the member. Such companies may be private or public.

Private company v public company

There will be differences between a private company and a public company. The differences can depend on the company law legislation of a particular country. The following table summarises the difference between a private company and a public company in the UK.

	Public companies	Private (limited) companies
Definition	Registered as a public company.	Any company that is not a public company.
Name	Ends with plc or public limited company.	Ends with Ltd or limited.
Capital	In order to trade, must have allotted shares of at least £50,000.	No minimum (or maximum) requirements.
Raising capital	May raise capital by advertising its shares as available for public subscription. This can be through a Stock Exchange.	Prohibited from offering its shares to the public.
Start of trading	Must obtain trading certificate from registrar before commencing trading.	Can begin from date of incorporation.
Directors	Minimum two.	Minimum one.
Secretary	Must have one. Must be qualified.	Need not have one.
Accounts	Must file accounts within 6 months.	Need not lay accounts before general meeting. Must file within 9 months.
Audit	Accounts must be audited.	Audit not required if meets exemption criteria.
Annual General Meeting (AGM)	Must be held each year.	Need not hold an AGM.

5 Company formation

In order to form a company a procedure will need to be followed. Normally a number of documents will need to be submitted to a central registration office (e.g. in England the office of the Registrar of Companies) which includes the following type of information:

- the proposed name of the company

- the memorandum of association which records the intention of each initial subscriber to form a new limited company

- the type of company (e.g. private or public)

- details of the registered office (the address for delivery of legal documents which may need to be served on the company)

- the share capital (e.g. number and class of shares and their nominal value)

- the names of proposed directors and their consent to act

- the names of the first shareholders

- a registration fee.

If this information is satisfactory, then a certificate of incorporation or similar document is issued and the company exists from the date on that certificate.

Off-the-shelf companies

Rather than forming a new company themselves, those wishing to set up a company may buy one 'ready made' or 'off-the-shelf' from a company formation dealer.

The dealer will hold in stock a number of ready made companies with generally non-descriptive names. The company can either trade with an existing name, or have the existing name changed to one of the purchaser's choice, subject to availability.

Buying off the shelf has a number of advantages as follows:

- it may be cheaper and simpler

- the company may be able to trade immediately

- as the company exists, it can enter into contracts immediately.

6   Articles of association

Introduction

The Articles of Association (also known as the Articles of Incorporation or Memorandum of Incorporation in some jurisdictions) form part of the company's internal constitution along with the memorandum of association (in cases where a memorandum is required).

The Articles of Association:

- set out the manner in which the company is to be governed and

- regulate the relationship between the company, its shareholders and its directors.

Articles should contain rules on a number of areas, the most important of which are as follows:

- Appointment and dismissal of directors.

- Powers, responsibilities and liabilities of directors.

- Directors' meetings.

- Members' rights.

- Members' meetings.

- Payment of dividends.

- Communication with members.

- Issue of shares.

- Documents and records.

Companies often draft their own articles although in some jurisdictions the company can choose to adopt articles prescribed by law. These articles can usually be amended by the members although the law often prescribes that a certain percentage of members must approve any such amendment.

Legal effect of company's constitutional documents

Generally the provisions of a company's constitution bind the company and its members to the same extent as if there were covenants on the part of the company and of each member to observe those provisions. This means that the articles form a contract between the company and its members, and between the members themselves, even if they do not sign them. They do not however bind the company to third parties.

7   Advantages and disadvantages of companies limited by shares

Detailed below are the principal advantages and disadvantages of operating a business through the medium of a company limited by shares that are found in many jurisdictions.

Advantages

- Legal entity – separate from its members.

- Liability – the company is liable itself on its contracts.

- Limit on liability – the member's liability is limited to the amount he or she agreed to pay for the shares; the liability of the company is unlimited.

- Ownership – the company owns its assets and ownership is not affected by any change in members (perpetual succession of the company).

- Transferability of shares – members' shares are freely transferrable (subject to any provision in the articles).

Disadvantages

- Formation – detailed documents and administration procedures required on registration.

- Disclosure and loss of privacy – much information about the company, its officers and its financial affairs must be kept and much of this may have to be open for public inspection.

- Cost – complying with all the administrative requirements and the possible need for an audit.

- Management – a member cannot be directly involved in the management of the company unless he or she is also a director.

- Dissolution – formal procedure required.

8   Test your understanding questions

Test your understanding 1

Which of the following is an example of an artificial legal person?

A   A sole trader

B   A general partnership

C   A company

D   None of the above

Test your understanding 2

What are the characteristics of an LLP?

Test your understanding 3

A partnership is a significant form of business organisation.

Which one of the following statements is correct?

A   A partnership is an example of an incorporated business
organisation

B   A partnership is recognised in law as an artificial legal person

C   Partners generally benefit from limited liability for any debts
incurred as a result of their business activities

D   None of the above

Test your understanding 4

What does 'lifting the veil of incorporation' mean?

Test your understanding 5

What are the articles of association?

Test your understanding answers

Test your understanding 1

C

A company is an artificial legal person.

Test your understanding 2

An artificial legal entity with 'perpetual succession'.

It can hold property in its own right, enter into contracts in its own name, sue and be sued.

The liability of the members is limited to the amount of capital they have agreed to contribute.

Test your understanding 3

D

Test your understanding 4

'Lifting the veil of incorporation' means that in certain circumstances the courts can look through the company to the identity of the shareholders.

Test your understanding 5

The articles of association form part of the company's internal constitution. They set out the manner in which the company is to be governed and regulate the relationship between the company, its shareholders and its directors.

Mock Assessment

Chapter learning objectives

This section is intended for use when you have completed your study and initial revision. It contains a complete mock assessment.

This should be attempted as an exam conditions, timed mock. This will give you valuable experience that will assist you with your time management and examination strategy.

Certificate Level

Fundamentals of Ethics, Corporate Governance and Business Law

Instructions: attempt all 85 questions.

Time allowed 2 hours.

Test your understanding 1

Which of the following describes the aim of corporate governance?

A   To ensure that companies are well run in the interests of their shareholders and the wider community

B   To ensure the wealth of companies contributes to the health of the economies where their shares are traded

C   To ensure that companies have a positive impact on the environment, stakeholders and the wider society

D   None of the above

Test your understanding 2

Which corporate governance report focused specifically on the role of non-executive directors?

A   Greenbury report

B   Turnbull report

C   Higgs report

D   Smith report

Test your understanding 3

In which one of the following instances will misrepresentation generally not be recognised?

A   Where there has been a false statement of fact

B   In a contract of utmost good faith, full disclosure is not made

C   Information ceases to be accurate because of changed circumstances

D   Where the representee was unaware of the false statement

Test your understanding 4

The following advertisement appeared in a farming magazine.

'Plough for sale. Little used, very good condition £1,000.'

How would this statement be defined at law?

A Advertising puff

B Offer to sell

C Invitation to treat

D Invitation to buy

Test your understanding 5

An offer was made by A to sell goods on the 1st April for £2,000. B the offeree telephoned A on the 5th April offering to pay £1,800 for the goods. On the 8th April, A offered to sell the goods to C for £1,900, and C accepted this offer on the same day. On the 7th April, B sent a letter to A which was received on the 10th April agreeing to pay the £2,000, the asked price for the goods.

A There is a contract between A and B created on the 7th April

B There is a contract between A and B created on the 10th April

C There is a contract between A and C

D There is no contract created

Test your understanding 6

A coat was displayed in a shop window with a price tag attached which read £10. The price tag should have read £100. X who saw this went into the shop and demanded the coat for £10.

Which one of the following is correct?

A As the window display is an offer, X can demand the coat at £10

B The window display is merely an invitation to treat and the shopkeeper does not have to sell the coat to X

C The shopkeeper can refuse to sell the coat for £10, but cannot refuse to sell the coat to X for £100 if X was prepared to pay this sum

D The shopkeeper would be bound to sell the coat to any customer prepared to pay this £100

Test your understanding 7

Which of the following statement/s is/are correct?

1   A contract term can be implied by statute

2   A contract term can be implied by a court on the basis of trade custom

A   1 only

B   2 only

C   Both 1 and 2

D   Neither 1 or 2

Test your understanding 8

Which one of the following statements is correct?

A   In a contract, a breach of a condition will result in the contract being terminated

B   In a contract, a breach of a condition is a breach of a term of fundamental importance to the contract

C   In a contract, a breach of warranty entitles the injured party to terminate the contract

D   In a contract, a breach of warranty can terminate a contract, but only on the basis of equity

Test your understanding 9

Which of the following statement/s is/are correct?

1   A limited liability partnership has legal personality

2   Individual members of a limited liability partnership will have contractual liability to creditors of the partnership

A   1 only

B   2 only

C   Both 1 and 2

D   Neither 1 or 2

Test your understanding 10

To which type of company is the UK Corporate Governance Code primarily directed?

A   All companies

B   All public companies

C   All private and public companies

D   All listed public companies

Test your understanding 11

Which of the following is not a recommendation of the UK Corporate Governance Code?

A   The board should ensure that workforce policies and practices are consistent with the company's values

B   The board should promote short-term profitability for the shareholders

C   There should be an annual evaluation of the board

D   No director should be involved in setting their own pay

Test your understanding 12

The two-tier board structure comprises a Supervisory Board and what other organ?

A   A board representing the employees

B   A board majority of non-executive directors

C   An all-executive board

D   A management board

Test your understanding 13

Which of the following is not an accurate description of what a company's code of ethics is likely to achieve?

A   It tells employees what is expected of them in terms of behaviour

B   It explains the approach and outlook of the organisation

C   It encourages employees to take a consistent approach to ethical issues

D   It eliminates the need for legislation

Test your understanding 14

Which of the following actions by a company would not encourage employees to speak up if they encounter potentially serious cases of unprofessional or unethical behaviour?

A   Introduce an employee helpline for ethics-related queries

B   State in the company's code of ethics that employees have a duty to speak up

C   Stress the importance of employees working together to meet ambitious sales targets

D   Develop a culture where it is safe and acceptable for employees to raise concerns

Test your understanding 15

Which of the following does not specifically relate to business ethics?

A   The financial viability of a business

B   The behaviour of the business and its employees

C   How a business conducts its relationships with its stakeholders

D   How a company does business, rather than what it does

Test your understanding 16

Which of the following is not one of the five personal qualities that CIMA expects of its members?

A   Reliability

B   Respect

C   Responsibility

D   Reflection

Test your understanding 17

While reviewing the work of one of your colleagues, you discover that he has made some extremely serious mistakes. When you discuss this with him, it becomes clear that he does not have the understanding of financial matters that he requires to be a competent accountant. This violates CIMA's fundamental principle of:

A   Integrity

B   Objectivity

C   Professional competence and due care

D   Confidentiality

Test your understanding 18

Where a transaction has been completely missed out from the ledger account what is this known as?

A   Error of principle

B   Error of commission

C   Error of omission

D   None of the above

Test your understanding 19

You are working abroad and find yourself in a situation where a particular element of the country's legislation is in conflict with the IFAC Code of Ethics. In this situation, you should:

A   Obey the law because it is mandatory to comply with legislation

B   Obey the ethics code because it is internationally binding

C   Obey the law because you have a public duty to uphold the law, but not to uphold ethics

D   Obey the ethics code because it is a requirement of your profession

Test your understanding 20

Which of the following relates specifically to accountability?

A   Taking responsibility for one's work and conclusions

B   Maintaining clear records that provide evidence to back up conclusions

C   Being answerable to queries in relation to one's work

D   All of the above

Test your understanding 21

Which of the following relates to an ethical issue?

A   Moving into a larger office as part of a plan to expand your business

B   Introducing a new monthly reporting process to maximise efficiency

C   Introducing a new IT system to ensure confidentiality of customer information

D   Recruiting a new finance director

Test your understanding 22

Which of the following would be of the least help in developing an effective corporate ethics programme?

A   Having a chairman and chief executive who champion ethics at every opportunity

B   Providing copies of the company's code of ethics to trusted personnel only to avoid the document falling into the hands of competitors

C   Incorporating ethical issues into new employee induction programmes

D   Talking to the company's key stakeholders about the social and environmental issues they believe to be important

Test your understanding 23

Which of the following correctly states the composition of an audit committee?

A   Executive directors only

B   Non-executive directors only

C   Executive directors and internal auditors

D   Non-executive directors and internal auditors

Test your understanding 24

In tackling ethical dilemmas, which of the following would not help you to find a solution?

A   Establishing the facts and the ethical issues involved

B   Referring to the CIMA and/or your company's code of ethics

C   Following an established internal procedure

D   Choosing to postpone tackling the issue due to pressure of deadlines

Test your understanding 25

One of your colleagues has just been passed over for promotion for the third time. She shows you evidence that only a small number of women have ever been promoted to positions of seniority within your company. This, she says, is an issue of:

A   Harassment

B   Discrimination

C   Conflict of interest

D   Bribery and corruption

Test your understanding 26

Which of the following is not an ethical issue for a bank?

A   Providing accurate information about terms and conditions when advertising interest rates for customer loans

B   Launching a premium account service for customers who are willing to pay a monthly charge for improved service

C   Money laundering

D   Disabled access to bank branches

Test your understanding 27

Which of the following ethical issues is most likely to be affected by new developments in information technology?

A   Data protection

B   Gifts and hospitality

C   Harassment

D   Health and safety

Test your understanding 28

In contract law, a misrepresentation is which one of the following?

A   An untrue statement of fact or opinion which induces another to contract

B   An untrue statement of fact, opinion or intention which induces another to contract

C   An untrue statement of fact or law which induces another to contract

D   An untrue statement of fact or intention which induces another to contract

Test your understanding 29

When deciding on whether a solution to an ethical dilemma is appropriate, which of the following questions is irrelevant?

A   Do I feel comfortable about others knowing about my decision?

B   Have I considered all parties who may be affected by my decision?

C   Would a reasonable third party consider my decision fair?

D   Is this the most appropriate decision considering my career aspirations?

Test your understanding 30

Which of the following board has members which are elected by shareholders at the annual general meeting?

A   Management board only

B   Supervisory board only

C   Both the management and supervisory board

D   Neither the management or supervisory board

Test your understanding 31

What is the objective of an external audit?

A   To protect the interests of minority shareholders

B   To detect fraud and other irregularities

C   To assess the effectiveness of the company's performance

D   To provide assurance on the directors' assertions about the financial statements

Test your understanding 32

Which of the following correctly describes the composition of a unitary board?

A   Executive directors only

B   Non-executive directors only

C   Both executive and non-executive directors

D   Non-executive directors and internal auditors

Test your understanding 33

Which of the following is incorrect in relation to the Sarbanes-Oxley Act ('the Act')?

A   The Act created the Public Company Accounting Oversight Board ('PCAOB')

B   The Act requires all US listed companies to have an audit committee

C   The Act restricts the additional services that an auditor can provide to an audit client

D   The Act requires directors to be professionally qualified to act as directors of public companies

Test your understanding 34

Who is ultimately responsible for ensuring that the financial statements are prepared in accordance with relevant legislation?

A   The external auditors

B   The internal auditors

C   The board of directors

D   The shareholders

Test your understanding 35

In relation to the UK Corporate Governance Code which of the following statements is correct?

A   The Code contains principles which, if broken, may give rise to civil liability only

B   The Code contains principles which, if broken, are punishable by relatively small fines

C   The Code contains principles which, if broken, only oblige the board to disclose the reasons for the breach

D   The Code contains principles which, if broken, have no consequences whatsoever

Test your understanding 36

Which one of the following statements is incorrect in relation to the interaction of corporate governance with business ethics and company law?

A   Corporate governance is primarily concerned with the effective control business efficacy and accountability of the management of public listed companies

B   Corporate governance does not affect private companies

C   Corporate governance business ethics and company law are made up of entirely separate principles

D   The term 'stakeholders' is wider than shareholders and employees

Test your understanding 37

Which of the following is not a principle of the OECD framework of governance?

A   Disclosure and transparency

B   Innovation and adaptability

C   Responsibilities of the board

D   Stakeholder's role and rights

Test your understanding 38

Which of the following error/s would affect calculation of profit?

1   Error of commission

2   Error of principle

A   1 only

B   2 only

C   Both 1 and 2

D   Neither 1 or 2

Test your understanding 39

What is ethical conduct for a CIMA accountant?

A   Doing what you think is right for society

B   Thinking that what you are doing is socially right

C   Thinking about the social consequences of what you do before you do it

D   Doing things that you believe comply with the CIMA Code

Test your understanding 40

What is detection risk?

A   That the company's control system will fail to detect and correct material errors in the processing of transactions

B   That the auditor's procedures will not detect material errors which exist in the financial statements

C   The susceptibility of financial statement transactions and balances to material errors which may or may not be detected

D   None of the above

Test your understanding 41

Which of the following is a correct statement about CIMA's Code of Ethics?

A   It covers all ethical eventualities

B   It covers unusual situations in practice which are unlikely to give rise to ethical problems

C   It gives the general principles to guide behaviour, rather than any specific guidance on how to act in particular circumstances

D   It can only be understood if read in conjunction with the IFAC Code

Test your understanding 42

Which of these is correct?

The importance of the ethical rule is to be judged by the:

A   cost of breach to the individual bound by that rule

B   social consequences for breach of the rule

C   impact on the profession of the rule

D   the context within which it is applied

Test your understanding 43

Which of these is not a fundamental ethical principle?

A   Integrity

B   Objectivity

C   Professional competence and due care

D   Independence

Test your understanding 44

A project that your manager is keen on looks set to have problems showing a profit in the first year. Thereafter, it is projected to make a healthy margin. You are aware of the way in which the system has gaps, which could hide the weak performance in the first year and could be disguised, and your manager asks you what they are and whether you can implement them. Do you:

A   Tell the manager that the company systems do not permit any variance from the accounting method that would show up the weakness?

B   Say that you know how to help, but you can't because you don't think it's right to give false information?

C   Prepare the financial reports in the way the manager requests, but get the manager to send you an e-mail confirming the manager asked you for this unrepresentative report?

D   Do what the manager says, because they are the client?

Test your understanding 45

Which of the following is not one of the personal qualities and virtues specifically sought by CIMA?

A   Courtesy

B   Timeliness

C   Respect

D   Selflessness

Test your understanding 46

Which of the following statement/s is/are correct in relation to CIMA's proposals for better corporate governance?

1   There should be more disclosure

2   There should be better disclosure

3   Disclosure should be adapted to the circumstances of the company

A   1 and 2

B   1 and 3

C   2 and 3

D   3 only

Test your understanding 47

Your employer is having liquidity problems and has reached its overdraft limit. The finance director has asked you to review the company's accounting policies to see if a change could improve the presentation of the financial accounts, which are supplied on a monthly basis to the bank. From an ethical perspective, what is the most appropriate action for you to take?

A   Seek advice from your professional body

B   Do as requested and seek advice afterwards

C   Do as requested

D   Go off sick

Test your understanding 48

Which of the following is not one of the Seven Principles of Public Life issued by the Committee on Standards in Public Life?

A   Courtesy

B   Openness

C   Integrity

D   Leadership

Test your understanding 49

Why should an accountant continually develop?

A   Because management accounting changes so fast that you need to keep up with it to stay marketable for employment

B   Because continual development means that the client always gets a better service every time he or she uses your services

C   Because professional competence rests on checking what you do know, adding to knowledge and skills and challenging habitual working practices

D   Because management accounting needs to reflect the evolving climate in business and finance

Test your understanding 50

You believe that one of your colleagues has knowingly provided misleading information. If your belief is true, which of CIMA's fundamental principles has your colleague breached?

A   Professional competence and due care

B   Integrity

C   Objectivity

D   Confidentiality

Test your understanding 51

Which of the following is a good indicator of accountability?

A   Having regular reviews with your line manager to explain how you are working

B   Keeping accurate records in an orderly way

C   Always explaining your decisions when you make them

D   Being an able accountant

Test your understanding 52

Which is the best explanation of social responsibility?

A   Social responsibility means the accountant is responsible to all of society equally

B   Social responsibility means that the accountant should do additional things to support social initiatives

C   Social responsibility means that the accountant has to be squeaky clean in his or her social as well as professional life

D   Social responsibility means that the accountant should always be aware of the broader social consequences of his or her actions

Test your understanding 53

In relation to a value for money audit, which term does the following statement define?

'Achievement of objectives'.

A   Economy

B   Efficiency

C   Effectiveness

D   Efficacy

Test your understanding 54

An accountant who answers accusations that their work has failed to meet professional standards demonstrates which concept?

A   Accountability

B   Reliability

C   Social responsibility

D   Independence

Test your understanding 55

Which of the following is not a board committee?

A   Audit committee

B   Remuneration committee

C   Nomination committee

D   Corporate social responsibility committee

Test your understanding 56

Which of the following is correct?

A   The IFAC Codes of conduct deal with accountants working internationally, while CIMA only applies to business done in Britain

B   The CIMA Code is inferior to IFAC's Code

C   The IFAC Code reflects the standards laid down by CIMA

D   The IFAC Code is reflected in the CIMA Code

Test your understanding 57

Which of the following is not an advantage of a company limited by shares?

A   The company is liable on its own contracts

B   The member's liability is limited to the amount he or she agreed to pay for the shares

C   The company is not affected by any change in members

D   There are less disclosure requirements than for a sole trader

Test your understanding 58

Why do we need codes of professional ethics?

A   To resolve disputes

B   To punish bad accountants

C   To protect the reputation of the profession

D   To improve the quality of service to the public

Test your understanding 59

Which statement is the most accurate of the statements?

A   Laws can never be broken, even if they breach ethics

B   Ethical breaches always have to be justified, even if they result from the breach of a law

C   Legal breaches often result in ethical breaches

D   Ethical breaches often result in legal breaches

Test your understanding 60

The articles of association are a contract between:

A   The company and its members

B   The company and its stakeholders

C   The company and third parties

D   None of the above

Test your understanding 61

Which of the following statements most accurately expresses different approaches to ethical regulations?

A   Breaches of ethics have less serious consequences than breaches of the criminal law

B   Ethical frameworks let the individual decide about how they should act in particular situations

C   Regulations provide a 'thou shall not' approach to behaviour, whereas framework approaches encourage positive behaviour in support of ethical conduct

D   The framework approach is best suited to practical problem-solving in ethics

Test your understanding 62

How does the framework-based approach to ethics differ from the rules-based approach?

A   The framework-based approach uses legal language

B   The framework-based approach requires a detailed rule book

C   The framework-based approach sets out rules covering all eventualities

D   The framework-based approach sets out general guidelines

Test your understanding 63

Which of the following would not need to be provided to form a company?

A   The proposed name of the company

B   The type of company

C   The proposed start date of trading

D   Details of the registered office

Test your understanding 64

What is meant by the expression 'lifting the veil of incorporation'?

A   The company is treated as if it were fully liable for all its debts

B   The shareholders are treated as though they were carrying on business in partnership

C   The directors are treated as partners and are fully liable for the company's debts

D   The company is treated as if it were not a separate person at law

Test your understanding 65

Which of the following is not a type of stakeholder?

A   Associated

B   Internal

C   Connected

D   External

Test your understanding 66

In which one of the following instances will it be deemed to be an automatic unfair dismissal?

A   Where an employee brings a court action against the employer in good faith to enforce a statutory right, where no right in fact exists

B   Where an employee is selected for redundancy contrary to an agreed arrangement of custom, without good reason

C   Where an employee fails to comply with orders on the basis of valid health and safety grounds

D   Where an employee is pregnant

Test your understanding 67

Which of the following use a rules-based approach to corporate governance?

1   King IV

2   UK Corporate Governance Code

3   Sarbanes-Oxley

A   1 and 2

B   2 and 3

C   1 and 3

D   3 only

Test your understanding 68

Where a dismissed employee claims wrongful dismissal, which of the following statement/s is/are correct?

1   The claim can be based on dismissal without proper notice

2   The claim will essentially be for breach of contract

A   1 only

B   2 only

C   Both 1 and 2

D   Neither 1 or 2

Test your understanding 69

Employers owe certain implied duties to employees. In which of the following instances, does a duty to provide work not exist?

A   Where the employee's remuneration depends upon the work done

B   Where the employee needs work to maintain reputation

C   Where the employee needs work to maintain familiarity with technical change

D   Where the employee is participating in an ongoing staff training programme

Test your understanding 70

In which country was King IV introduced?

A   UK

B   USA

C   South Africa

D   Canada

Test your understanding 71

Which of the following is invalid consideration?

1   A promise to perform an existing contractual obligation

2   A promise to perform an existing statutory obligation

A   1 only

B   2 only

C   Both 1 and 2

D   Neither 1 or 2

Test your understanding 72

Which of the following focused on directors' remuneration in the UK?

A   Hampel report

B   Turnbull report

C   Greenbury report

D   Tyson report

Test your understanding 73

Ria writes to Sarah offering to buy Sarah's boat for £500. In her letter, she writes 'If I don't hear from you, I shall consider it mine and pick it up on Friday'. Which of the following best describes the legal position as to whether or not a contract exists?

A   There is a contract because Ria waived the need for acceptance

B   There is a contract because Sarah complied with Ria's terms exactly

C   There is a contract because acceptance can be inferred from Sarah's conduct

D   There is no contract because there is no positive act to indicate acceptance

Test your understanding 74

Which of the following statements with regards to misrepresentation is incorrect?

A   The statement made must have been intended to be acted upon

B   The statement made must have induced the other party to enter into the contract

C   The statement made must be a false statement of fact or law

D   The contract is automatically void

Test your understanding 75

Which of the following statement/s is/are correct?

1   An external audit report has a formal reporting structure

2   An internal audit report has a formal reporting structure

A   1 only

B   2 only

C   Both 1 and 2

D   Neither 1 or 2

Test your understanding 76

Which one of the following is incorrect?

A   A condition is a term that the parties intended to be of fundamental importance

B   A warranty is a term that the parties did not intend to be of fundamental importance

C   If a condition is breached, the contract is automatically terminated

D   If a warranty is breached, the innocent party cannot treat the contract as discharged

Test your understanding 77

In relation to whistleblowing to whom can a disclosure only be made in extreme circumstances?

A   Legal adviser

B   Government minister

C   Media

D   Internal department

Test your understanding 78

Which of the following is not an advantage of a company outsourcing its internal audit function?

A   There will always be a reduction in costs

B   Provides access to specialist skills

C   Can provide access to an internal audit team immediately

D   Reduced management time in administering an in-house department

Test your understanding 79

If you are offered an expensive gift from a client which threat arises?

A   Intimidation

B   Advocacy

C   Self-review

D   Self-interest

Test your understanding 80

Which of the following is correct in relation to a company limited by shares?

A   A company has management of the company separate from ownership

B   A company does not have perpetual succession

C   A private company is not a separate legal person distinct from its shareholders

D   None of the above

Test your understanding 81

Which of the following business organisation is appropriate for a high-risk business?

A   Sole trader

B   General partnership

C   A company limited by shares

D   None of the above

Test your understanding 82

Which of the following is/are an element of audit risk?

1   The risk that the financial statements contain a material misstatement

2   The risk that the auditor fails to detect any misstatement

A   1 only

B   2 only

C   Both 1 and 2

D   Neither 1 or 2

Test your understanding 83

Which of the following statement/s is/are correct?

1 A company may enter into any contract in its own name

2 A company has restrictions on its business purpose

A 1 only

B 2 only

C Both 1 and 2

D Neither 1 or 2

Test your understanding 84

Which of the following statement/s regarding off-the-shelf companies is/are correct?

1 They may be cheaper and simpler than incorporating a new company

2 They cannot enter into contracts immediately

A 1 only

B 2 only

C Both 1 and 2

D Neither 1 or 2

Test your understanding 85

Which of the following should be included in an audit engagement letter?

1 Objective and scope of the audit

2 Results of previous audits

3 Management's responsibilities

A 1 and 2

B 1 and 3

C 2 and 3

D 2 only

Test your understanding answers

Test your understanding 1

A

Test your understanding 2

C

Test your understanding 3

D

Test your understanding 4

C

Test your understanding 5

C

Test your understanding 6

B

Test your understanding 7

C

Test your understanding 8

B

Test your understanding 9

A

Test your understanding 10

D

Test your understanding 11

B

Test your understanding 12

D

Test your understanding 13

D

Test your understanding 14

C

Test your understanding 15

A

Test your understanding 16

D

Test your understanding 17

C

Test your understanding 18

C

Test your understanding 19

A

Test your understanding 20

D

Test your understanding 21

C

Test your understanding 22

B

Test your understanding 23

B

Test your understanding 24

D

Test your understanding 25

B

Test your understanding 26

B

Test your understanding 27

A

Test your understanding 28

C

Test your understanding 29

D

Test your understanding 30

B

Test your understanding 31

D

Test your understanding 32

C

Test your understanding 33

D

Test your understanding 34

C

Test your understanding 35

C

Test your understanding 36

C

Test your understanding 37

B

Test your understanding 38

B

Test your understanding 39

D

Test your understanding 40

B

Test your understanding 41

C

Test your understanding 42

D

Test your understanding 43

D

Test your understanding 44

B

Test your understanding 45

D

Test your understanding 46

C

Test your understanding 47

A

Test your understanding 48

A

Test your understanding 49

C

Test your understanding 50

B

Test your understanding 51

C

Test your understanding 52

D

Test your understanding 53

C

Test your understanding 54

A

Test your understanding 55

D

Test your understanding 56

D

Test your understanding 57

D

Test your understanding 58

D

Test your understanding 59

A

Test your understanding 60

A

Test your understanding 61

D

Test your understanding 62

D

Test your understanding 63

C

Test your understanding 64

D

Test your understanding 65

A

Test your understanding 66

D

Test your understanding 67

D

Test your understanding 68

C

Test your understanding 69

D

Test your understanding 70

C

Test your understanding 71

C

Test your understanding 72

C

Test your understanding 73

D

Test your understanding 74

D

Test your understanding 75

A

Test your understanding 76

C

Test your understanding 77

C

Test your understanding 78

A

Test your understanding 79

D

Test your understanding 80

A

Test your understanding 81

C

Test your understanding 82

A

Test your understanding 83

A

Test your understanding 84

A

Test your understanding 85

B

Appendix

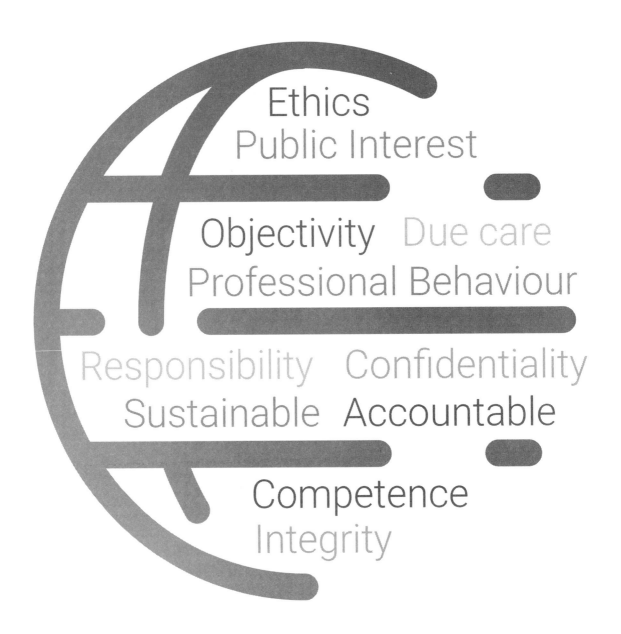

Ethics
Public Interest
Objectivity Due care
Professional Behaviour
Responsibility Confidentiality
Sustainable Accountable
Competence
Integrity

CIMA Code of Ethics

For Professional Accountants.

Issued January 2020

Contents

Part 3
Professional accountants in public practice

Annex 1 – Separate document

Part 4A independence for audit and review engagement

Part 4B independence for assurance engagements other than audit and review engagements

For Annex 1 of the Code, please refer directly to the full IFAC International Code of Ethics for Professional Accountants.

CIMA preface

As chartered management accountants, CIMA members (and registered students) throughout the world have a duty to observe the highest standards of conduct and integrity, and to uphold the good standing and reputation of the profession. They must also refrain from any conduct which might discredit the profession. Members and registered students must have regard to these guidelines irrespective of their field of activity, of their contract of employment or of any other professional memberships they may hold.

CIMA upholds the aims and principles of equal opportunities and fundamental human rights worldwide, including the handling of personal information. The Institute promotes the highest ethical and business standards and encourages its members to be good and responsible professionals. Good ethical behaviour may be above that required by the law. In a highly competitive, complex business world, it is essential that CIMA members sustain their integrity and remember the trust and confidence that is placed on them by whoever relies on their objectivity and professionalism. Members must avoid actions or situations which are inconsistent with their professional obligations. They should also be guided not merely by the terms but by the spirit of this Code.

CIMA members should conduct themselves with courtesy and consideration towards all with whom they have professional dealings and should not behave in a manner which could be considered offensive or discriminatory.

To ensure that CIMA members protect the good standing and reputation of the profession, members must report the fact to the Institute if they are convicted or disqualified from acting as an officer of a company or if they are subject to any sanction resulting from disciplinary action taken by any other body or authority.

CIMA has adopted the following Code of Ethics. Parts 1 and 3 of this Code are based on the IFAC[1] Code of Ethics that was developed with the help of input from CIMA and the global accountancy profession. Part 2 of the Code was developed in cooperation with the American Institute of CPAs (AICPA). The AICPA and CIMA joined together to create a designation for management accountants, the Chartered Global Management Accountant® (CGMA). The CGMA designation is designed to elevate management accounting and further emphasise its importance for businesses worldwide. Part 2 of the Code is designed to provide guidance to all CIMA members around the world who are members in business and professional accountants in business and, those who hold the CGMA credential. When a CGMA is also a member in public practice the CGMA should also comply with the applicable guidance of the CIMA Code of Ethics and apply the most restrictive provisions.

If a member cannot resolve an ethical issue by following this Code by consulting the ethics information on CIMA's website or by seeking guidance from CIMA's ethics helpline, they should seek legal advice as to both their legal rights and any obligations they may have. The CIMA Charter, Byelaws and Regulations give definitive rules on many matters.

For further information see: cimaglobal.com/ethics

Note: The CIMA Code of Ethics is a Law of the Institute (to which all members and registered students are required to comply) for the purpose of the definition of "misconduct" in Byelaw 1.

[1]International Federation of Accountants.

Parts 1 - 3 and Annex 1 of the CIMA Code of Ethics are based on the IFAC Handbook of the Code of Ethics for Professional Accountants, of the International Ethics Standards Board of Accountants (IESBA), published by IFAC in July 2018. Copy right © July 2018 by the International Federation of Accountants (IFAC). All rights reserved. Used with permission of IFAC. Contact Permissions@ifac.org for permission to reproduce, store or transmit, or to make similar uses of this document.

CIMA Code at a glance

How the Code is structured

Part 1: Complying with the Code, fundamental principles, and conceptual framework

Part 1 establishes the fundamental principles of professional ethics for professional accountants. It also provides a conceptual framework that they shall use to identify, evaluate and apply safeguards to eliminate threats to compliance with the fundamental principles.

Part 1 is applicable to all professional accountants. The five fundamental principles listed in Part 1 are Integrity (111), Objectivity (112), Professional competence and due care (113), Confidentiality (114), and Professional behaviour (115).

Part 2: Professional accountants in business (including CGMA designation holders)

Part 2 sets out additional material that applies to professional accountants in business when performing professional activities. Part 2 of the Code was developed in cooperation with the American Institute of CPAs (AICPA); and, like Parts 1 and 3, the elements of the updated Part 2 that apply to CIMA members and students continue to reflect fundamental principles and conceptual framework approach.

Professional accountants in business include professional accountants employed, engaged or contracted in an executive or non-executive capacity in, for example:

• Commerce, industry or service

• The public sector

• Education

• The not-for-profit sector

• Regulatory or professional bodies.

Part 2 is also applicable to individuals who are professional accountants in public practice when performing professional activities pursuant to their relationship with the firm, whether as a contractor, employee, or owner.

Part 2 section 210 addresses ethical conflicts, and includes an interpretation under CIMA's Integrity and Objectivity Principles, and AICPA's Integrity and Objectivity Rule. Section 220 addresses conflicts of interest, including how they are identified, evaluated and disclosed. Offering or accepting gifts, entertainment and other forms of inducements are found in section 230. Preparing and reporting information (240) is addressed with subheadings including "knowing misrepresentations in the preparation of financial

statements or records", "subordination of judgment", and "obligation of a member to their employer's external accountant".

Information related to educational services can be found in section 250. Section 260 highlights the principle of Professional competence and due care and AICPA's General Standards Rule, and includes information around submission of financial statements, accounting principles, and responsibility for affirming that financial statements are in conformity with the applicable financial reporting framework.

CIMA's Professional Behaviour and Confidentiality Principles, and AICPA's Acts Discreditable Rule are addressed in section 270, with subheadings including "discrimination and harassment in employment practices", "solicitation or disclosure of CPA/CIMA examination questions and answers", "failure to file a tax return or pay a tax liability", "negligence in the preparation of financial statements or records", "governmental bodies, commissions, or other regulatory agencies", "indemnification and limitation of liability provisions", "confidential information obtained from employment or volunteer activities", and "false, misleading or deceptive acts in promoting or marketing professional services".

A new section, Section 280, addresses pressure to breach the rules or fundamental principles, and Section 290 sets out requirements and application material for professional accountants in business in responding to non-compliance with laws and regulations (NOCLAR). The provisions in Section 290 only apply to CIMA members including those who hold the CGMA credential (or are entitled to do so) and do not apply to AICPA members who hold the CGMA credential (or are entitled to do so).

Part 3: Professional accountants in public practice

Part 3 sets out additional material that applies to professional accountants in public practice when providing professional services.

It provides examples of threats that could be encountered and how such threats might be evaluated and addressed. Requirements relating to communicating with those charged with governance is also covered (300.9).

Part 3 addresses conflicts of interest (310), professional appointments including client and engagement acceptance and changes in a professional appointment (320), second opinions (321), fees and other types of remuneration (330), inducements including gifts and hospitality (340), custody of client assets (350), and responding to non-compliance with laws and regulations (360).

Annex 1

Part 4a — Independence for audit and review engagements

Part 4b — Independence for assurance engagements other than audit and review engagements

These Parts collectively form the *International Independence Standards*, and set out additional material that applies to professional accountants in public practice when providing assurance services.

For Annex 1 of the Code, please refer directly to the full IFAC International Code of Ethics for Professional Accountants.

Glossary

The glossary contains defined terms (together with additional explanations where appropriate) and described terms which have a specific meaning in certain parts of the Code. The glossary also includes lists of abbreviations that are used in the Code and other standards to which the Code refers.

Section structure

The Code contains sections which address specific topics. Some sections contain subsections, dealing with specific aspects of those topics. Each section of the Code is structured, where appropriate, as follows:

- **Introduction** — Sets out the subject matter addressed within the section, and introduces the requirements and application material in the context of the conceptual framework. Introductory material contains information, including an explanation of terms used, which is important to the understanding and application of each Part and its sections.

- **Requirements** — Establish general and specific obligations with respect to the subject matter addressed.

- **Application material** — Provides context, explanations, suggestions for actions or matters to consider, illustrations and other guidance to assist in complying with the requirements.

How to use the Code

The fundamental principles, independence and conceptual framework

CIMA's Code of Ethics is made up of five fundamental principles:

- **Integrity:** Being straightforward, honest and truthful in all professional and business relationships. You should not be associated with any information that you believe contains a materially false or misleading statement, or which is misleading by omission.

- **Objectivity:** Not allowing bias, conflict of interest or the influence of other people to override your professional judgment.

- **Professional competence and due care:** An ongoing commitment to your level of professional knowledge and skill. Base this on current developments in practice, legislation and techniques. Those working under your authority must also have the appropriate training and supervision.

- **Confidentiality:** You should not disclose professional information unless you have specific permission or a legal or professional duty to do so.

- **Professional behaviour:** Comply with relevant laws and regulations. You must also avoid any action that could negatively affect the reputation of the profession.

The Code requires you to comply with these fundamental principles of ethics. The Code also requires you to apply the conceptual framework to identify, evaluate and address threats to compliance with the fundamental principles. Applying the conceptual framework requires exercising professional judgment, remaining alert for new information and to changes in facts and circumstances, and using the reasonable and informed third party test.

Threats to compliance with the fundamental principles fall into one or more of the following categories:

- **Self-interest threat:** Commonly called a "conflict of interest" which may inappropriately influence judgment or behaviour.

- **Self-review threat:** When you are required to evaluate the results of a previous judgment or service.

- **Advocacy threat:** Arising if promoting a position or opinion to the point that your subsequent objectivity is compromised.

- **Familiarity threat:** When you become so sympathetic to the interests of others as a result of a close relationship that your professional judgment becomes compromised.

- **Intimidation threat:** When you are deterred from acting objectively by actual or perceived pressure or influence.

The conceptual framework recognises that the existence of conditions, policies and procedures established by the profession, legislation, regulation, the firm, or the employing organisation might affect the identification of threats. Those conditions, policies and procedures might also be a relevant factor in your evaluation of whether a threat is at an acceptable level. When threats are not at an acceptable level, the conceptual framework requires you to address those threats. Applying safeguards is one way that threats might be reduced. Safeguards are actions you take individually or in combination that effectively reduce threats to an acceptable level.

Complying with the Code requires knowing, understanding and applying:

- All of the relevant provisions of a particular section in the context of Part 1, together with the additional material set out in Sections 200, 300, 400 and 900 as applicable.

- All of the relevant provisions of a particular section, for example, applying the provisions that are set out under the subheadings titled "General" and "All Audit Clients" together with additional specific provisions, including those set out under the subheadings titled "Audit Clients that are not Public Interest Entities" or "Audit Clients that are Public Interest Entities".

- All of the relevant provisions set out in a particular section together with any additional provisions set out in any relevant subsection.

Requirements and application material

Requirements and application material are to be read and applied with the objective of complying with the fundamental principles, applying the conceptual framework and, when performing audit, review and other assurance engagements, being independent.

Requirements

Requirements are designated with the letter "R" and, in most cases, include the word "shall". The word "shall" in the Code imposes an obligation on you or your firm to comply with the specific provision in which "shall" has been used.

In some situations, the Code provides a specific exception to a requirement. In such a situation, the provision is designated with the letter "R" but uses "may" or conditional wording.

When the word "may" is used in the Code, it denotes permission to take a particular action in certain circumstances, including as an exception to a requirement. It is not used to denote possibility.

When the word "might" is used in the Code, it denotes the possibility of a matter arising, an event occurring or a course of action being taken. The term does not ascribe any particular level of possibility or likelihood when used in conjunction with a threat, as the evaluation of the level of a threat depends on the facts and circumstances of any particular matter, event or course of action.

Application material

In addition to requirements, the Code contains application material that provides context relevant to a proper understanding of the Code. In particular, the application material is intended to help you to understand how to apply the conceptual framework to a particular set of circumstances and to understand and comply with a specific requirement. While such application material does not of itself impose a requirement, consideration of the material is necessary to the proper application of the requirements of the Code, including application of the conceptual framework. Application material is designated with the letter "A".

Where application material includes lists of examples, these lists are not intended to be exhaustive.

Part 1
Complying with the code, fundamental principles and conceptual framework

Section 100
Complying with the Code
General

100.1 A1   A distinguishing mark of the accountancy profession is its acceptance of the responsibility to act in the public interest. A professional accountant's responsibility is not exclusively to satisfy the needs of an individual client or employing organisation. Therefore, the Code contains requirements and application material to enable professional accountants to meet their responsibility to act in the public interest.

100.2 A1   Application material, designated with the letter "A", provides context, explanations, suggestions for actions or matters to consider, illustrations and other guidance relevant to a proper understanding of the Code. In particular, the application material is intended to help a professional accountant to understand how to apply the conceptual framework to a particular set of circumstances and to understand and comply with a specific requirement. While such application material does not of itself impose a requirement, consideration of the material is necessary to the proper application of the requirements of the Code, including the application of the conceptual framework.

R100.3   A professional accountant shall comply with the Code. There might be circumstances where laws or regulations preclude an accountant from complying with certain parts of the Code. In such circumstances, those laws and regulations prevail, and the accountant shall comply with all other parts of the Code.

100.3 A1   The principle of professional behaviour requires a professional accountant to comply with relevant laws and regulations. Some jurisdictions might have provisions that differ from or go beyond those set out in the Code. Accountants in those jurisdictions need to be aware of those differences and comply with the more stringent provisions unless prohibited by law or regulation.

100.3 A2   A professional accountant might encounter unusual circumstances in which the accountant believes that the result of applying a specific requirement of the Code would be disproportionate or might not be in the public interest. In those circumstances, the accountant is encouraged to consult with a professional or regulatory body.

Breaches of the Code

R100.4   Paragraphs R400.80 to R400.89 and R900.50 to R900.55 address a breach of International Independence Standards. A professional accountant who identifies a breach of any other provision of the Code shall evaluate the significance of the breach and its impact on the accountant's ability to comply with the fundamental principles. The accountant shall also:

(a) Take whatever actions might be available, as soon as possible, to address the consequences of the breach satisfactorily; and

(b) Determine whether to report the breach to the relevant parties.

100.4 A1   Relevant parties to whom such a breach might be reported include those who might have been affected by it, a professional or regulatory body or an oversight authority.

Section 110
The fundamental principles
General

110.1 A1   There are five fundamental principles of ethics for professional accountants:

(a) Integrity — to be straightforward and honest in all professional and business relationships

(b) Objectivity — not to compromise professional or business judgments because of bias, conflict of interest or undue influence of others.

(c) Professional competence and due care — to:

(i) Attain and maintain professional knowledge and skill at the level required to ensure that a client or employing organisation receives competent professional service, based on current technical and professional standards and relevant legislation; and

(ii) Act diligently and in accordance with applicable technical and professional standards.

(d) Confidentiality — to respect the confidentiality of information acquired as a result of professional and business relationships.

(e) Professional behaviour — to comply with relevant laws and regulations and avoid any conduct that the professional accountant knows or should know might discredit the profession.

R110.2 A professional accountant shall comply with each of the fundamental principles.

110.2 A1 The fundamental principles of ethics establish the standard of behaviour expected of a professional accountant. The conceptual framework establishes the approach which an accountant is required to apply to assist in complying with those fundamental principles. Subsections 111 to 115 set out requirements and application material related to each of the fundamental principles.

110.2 A2 A professional accountant might face a situation in which complying with one fundamental principle conflicts with complying with one or more other fundamental principles. In such a situation, the accountant might consider consulting, on an anonymous basis if necessary, with:

- Others within the firm or employing organisation.
- Those charged with governance.
- A professional body.
- A regulatory body.
- Legal Counsel.

However, such consultation does not relieve the accountant from the responsibility to exercise professional judgment to resolve the conflict or, if necessary, and unless prohibited by law or regulation, disassociate from the matter creating the conflict.

110.2 A3 The professional accountant is encouraged to document the substance of the issue, the details of any discussions, the decisions made, and the rationale for those decisions.

Section 111
Integrity

R111.1 A professional accountant shall comply with the principle of integrity, which requires an accountant to be straightforward and honest in all professional and business relationships.

111.1 A1 Integrity implies fair dealing and truthfulness.

R111.2 A professional accountant shall not knowingly be associated with reports, returns, communications or other information where the accountant believes that the information:

(a) Contains a materially false or misleading statement;

(b) Contains statements or information provided recklessly; or

(c) Omits or obscures required information where such omission or obscurity would be misleading.

111.2 A1 If a professional accountant provides a modified report in respect of such a report, return, communication or other information, the accountant is not in breach of paragraph R111.2.

R111.3 When a professional accountant becomes aware of having been associated with information described in paragraph R111.2, the accountant shall take steps to be disassociated from that information.

Section 112
Objectivity

R112.1 A professional accountant shall comply with the principle of objectivity, which requires an accountant not to compromise professional or business judgment because of bias, conflict of interest or undue influence of others.

R112.2 A professional accountant shall not undertake a professional activity if a circumstance or relationship unduly influences the accountant's professional judgment regarding that activity.

Section 113
Professional competence and due care

R113.1 A professional accountant shall comply with the principle of professional competence and due care, which requires an accountant to:

(a) Attain and maintain professional knowledge and skill at the level required to ensure that a client or employing organisation receives competent professional service, based on current technical and professional standards and relevant legislation; and;

(b) Act diligently and in accordance with applicable technical and professional standards.

113.1 A1 Serving clients and employing organisations with professional competence requires the exercise of sound judgment in applying professional knowledge and skill when undertaking professional activities.

113.1 A2 Maintaining professional competence requires a continuing awareness and an understanding of relevant technical, professional and business developments. Continuing professional development enables a professional accountant to develop and maintain the capabilities to perform competently within the professional environment.

113.1 A3 Diligence encompasses the responsibility to act in accordance with the requirements of an assignment, carefully, thoroughly and on a timely basis.

R113.2 In complying with the principle of professional competence and due care, a professional accountant shall take reasonable steps to ensure that those working in a professional capacity under the accountant's authority have appropriate training and supervision.

R113.3 Where appropriate, a professional accountant shall make clients, the employing organisation, or other users of the accountant's professional services or activities, aware of the limitations inherent in the services or activities.

Section 114
Confidentiality

R114.1 A professional accountant shall comply with the principle of confidentiality, which requires an accountant to respect the confidentiality of information acquired as a result of professional and business relationships. An accountant shall:

(a) Be alert to the possibility of inadvertent disclosure, including in a social environment, and particularly to a close business associate or an immediate or a close family member;

(b) Maintain confidentiality of information within the firm or employing organisation;

(c) Maintain confidentiality of information disclosed by a prospective client or employing organisation;

(d) Not disclose confidential information acquired as a result of professional and business relationships outside the firm or employing organisation without proper and specific authority, unless there is a legal or professional duty or right to disclose;

(e) Not use confidential information acquired as a result of professional and business relationships for the personal advantage of the accountant or for the advantage of a third party;

(f) Not use or disclose any confidential information, either acquired or received as a result of a professional or business relationship, after that relationship has ended; and;

(g) Take reasonable steps to ensure that personnel under the accountant's control, and individuals from whom advice and assistance are obtained, respect the accountant's duty of confidentiality.

144.1 A1 Confidentiality serves the public interest because it facilitates the free flow of information from the professional accountant's client or employing organisation to the accountant in the knowledge that the information will not be disclosed to a third party. Nevertheless, the following are circumstances where professional accountants are or might be required to disclose confidential information or when such disclosure might be appropriate:

(a) Disclosure is required by law, for example:

(i) Production of documents or other provision of evidence in the course of legal proceedings; or

(ii) Disclosure to the appropriate public authorities of infringements of the law that come to light;

(b) Disclosure is permitted by law and is authorised by the client or the employing organisation; and

(c) There is a professional duty or right to disclose, when not prohibited by law:

(i) To comply with the quality review of a professional body;

(ii) To respond to an inquiry or investigation by a professional or regulatory body;

(iii) To protect the professional interests of a professional accountant in legal proceedings; or

(iv) To comply with technical and professional standards, including ethics requirements.

114.1 A2 In deciding whether to disclose confidential information, factors to consider, depending on the circumstances, include:

• Whether the interests of any parties, including third parties whose interests might be affected, could be harmed if the client or employing organisation consents to the disclosure of information by the professional accountant.

• Whether all of the relevant information is known and substantiated, to the extent practicable. Factors affecting the decision to disclose include:

• Unsubstantiated facts.

• Incomplete information.

• Unsubstantiated conclusions.

• The proposed type of communication, and to whom it is addressed.

• Whether the parties to whom the communication is addressed are appropriate recipients.

R114.2 A professional accountant shall continue to comply with the principle of confidentiality even after the end of the relationship between the accountant and a client or employing organisation. When changing employment or acquiring a new client, the accountant is entitled to use prior experience but shall not use or disclose any confidential information acquired or received as a result of a professional or business relationship.

Section 115
Professional behaviour

R115.1 A professional accountant shall comply with the principle of professional behaviour, which requires an accountant to comply with relevant laws and regulations and avoid any conduct that the accountant knows or should know might discredit the profession. A professional accountant shall not knowingly engage in any business, occupation or activity that impairs or might impair the integrity, objectivity or good reputation of the profession, and as a result would be incompatible with the fundamental principles.

115.1 A1 Conduct that might discredit the profession includes conduct that a reasonable and informed third party would be likely to conclude adversely affects the good reputation of the profession.

R115.2 When undertaking marketing or promotional activities, a professional accountant shall not bring the profession into disrepute. A professional accountant shall be honest and truthful and shall not make:

(a) Exaggerated claims for the services offered by, or the qualifications or experience of, the accountant; or

(b) Disparaging references or unsubstantiated comparisons to the work of others.

115.2 A1 If a professional accountant is in doubt about whether a form of advertising or marketing is appropriate, the accountant is encouraged to consult with the relevant professional body.

Section 120
The conceptual framework
Introduction

120.1 The circumstances in which professional accountants operate might create threats to compliance with the fundamental principles. Section 120 sets out requirements and application material, including a conceptual framework, to assist accountants in complying with the fundamental principles and meeting their responsibility to act in the public interest. Such requirements and application material accommodate the wide range of facts and circumstances, including the various professional activities, interests and relationships that create threats to compliance with the fundamental principles. In addition, they deter accountants from concluding that a situation is permitted solely because that situation is not specifically prohibited by the Code.

120.2 The conceptual framework specifies an approach for a professional accountant to:

(a) Identify threats to compliance with the fundamental principles;

(b) Evaluate the threats identified; and

(c) Address the threats by eliminating or reducing them to an acceptable level.

Requirements and application material
General

R120.3 The professional accountant shall apply the conceptual framework to identify, evaluate and address threats to compliance with the fundamental principles set out in Section 110.

120.3 A1 Additional requirements and application material that are relevant to the application of the conceptual framework are set out in:

(a) Part 2 – Professional Accountants in Business (including CGMA designation holders)

(b) Part 3 – Professional Accountants in Public Practice; and

(c) International Independence Standards, as follows:

(i) Part 4A – Independence for Audit and Review Engagements; and

(ii) Part 4B – Independence for Assurance Engagements Other than Audit and Review Engagements.

R120.4 When dealing with an ethics issue, the professional accountant shall consider the context in which the issue has arisen or might arise. Where an individual who is a professional accountant in public practice is performing professional activities pursuant to the accountant's relationship with the firm, whether as a contractor, employee or owner, the individual shall comply with the provisions in Part 2 that apply to these circumstances.

R120.5 When applying the conceptual framework, the professional accountant shall:

(a) Exercise professional judgment;

(b) Remain alert for new information and to changes in facts and circumstances; and

(c) Use the reasonable and informed third party test described in paragraph 120.5 A4.

Exercise of professional judgment

120.5 A1 Professional judgment involves the application of relevant training, professional knowledge, skill and experience commensurate with the facts and circumstances, including the nature and scope of the particular professional activities, and the interests and relationships involved. In relation to undertaking professional activities, the exercise of professional judgment is required when the professional accountant applies the conceptual framework in order to make informed decisions about the courses of actions available, and to determine whether such decisions are appropriate in the circumstances.

120.5 A2 An understanding of known facts and circumstances is a prerequisite to the proper application of the conceptual framework. Determining the actions necessary to obtain this understanding and coming to a conclusion about whether the fundamental principles have been complied with also require the exercise of professional judgment.

120.5 A3 In exercising professional judgment to obtain this understanding, the professional accountant might consider, among other matters, whether:

• There is reason to be concerned that potentially relevant information might be missing from the facts and circumstances known to the accountant.

• There is an inconsistency between the known facts and circumstances and the accountant's expectations.

• The accountant's expertise and experience are sufficient to reach a conclusion.

• There is a need to consult with others with relevant expertise or experience.

• The information provides a reasonable basis on which to reach a conclusion.

• The accountant's own preconception or bias might be affecting the accountant's exercise of professional judgment.

• There might be other reasonable conclusions that could be reached from the available information.

Reasonable and informed third party

120.5 A4 The reasonable and informed third party test is a consideration by the professional accountant about whether the same conclusions would likely be reached by another party. Such consideration is made from the perspective of a reasonable and informed third party, who weighs all the relevant facts and circumstances that the accountant knows, or could reasonably be expected to know, at the time the conclusions are made. The reasonable and informed third party does not need to be an accountant, but would possess the relevant knowledge and experience to understand and evaluate the appropriateness of the accountant's conclusions in an impartial manner.

Identifying threats

R120.6 The professional accountant shall identify threats to compliance with the fundamental principles.

120.6 A1 An understanding of the facts and circumstances, including any professional activities, interests and relationships that might compromise compliance with the fundamental principles, is a prerequisite to the professional accountant's identification of threats to such compliance. The existence of certain conditions, policies and procedures established by the profession, legislation, regulation, the firm, or the employing organisation that can enhance the accountant acting ethically might also help identify threats to compliance with the fundamental principles. Paragraph 120.8 A2 includes general examples of such conditions, policies and procedures which are also factors that are relevant in evaluating the level of threats.

120.6 A2 Threats to compliance with the fundamental principles might be created by a broad range of facts and circumstances. It is not possible to define every situation that creates threats. In addition, the nature of engagements and work assignments might differ and, consequently, different types of threats might be created.

120.6 A3 Threats to compliance with the fundamental principles fall into one or more of the following categories:

(a) Self-interest threat – the threat that a financial or other interest will inappropriately influence a professional accountant's judgment or behaviour;

(b) Self-review threat – the threat that a professional accountant will not appropriately evaluate the results of a previous judgment made; or an activity performed by the accountant, or by another individual within the accountant's firm or employing organisation, on which the accountant will rely when forming a judgment as part of the performing a current activity;

(c) Advocacy threat – the threat that a professional accountant will promote a client's or employing organisation's position to the point that the accountant's objectivity is compromised;

(d) Familiarity threat – the threat that due to a long or close relationship with a client, or employing organisation, a professional accountant will be too sympathetic to their interests or too accepting of their work; and

(e) Intimidation threat – the threat that a professional accountant will be deterred from acting objectively because of actual or perceived pressures, including attempts to exercise undue influence over the accountant.

120.6 A4 A circumstance might create more than one threat, and a threat might affect compliance with more than one fundamental principle.

Evaluating threats

R120.7 When the professional accountant identifies a threat to compliance with the fundamental principles, the accountant shall evaluate whether such a threat is at an acceptable level.

Acceptable level

120.7 A1 An acceptable level is a level at which a professional accountant using the reasonable and informed third party test would likely conclude that the accountant complies with the fundamental principles.

Factors relevant in evaluating the level of threats

120.8 A1 The consideration of qualitative as well as quantitative factors is relevant in the professional accountant's evaluation of threats, as is the combined effect of multiple threats, if applicable.

120.8 A2 The existence of conditions, policies and procedures described in paragraph 120.6 A1 might also be factors that are relevant in evaluating the level of threats to compliance with fundamental principles. Examples of such conditions, policies and procedures include:

- Corporate governance requirements.
- Educational, training and experience requirements for the profession.
- Effective complaint systems which enable the professional accountant and the general public to draw attention to unethical behaviour.
- An explicitly stated duty to report breaches of ethics requirements.
- Professional or regulatory monitoring and disciplinary procedures.

Consideration of new information or changes in facts and circumstances

R120.9 If the professional accountant becomes aware of new information or changes in facts and circumstances that might impact whether a threat has been eliminated or reduced to an acceptable level, the accountant shall re-evaluate and address that threat accordingly.

120.9 A1 Remaining alert throughout the professional activity assists the professional accountant in determining whether new information has emerged or changes in facts and circumstances have occurred that:

(a) Impact the level of a threat; or

(b) Affect the accountant's conclusions about whether safeguards applied continue to be appropriate to address identified threats.

120.9 A2 If new information results in the identification of a new threat, the professional accountant is required to evaluate and, as appropriate, address this threat. (Ref: Paras. R120.7 and R120.10).

Addressing threats

R120.10 If the professional accountant determines that the identified threats to compliance with the fundamental principles are not at an acceptable level, the accountant shall address the threats by eliminating them or reducing them to an acceptable level. The accountant shall do so by:

(a) Eliminating the circumstances, including interests or relationships, that are creating the threats;

(b) Applying safeguards, where available and capable of being applied, to reduce the threats to an acceptable level; or

(c) Declining or ending the specific professional activity.

120.10 A1 Depending on the facts and circumstances, a threat might be addressed by eliminating the circumstance creating the threat. However, there are some situations in which threats can only be addressed by declining or ending the specific professional activity. This is because the circumstances that created the threats cannot be eliminated and safeguards are not capable of being applied to reduce the threat to an acceptable level.

Safeguards

120.10 A2 Safeguards are actions, individually or in combination that the professional accountant takes that effectively reduce threats to compliance with the fundamental principles to an acceptable level.

Consideration of significant judgment made and overall conclusions reached

R120.11 The professional accountant shall form an overall conclusion about whether the actions that the accountant takes, or intends to take, to address the threats created will eliminate those threats or reduce them to an acceptable level. In forming the overall conclusion, the accountant shall:

(a) Review any significant judgments made or conclusions reached; and

(b) Use the reasonable and informed third party test.

Considerations for audits, reviews and other assurance engagements

Independence

120.12 A1 Professional accountants in public practice are required by International Independence Standards to be independent when performing audits, reviews, or other assurance engagements. Independence is linked to the fundamental principles of objectivity and integrity. It comprises:

(a) Independence of mind – the state of mind that permits the expression of a conclusion without being affected by influences that compromise professional judgment, thereby allowing an individual to act with integrity, and exercise objectivity and professional skepticism.

(b) Independence in appearance – the avoidance of facts and circumstances that are so significant that a reasonable and informed third party would be likely to conclude that a firm's or an audit or assurance team member's integrity, objectivity or professional skepticism has been compromised.

120.12 A2 International Independence Standards set out requirements and application material on how to apply the conceptual framework to maintain independence when performing audits, reviews or other assurance engagements. Professional accountants and firms are required to comply with these standards in order to be independent when conducting such engagements. The conceptual framework to identify, evaluate and address threats to compliance with the fundamental principles applies in the same way to compliance with independence requirements. The categories of threats to compliance with the fundamental principles described in paragraph 120.6 A3 are also the categories of threats to compliance with independence requirements.

Professional skepticism

120.13 A1 Under auditing, review and other assurance standards, including those by the IAASB, professional accountants in public practice are required to exercise professional skepticism when planning and performing audits, reviews and other assurance engagements. Professional skepticism and the fundamental principles that are described in Section 110 are inter-related concepts.

120.13 A2 In an audit of financial statements, compliance with the fundamental principles, individually and collectively, supports the exercise of professional skepticism, as shown in the following examples:

• Integrity requires the professional accountant to be straightforward and honest. For example, the accountant complies with the principle of integrity by:

(a) Being straightforward and honest when raising concerns about a position taken by a client; and

(b) Pursuing inquiries about inconsistent information and seeking further audit evidence to address concerns about statements that might be materially false or misleading in order to make informed decisions about the appropriate could of action in the circumstances.

In doing so, the accountant demonstrates the critical assessment of audit evidence that contributes to the exercise of professional skepticism.

• Objectivity requires the professional accountant not to compromise professional or business judgment because of bias, conflict of interest or the undue influence of others. For example, the accountant complies with the principle of objectivity by:

(a) Recognizing circumstances or relationships such as familiarity with the client, that might compromise the accountant's professional or business judgment; and

(b) Considering the impact of such circumstances and relationships on the accountant's judgment when evaluating the sufficiency and appropriateness of audit evidence related to a matter material to the client's financial statements.

In doing so, the accountant behaves in a manner that contributes to the exercise of professional skepticism.

• Professional competence and due care requires the professional accountant to have professional knowledge and skill at the level required to ensure the provision of competent professional service, and to act diligently in accordance with applicable standards, laws and regulations. For example, the accountant complies with the principle of professional competence and due care by:

(a) Applying knowledge that is relevant to a particular client's industry and business activities in order to properly identify risks of material misstatement;

(b) Designing and performing appropriate audit procedures; and

(c) Applying relevant knowledge when critically assessing whether audit evidence is sufficient and appropriate in the circumstances.

In doing so, the accountant behaves in a manner that contributes to the exercise of professional skepticism.

Part 2
Professional accountants In business (Including CGMA® designation holders)

Section 200

Applying the conceptual framework – professional accountants in business (including CGMA designation holders)

Introduction

200.1   This Part of the Code applies to "Members" as defined and referred to as:

    (a) Members in business (AICPA) who hold the CGMA credential;

    (b) All professional accountants in business (CIMA) including those who hold the CGMA credential (or are entitled to do so); and

    (c) An individual who is a professional accountant in public practice (CIMA) when performing professional activities pursuant to the accountant's relationship with the accountant's firm, whether as a contractor, employee or owner. More information on when Part 2 is applicable to professional accountants in public practice (CIMA) is set out in paragraphs R120.4, R300.5, and 300.5 A1.

200.2   Investors, creditors, employing organisations and other sectors of the business community, as well as governments and the general public, might rely on the work of members.

200.3   Members might be solely or jointly responsible for the preparation and reporting of financial and other information, on which both their employing organisations and third parties might rely. Members may also carry out a range of other activities, including:

- Providing effective financial management and competent advice on a variety of business-related matters. These may include forecasts, estimates, and projections and the assumptions upon which they are based being transparent and credible;

- Providing robust business case information, supporting decisions and capital allocation; and

- Providing assessment of effective and sufficient IT controls and procedures as part of implementing or improving financial and non-financial reporting systems.

200.4   A member might be an employee, contractor, partner, director (executive or non-executive), owner-manager, or volunteer of an employing organisation, engaged in commerce, industry or service, the public sector, education, the not-for-profit, or regulatory or professional bodies. The legal form of the relationship of the member with the employing organisation has no bearing on the ethical responsibilities placed on the member.

Conceptual framework for members in business

200.5   Members may encounter various relationships or circumstances that create threats to the member's compliance with the rules and fundamental principles. The rules, fundamental principles and interpretations seek to address many situations; however, they cannot address all relationships or circumstances that may arise. Thus, in the absence of an interpretation that addresses a particular relationship or circumstance, a member should evaluate whether that relationship or circumstance would lead a reasonable and informed third party who is aware of the relevant information to conclude that there is a threat to the member's compliance with the rules and fundamental principles that is not at an acceptable level. When making that evaluation, the member should apply the conceptual framework approach as outlined in this interpretation. The conceptual framework requires members to be alert for such facts and circumstances.

200.6   The CGMA Code specifies that in some circumstances, no safeguards can reduce a threat to an acceptable level. For example, the Code specifies that a member may not subordinate the member's professional judgment to others without violating the Integrity and Objectivity Rule and Principles. A member may not use the conceptual framework to overcome this or any other prohibition or requirement in the Code.

Requirements and application material

General

R200.7   Under the conceptual framework approach, members shall identify, evaluate and address threats to compliance with the rules and fundamental principles. Members should evaluate identified threats both individually and in the aggregate because threats can have a cumulative effect on a member's compliance with the rules and fundamental principles.

200.7 A1   Members have a responsibility to further the legitimate objectives of the member's employing organisation. The Code does not seek to hinder members from fulfilling that responsibility, but addresses circumstances in which compliance with the rules and fundamental principles might be compromised.

200.7 A2   Members may promote the position of the employing organisation when furthering legitimate goals and objectives of their employing organisation, provided that any statements made are neither false nor misleading. Such actions usually would not create an advocacy threat.

200.7 A3 The more senior the position of a member, the greater will be the ability and opportunity to access information, and to influence policies, decisions made and actions taken by others involved with the employing organisation. To the extent that they are able to do so, taking into account their position and seniority in the organisation, members are expected to encourage and promote an ethics-based culture in the organisation. Examples of actions that might be taken include the introduction, implementation and oversight of:

- Ethics education and training programs;
- Ethics and whistle-blowing policies;
- Policies and procedures designed to prevent non-compliance with laws and regulations.

Identifying threats

R200.8 The relationships or circumstances that a member encounters in various engagements and work assignments or positions will often create different threats to complying with the rules. When a member encounters a relationship or circumstance that is not specifically addressed by a rule, fundamental principle or an interpretation, under this approach, the member shall determine whether the relationship or circumstance creates one or more threats, such as those identified in paragraphs .07–.12 that follow. The existence of a threat does not mean that the member is not in compliance with the rules and fundamental principles; however, the member should evaluate the significance of the threat.

200.8 A1 Threats to compliance with the rules and fundamental principles might be created by a broad range of facts and circumstances. Many threats fall into one or more of the following six broad categories: adverse interest, advocacy, familiarity, self-interest, self-review, and undue influence (also referred to as "intimidation threat").

200.8 A2 Examples of threats associated with a specific relationship or circumstance are identified in the interpretations of the Code. Paragraphs 200.7 A3 – 200.7 A12 of this section define and provide examples, which are not all inclusive, of each of these threat categories.

200.8 A3 **Adverse interest threat.** The threat that a member will not act with objectivity, because the member's interests are opposed to the interests of the employing organisation. Examples of adverse interest threats include the following:

(a) A member has charged, or expressed an intention to charge, the employing organisation with violations of law.

(b) A member or the member's immediate family or close family has a financial or another relationship with a vendor, customer, competitor, or potential acquisition of the employing organisation.

(c) A member has sued or expressed an intention to sue the employing organisation or its officers, directors, or employees.

200.7 A4 **Advocacy threat.** The threat that a member will promote an organisation's interests or position to the point that their objectivity is compromised. Examples of advocacy threats include the following:

(a) Obtaining favorable financing or additional capital is dependent upon the information that the member includes in, or excludes from, a prospectus, an offering, a business plan, a financing application, or a regulatory filing.

(b) The member gives or fails to give information that the member knows will unduly influence the conclusions reached by an external service provider or other third party.

200.8 A4 **Familiarity threat**. The threat that, due to a long or close relationship with a person or an employing organisation, a member will become too sympathetic to their interests or too accepting of the person's work or organisation's product or service. Examples of familiarity threats include the following:

(a) A member uses an immediate family's or close family's company as a supplier to the employing organisation.

(b) A member accepts an individual's work product with little or no review because the individual has been producing an acceptable work product for an extended period of time.

(c) A member's immediate family or close family is employed as a member's subordinate.

200.8 A6 **Self-interest threat**. The threat that a member could benefit, financially or otherwise, from an interest in, or relationship with, the employing organisation or persons associated with the employing organisation. Examples of self-interest threats include the following:

(a) A member's immediate family or close family has a financial interest in the employing organisation.

(b) A member holds a financial interest (for example, shares or share options) in, or receives a loan or guarantee from, the employing organisation, and the value of that financial interest is directly affected by the Member's decisions.

(c) A member is eligible for a profit or other performance-related bonus, and the value of that bonus is directly affected by the Member's decisions.

(d) A member being offered a gift or special treatment from a supplier of the employing organisation.

200.8 A7 **Self-review threat**. The threat that a member will not appropriately evaluate the results of a previous judgment made or service performed or supervised by the member, or an individual in the employing organisation, and that the member will rely on that service in forming a judgment as part of another service. Examples of self-review threats include the following:

(a) When performing an internal audit procedure, an internal auditor accepts work that they previously performed in a different position.

(b) The member accepts the work previously performed by the member, alone or with others that will be the basis for providing another professional service.

200.8 A7 **Undue influence threat** (also referred to as "intimidation threat"). The threat that a member will subordinate their judgment to that of an individual associated with the employing organisation or any relevant third party due to that individual's position, reputation or expertise, aggressive or dominant personality, or attempts to coerce or exercise excessive influence over the member. Examples of undue influence threats include the following:

(a) A member is pressured to become associated with misleading information.

(b) A member is pressured to deviate from a company policy.

(c) A member is pressured to change a conclusion regarding an accounting or a tax position.

(d) A member is pressured to hire an unqualified individual.

Evaluating threats

R200.9 In evaluating the significance of an identified threat, a member shall determine whether a threat is at an acceptable level.

200.9 A1 Members are encouraged to evaluate identified threats both individually and in the aggregate because threats can have a cumulative effect on a member's compliance with the rules and fundamental principles.

200.9 A2 A threat is at an acceptable level when a reasonable and informed third party who is aware of the relevant information would be expected to conclude that the threat would not compromise the member's compliance with the rules and fundamental principles.

200.9 A3 If the member evaluates the threat and concludes that a reasonable and informed third party who is aware of the relevant information would be expected to conclude that the threat does not compromise a member's compliance with the rules and fundamental principles, the threat is at an acceptable level and the member is not required to evaluate the threat any further under this conceptual framework approach.

200.9 A4 Members may consider both qualitative and quantitative factors when evaluating the significance of a threat, including the extent to which existing safeguards already reduce the threat to an acceptable level.

200.9 A5 A member's evaluation of the level of a threat might be impacted by the work environment within the employing organisation and its operating environment. For example:

• Leadership that stresses the importance of ethical behaviour and the expectation that employees will act in an ethical manner.

• Policies and procedures to empower and encourage employees to communicate ethics issues that concern them to senior levels of management without fear of retribution.

• Policies and procedures to implement and monitor the quality of employee performance.

• Systems of corporate oversight or other oversight structures and strong internal controls.

• Recruitment procedures emphasizing the importance of employing high calibre competent personnel.

• Timely communication of policies and procedures, including any changes to them, to all employees, and appropriate training and education on such policies and procedures.

• Ethics and Code of conduct policies.

Addressing threats

R200.10 If, in evaluating the significance of an identified threat, a member concludes that a threat is not at an acceptable level, the member shall address the threats by eliminating them or reducing them to an acceptable level. The member shall do so by:

(a) Eliminating the circumstances, including interests or relationships, that are creating the threats;

(b) Applying safeguards, where available and capable of being applied, to reduce the threats to an acceptable level; or

(c) Declining or ending the specific professional activity.

200.10 A1 Sections 210 to 270 describe certain threats that might arise during the course of performing professional activities and include examples of actions that might address such threats.

200.10 A2 Members might consider obtaining legal advice where they believe that unethical behaviour or actions by others have occurred, or will continue to occur, within the employing organisation.

200.10 A3 In extreme situations, if the circumstances that created the threats cannot be eliminated and safeguards are not available or capable of being applied to reduce the threat to an acceptable level, it might be appropriate for a member to resign from the employing organisation.

Communicating with those charged with governance

R200.11 When communicating with those charged with governance in accordance with the Code, a member shall determine the appropriate individual(s) within the employing organisation's governance structure with whom to communicate. If the member communicates with a subgroup of those charged with governance, the member shall determine whether communication with all of those charged with governance is also necessary so that they are adequately informed.

200.11 A1 In determining with whom to communicate, a member might consider:

(a) The nature and importance of the circumstances; and

(b) The matter to be communicated.

200.11 A2 Examples of a subgroup of those charged with governance include an audit committee or an individual of those charged with governance.

R200.12 If a member communicates with individuals who have management responsibilities as well as governance responsibilities, the member shall be satisfied that communication with those individuals adequately informs all of those in a governance role with whom the member would otherwise communicate.

200.12 A1 In some circumstances, all of those charged with governance are involved in managing the employing organisation, for example, a small business where a single owner manages the organisation and no one else has a governance role. In these cases, if matters are communicated with individual(s) with management responsibilities, and those individual(s) also have governance responsibilities, the member has satisfied the requirement to communicate with those charged with governance.

Section 210
Ethical conflicts
Introduction

R210.1 If an ethical conflict is encountered, a member should take steps to best achieve compliance with the rules, fundamental principles and law.

210.1 A1 An ethical conflict arises when a member encounters one or both of the following:

(a) Obstacles to following an appropriate course of action due to internal or external pressures

(b) Conflicts in applying relevant professional and legal standards

For example, a member suspects a fraud may have occurred, but reporting the suspected fraud would violate the member's responsibility to maintain the confidentiality of their employer's confidential information.

210.1 A2 In weighing alternative courses of action, a member might consider factors such as the following:

(a) Relevant facts and circumstances, including applicable rules, laws, or regulations.

(b) Ethical issues involved.

(c) Established internal procedures.

210.1 A3 A member should be prepared to justify any departures they believe are appropriate in applying the relevant rules, fundamental principles and law.

210.1 A4 If a member is unable to resolve the conflict in a way that permitted compliance with the applicable rules, fundamental principles and law, the member may have to address the consequences of any violations.

210.1 A5 Before pursuing a course of action, a member might consult with appropriate persons within the organisation that employs the member.

210.1 A6   If a member decides not to consult with appropriate persons within the employing organisation, and the conflict remains unresolved after pursuing the selected course of action, the member should consider either consulting with other individuals for help in reaching a resolution or obtaining advice from an appropriate professional body or legal counsel. The member also should consider documenting the substance of the issue, the parties with whom the issue was discussed, details of any discussions held, and any decisions made concerning the issue.

210.1 A7   If the ethical conflict remains unresolved, the member will in all likelihood be in violation of one or more rules or fundamental principles if they remain associated with the matter creating the conflict. Accordingly, the member should consider their continuing relationship with the specific assignment or employer. any decisions made concerning the issue.

Integrity and objectivity

R210.2   Integrity and Objectivity Rule (AICPA): In the performance of any professional service, a member shall maintain objectivity and integrity, shall be free of conflicts of interest, and shall not knowingly misrepresent facts or subordinate their judgment to others.

R210.3   Integrity Principle (CIMA): The fundamental principle of integrity imposes an obligation on all members to be straightforward and honest in all professional and business relationships.

Objectivity Principle (CIMA): The fundamental principle of objectivity imposes an obligation on all members not to compromise their professional or business judgment because of bias, conflict of interest or the undue influence of others.

R210.4   In the absence of an interpretation of the Integrity and Objectivity Rule (AICPA) and the Integrity and Objectivity Principles (CIMA) that addresses a particular relationship or circumstance, a member should apply the "Conceptual Framework for Members in Business" (200.3 – 200.4).

R210.5   A member will be considered in violation of the Integrity and Objectivity Rule and the Integrity and Objectivity Principles if the member cannot demonstrate that they identified, evaluated and addressed threats to compliance with the rules and fundamental principles.

210.5 A1   A member should consider the guidance in Paragraphs R210.1 and 210.1 A1 – 210.1 A7 when addressing ethical conflicts that might arise when the member encounters obstacles to following an appropriate course of action. Such obstacles may be due to internal or external pressures or to conflicts in applying relevant professional and legal standards, or both.

Section 220
Conflicts of interest
Conflicts of interest for members in business

220.1   Members are required to comply with the rules and fundamental principles and apply the conceptual framework set out in Section 200 to identify, evaluate and address threats.

220.2   A member in business may be faced with a conflict of interest when undertaking a professional service. In determining whether a professional service, relationship, or matter would result in a conflict of interest, a member should use professional judgment, taking into account whether a reasonable and informed third party who is aware of the relevant information would conclude that a conflict of interest exists.

220.3   A conflict of interest creates adverse interest and self-interest threats to the member's compliance with the "Integrity and Objectivity Rule" and the Integrity and Objectivity principles. For example, threats may be created when:

   (a) a member undertakes a professional service related to a particular matter involving two or more parties whose interests with respect to that matter are in conflict; or

   (b) the interests of a member with respect to a particular matter and the interests of a party for whom the member undertakes a professional service related to that matter are in conflict.

220.4   A party may include an employing organisation, a vendor, a customer, a lender, a shareholder, or another party.

Requirements and application material
General

R220.5   A member shall not allow a conflict of interest to compromise professional or business judgment.

220.5 A1   The following are examples of situations in which conflicts of interest may arise:

   • Serving in a management or governance position for two employing organisations and acquiring confidential information from one employing organisation that could be used by the member to the advantage or disadvantage of the other employing organisation.

- Undertaking a professional service for each of two parties in a partnership employing the member to assist in dissolving their partnership.
- Preparing financial information for certain members of management of the employing organisation who are seeking to undertake a management buy-out.
- Being responsible for selecting a vendor for the member's employing organisation when the member or their immediate or close family relative could benefit financially from the transaction.
- Serving in a governance capacity or influencing an employing organisation that is approving certain investments for the company in which one of those specific investments will increase the value of the personal investment portfolio of the member or their immediate or close family relative.

Identification of a conflict of interest

R220.6 A member shall take reasonable steps to identify circumstances that might create a conflict of interest, and therefore a threat to compliance with one or more of the rules and fundamental principles. Such steps shall include identifying:

(a) The nature of the relevant interests and relationships between the parties involved; and

(b) The activity and its implication for relevant parties.

R220.7 A member shall remain alert to changes over time in the nature of the activities, interests and relationships that might create a conflict of interest while performing a professional activity.

Evaluation of a conflict of interest

220.8 A1 When an actual conflict of interest has been identified, the member should evaluate the significance of the threat created by the conflict of interest to determine if the threat is at an acceptable level. Members should consider both qualitative and quantitative factors when evaluating the significance of the threat, including the extent to which existing safeguards already reduce the threat to an acceptable level.

220.8 A2 In evaluating the significance of an identified threat, members should consider the following:

(a) The significance of relevant interests or relationships.

(b) The significance of the threats created by undertaking the professional service or services. In general, the more direct the connection between the member and the matter on which the parties' interests are in conflict, the more likely the level of the threat is not at an acceptable level.

220.8 A3 If a member concludes that the threat is not at an acceptable level, the member should apply safeguards to reduce the threat to an acceptable level. Examples of actions that might be safeguards to address threats created by conflicts of interest include:

(a) Restructuring or segregating certain responsibilities and duties.

(b) Obtaining appropriate oversight, for example, acting under the supervision of an executive or non-executive director.

(c) Consulting with third parties, such as a professional body, legal counsel, or another professional accountant.

220.8 A4 Examples of actions that might eliminate threats created by conflicts of interest include:

(a) Withdrawing from the decision-making process related to the matter giving rise to the conflict of interest

(b) Declining to perform or discontinue the professional services that would result in the conflict of interest

(c) Terminating the relevant relationships or disposing of the relevant interests.

Disclosure of a conflict of interest and consent

220.9 A1 It is generally necessary to:

(a) Disclose the nature of the conflict of interest and how any threats created were addressed to the relevant parties, including to the appropriate levels within the employing organisation affected by a conflict; and

(b) Obtain consent from the relevant parties for the professional accountant to undertake the professional activity when safeguards are applied to address the threat.

220.9 A2 Consent might be implied by a party's conduct in circumstances where the member has sufficient evidence to conclude that the parties know the circumstances at the outset and have accepted the conflict of interest if they do not raise an objection to the existence of the conflict.

220.9 A3 If such disclosure or consent is not in writing, the member is encouraged to document:

(a) The nature of the circumstances giving rise to the conflict of interest;

(b) The safeguards applied to address the threats when applicable; and

(c) The consent obtained.

220.9 A4 When addressing a conflict of interest, a member is encouraged to seek guidance from within the employing organisation or from others, such as a professional body, legal counsel, or another professional accountant. When making disclosures and seeking guidance of third parties, the member should remain alert to the requirements of the "Confidential Information Obtained From Employment or Volunteer Activities", interpretation of the "Acts Discreditable Rule" and the Integrity and Objectivity principles (270.1 and R210.3). In addition, federal, state, or local statutes, or regulations concerning confidentiality of employer information may be more restrictive than the requirements contained in the CGMA Code.

220.9 A5 A member may encounter other threats to compliance with the "Integrity and Objectivity Rule" and the Integrity and Objectivity principles. This may occur, for example, when preparing or reporting financial information as a result of undue pressure from others within the employing organisation or financial, business or personal relationships that close relatives or immediate family of the member have with the employing organisation. Guidance on managing such threats is covered by the "Knowing Misrepresentations in the Preparation of Financial Statements or Records", interpretation (240.3 – 240.4) and the "Subordination of Judgment by a Member", interpretation (240.11 A1 – A11).

Section 230
Inducements, including gifts and hospitality
Introduction

230.1 Members are required to comply with the rules and fundamental principles and apply the conceptual framework set out in Section 200 to identify, evaluate and address threats.

230.2 For purposes of this interpretation, a customer or vendor of the member's employer includes a representative of the customer or vendor.

230.3 When a member offers to, or accepts gifts or entertainment from, a customer or vendor of the member's employer, self-interest, familiarity, or undue influence threats to the member's compliance with the rules and fundamental principles, in particular the "Integrity and Objectivity Rule" and the Integrity and Objectivity principles, may exist.

Requirements and application material
General

230.4 A1 An inducement is an object, situation, or action that is used as a means to influence another individual's behaviour, but not necessarily with the intent to improperly influence that individual's behaviour. Inducements can range from minor acts of hospitality between business colleagues to acts that result in non-compliance with laws and regulations. An inducement can take many different forms, for example:

- Gifts.
- Hospitality.
- Entertainment.
- Political or charitable donations.
- Appeals to friendship and loyalty.
- Employment or other commercial opportunities.
- Preferential treatment, rights or privileges.

Inducements prohibited by laws and regulations

R230.5 In many jurisdictions, there are laws and regulations, such as those related to bribery and corruption, that prohibit the offering or accepting of inducements in certain circumstances. A member shall obtain an understanding of relevant laws and regulations that may apply to the member's employer or the customer or vendor, and comply with them when they encounter such circumstances.

Inducements not prohibited by laws and regulations

230.6 A1 The offering or accepting of inducements that is not prohibited by laws and regulations might still create threats to compliance with the "Integrity and Objectivity Rule" and the Integrity and Objectivity fundamental principles.

Inducements with intent to improperly influence behaviour

R230.7 A member shall not offer, or encourage others to offer, any inducement from a customer or vendor of the member's employer that is made, or which the member considers a reasonable and informed third party would be likely to conclude is made, with the intent to improperly influence the behaviour of the recipient or of another individual, or that violates the policies of the member's employer or the customer or vendor.

R230.8 A member shall not accept, or encourage others to accept, any inducement from a customer or vendor of the member's employer that is made, or which the member considers a reasonable and informed third party would be likely to conclude is made, with the intent to improperly influence the behaviour of the recipient or of another individual, or that violates the policies of the member's employer or the customer or vendor.

R230.8 A member shall not accept, or encourage others to accept, any inducement from a customer or vendor of the member's employer that is made, or which the member considers a reasonable and informed third party would be likely to conclude is made, with the intent to improperly influence the behaviour of the recipient or of another individual, or that violates the policies of the member's employer or the customer or vendor.

230.9 A1 An inducement is considered as improperly influencing an individual's behaviour if it causes the individual to act in an unethical manner. Such improper influence can be directed either towards the recipient or towards another individual who has some relationship with the recipient. The rules and fundamental principles are appropriate frames of reference for a member in considering what constitutes unethical behaviour on the part of the member and, if necessary by analogy, other individuals.

230.9 A2 A breach of the "Integrity and Objectivity Rule" and the "Integrity Principle" arises when a member offers or accepts, or encourages others to offer or accept, an inducement where the intent is to improperly influence the behaviour of the recipient or of another individual.

230.9 A3 The determination of whether there is actual or perceived intent to improperly influence behaviour requires the exercise of professional judgment. Relevant factor to consider might include:

- The nature, frequency, value and cumulative effect of the inducement.
- Timing of when the inducement is offered relative to any action or decision that it might influence.
- Whether the inducement is a customary or cultural practice in the circumstances, for example, offering a gift on the occasion of a religious holiday or wedding.
- Whether the inducement is an ancillary part of a professional activity, for example, offering or accepting lunch in connection with a business meeting.
- Whether the offer of the inducement is limited to an individual recipient or available to a broader group. The broader group might be internal or external to the employing organisation, such as other customers or vendors.

- The roles and positions of the individuals offering or being offered the inducement.
- Whether the member knows, or has reason to believe, that accepting the inducement would breach the policies and procedures of the counterparty's employing organisation.
- The degree of transparency with which the inducement is offered.
- Whether the inducement was required or requested by the recipient.
- The known previous behaviour or reputation of the offeror.

Consideration of further actions

230.10 A1 If a member becomes aware of an inducement offered with actual or perceived intent to improperly influence behaviour, threats to compliance with the "Integrity and Objectivity Rule" and the "Integrity Principle" might still be created even if the requirements in paragraphs R230.7 and R230.8 are met.

230.10 A2 Examples of actions that might be safeguards to address such threats include:

- Informing senior management or those charged with governance of the employing organisation of the member or the offeror regarding the offer.
- Amending or terminating the business relationship with the offeror.

Inducements with no intent to improperly influence behaviour

230.11 A1 The requirements and application material set out in the conceptual framework apply when a member has concluded there is no actual or perceived intent to improperly influence the behaviour of the recipient or of another individual.

230.11 A2 If such an inducement is trivial and inconsequential, any threats created will be at an acceptable level.

230.11 A3 Examples of circumstances where offering or accepting such an inducement might create threats even if the member has concluded there is no actual or perceived intent to improperly influence behaviour include:

- Self-interest threats
  - A member is offered part-time employment by a customer or vendor.
- Familiarity threats
  - A member regularly takes a customer or vendor to sporting events.
- Undue influence (Intimidation) threats
  - A member accepts hospitality, the nature of which could be perceived to be inappropriate were it to be publicly disclosed.

230.11 A4 Relevant factors in evaluating the level of such threats created by offering or accepting such an inducement include the same factors set out in paragraph 230.9 A3 for determining intent.

230.11 A5 Examples of actions that might eliminate threats created by offering or accepting such an inducement include:

- Declining or not offering the inducement.
- Transferring responsibility for any business-related decision involving the counterparty to another individual who has the member has no reason to believe would be, or would be perceived to be, improperly influenced in making the decision.

230.11 A6 Examples of actions that might be safeguards to address such threats created by offering or accepting such an inducement include:

- Being transparent with senior management or those charged with governance of the employing organisation of the member or of the counterparty about offering or accepting an inducement.
- Registering the inducement in a log maintained by the employing organisation of the member or the counterparty.
- Having an appropriate reviewer, who is not otherwise involved in undertaking the professional activity, review any work performed or decisions made by the member with respect to the individual or organisation from which the member accepted the inducement.
- Donating the inducement to charity after receipt and appropriately disclosing the donation, for example, to those charged with governance or the individual who offered the inducement.
- Reimbursing the cost of the inducement, such as hospitality, received.
- As soon as possible, returning the inducement, such as a gift, after it was initially accepted.

Immediate or close family relatives

R230.12 A member shall remain alert to potential threats to the member's compliance with the rules and fundamental principles, in particular the "Integrity and Objectivity Rule" and the Integrity and Objectivity Principles, created by the offering of an inducement:

(a) By an immediate or close family relative of the member to a counterparty with whom the member has a professional relationship; or

(b) To an immediate or close family relative of the member by a counterparty with whom the member has a professional relationship.

230.12 A1 For example, self-interest threats are created when an inducement is made in an attempt to unduly influence actions or decisions, encourage illegal or unethical behaviour, or obtain confidential information, and undue influence (intimidation) threats are created if such an inducement is offered or accepted and it is followed by threats to make that offer public and damage the reputation of either the member or an immediate or close family relative to the member.

R230.13 Where the member becomes aware of an inducement being offered to or made by an immediate or close family relative and concludes there is intent to improperly influence the behaviour of the member or of the counterparty, or considers a reasonable and informed third party would be likely to conclude such intent exists, the member shall advise the immediate or close family relative not to offer or accept the inducement.

230.13 A1 The factors set out in paragraph 230.9 A3 are relevant in determining whether there is actual or perceived intent to improperly influence the behaviour of the member or of the counterparty. Another factor that is relevant is the nature or closeness of the relationship, between:

(a) The member and the immediate or close family relative;

(b) The immediate or close family relative and the counterparty; and

(c) The member and the counterparty.

For example, the offer of employment, outside of the normal recruitment process, to the spouse of the member by a counterparty with whom the member is negotiating a significant contract might indicate such intent.

230.13 A2 The application material in paragraph 230.10 A2 is also relevant in addressing threats that might be created when there is actual or perceived intent to improperly influence the behaviour of the member or of the counterparty even if the immediate or close family relative has followed the advice given pursuant to paragraph R230.13.

Application of the conceptual framework for members in business

230.14 A1 Where the member becomes aware of an inducement offered in the circumstances addressed in paragraph R230.12, threats to compliance with the rules and fundamental principles might be created where:

(a) The immediate or close family relative offers or accepts the inducement contrary to the advice of the member pursuant to paragraph 230.13; or

(b) The member does not have reason to believe an actual or perceived intent to improperly influence the behaviour of the member or of the counterparty exists.

230.14 A2 The application material in paragraphs 230.11 A1 to 230.11 A6 is relevant for the purposes of identifying, evaluating and addressing such threats. Factors that are relevant in evaluating the level of threats in these circumstances also include the nature and closeness of the relationships set out in paragraph 230.13 A1.

Other Considerations

230.15 A1 [CIMA ONLY] If a member encounters or is made aware of inducements that might result in non-compliance or suspected non-compliance with laws and regulations by other individuals working for or under the direction of the employing organisation, the requirements and application material set out in Section 290 apply.

230.15 A2 If a member faces pressure to offer or accept inducements that might create threats to compliance with the rules and fundamental principles, the requirements and application material in Section 280 apply.

Section 240
Preparation and presentation of information
Introduction

240.1 Members at all levels are required to comply with the rules and fundamental principles and apply the conceptual framework set out in Section 200 to identify, evaluate and address threats.

240.2 Preparing or presenting information might create self-interest, familiarity, undue influence or other threats to compliance with one of more the rules and fundamental principles, such as the "Integrity and Objectivity Rule" and the Integrity and Objectivity fundamental principles.

Requirements and application material
Knowing Misrepresentations in the Preparation of Financial Statements or Records

240.3 A1 Members in business are often involved in the preparation and reporting of information that may either be made public or used by others inside or outside the employing organisation.

240.3 A2 Stakeholders to whom, or for whom, such information is prepared or presented, include:

- Management and those charged with governance.
- Investors and lenders or other creditors.
- Regulatory bodies.

240.3 A3 Information might assist stakeholders in understanding and evaluating aspects of the employing organisation's state of affairs and in making decisions concerning the organisation. Information may include financial or non-financial or management information that might be made public or used for internal purposes. Examples include:

- Operating and performance reports.
- Decision support analyses.
- Budgets and forecasts.
- Information provided to the internal and external auditors.
- Risk analyses.
- General and special purpose financial statements.
- Tax returns.
- Reports filed with regulatory bodies for legal and compliance purposes.

240.3 A4 For the purposes of this section, preparing or presenting information includes recording, maintaining, approving, and reporting information.

R240.4 When preparing or presenting information, a member shall do so in accordance with the "Integrity and Objectivity Rule" and the Integrity and Objectivity fundamental principle, and shall:

(a) Prepare or present the information in accordance with a relevant reporting framework where applicable;

(b) Prepare or present the information in a manner that is intended neither to mislead nor to influence contractual or regulatory outcomes inappropriately;

(c) Exercising professional judgment to:

(i) Represent the facts accurately and completely in all material respects;

(ii) Describe clearly the true nature of business transactions or activities; and

(iii) Classify and record information in a timely and proper manner; and

(d) Not omit anything with the intention of rendering the information misleading or of influencing contractual or regulatory outcomes inappropriately.

240.4 A1 An example of influencing a contractual or regulatory outcome inappropriately is using an unrealistic estimate with the intention of avoiding violation of a contractual requirement such as a debt covenant or of a regulatory requirement such as a capital requirement for a financial institution.

240.4 A2 Threats to compliance with the "Integrity and Objectivity Rule" and the Integrity and Objectivity fundamental principles would not be at an acceptable level and could not be reduced to an acceptable level by the application of safeguards, and the member would be considered to have knowingly misrepresented facts in violation of the "Integrity and Objectivity Rule" and the Integrity and Objectivity fundamental principles, if the member:

(a) Makes, or permits or directs another to make, materially false and misleading entries in an entity's financial statements or records;

(b) Fails to correct an entity's financial statements or records that are materially false and misleading when the member has the authority to record the entries; or

(c) Signs, or permits or directs another to sign, a document containing materially false and misleading information.

Use of discretion in preparing or presenting information

R240.5 Preparing or presenting information might require the exercise of discretion in making professional judgments. A member shall not exercise such discretion with the intention of misleading others or influencing contractual or regulatory outcomes inappropriately.

240.5 A1 Examples of ways in which discretion might be misused to achieve inappropriate outcomes include:

• Determining estimates, for example, determining fair value estimates in order to misrepresent profit or loss.

• Selecting or changing an accounting policy or method among two or more alternatives permitted under the applicable financial reporting framework, for example, selecting a policy for accounting for long-term contracts in order to misrepresent profit or loss.

• Determining the timing of transactions, for example, timing the sale of an asset near the end of the fiscal year in order to mislead.

• Determining the structuring of transactions, for example, structuring financing transactions in order to misrepresent assets and liabilities or classification of cash flows.

• Selecting disclosures, for example omitting or obscuring information relating to financial or operating risk in order to mislead.

R240.6 When performing professional activities, especially those that do not require compliance with a relevant reporting framework, a member shall exercise professional judgment to identify and consider:

(a) The purpose for which the information is to be used;

(b) The context within which it is given; and

(c) The audience to whom it is addressed.

240.6 A1 For example, when preparing or presenting pro forma reports, budgets or forecasts, the inclusion of relevant estimates, approximations and assumptions, where appropriate, would enable those who might rely on such information to form their own judgments.

240.6 A2 A member might also consider clarifying the intended audience, context and purpose of the information to be presented.

Relying on the work of others

R240.7 A member who intends to rely on the work of others, either internal or external to the employing organisation, shall exercise professional judgment to determine what steps to take, if any, in order to fulfill the responsibilities set out in paragraph R240.4.

240.7 A1 Factors to consider in determining whether reliance on others is reasonable include:

• The reputation and expertise of, and resources available to, the other individual or organisation.

• Whether the other individual is subject to applicable professional and ethics standards.

Such information might be gained from prior association with, or from consulting others about, the other individual or organisation.

Addressing information that is or might be misleading

R240.8 When a member knows or has reason to believe that the information with which the member is associated is misleading, the member shall take appropriate actions to seek to resolve the matter.

240.8 A1 Actions that might be appropriate include:

• Discussing concerns that the information is misleading with the member's superior and/or the appropriate level(s) of management within the member's employing organisation or those charged with governance, and requesting such individuals to take appropriate action to resolve the matter. Such action might include:

  • Having the information corrected.

  • If the information has already been disclosed to the intended users, informing them of the correct information.

• Consulting the policies and procedures of the employing organisation (for example, an ethics or whistle-blowing policy) regarding how to address such matters internally.

240.8 A2 The member might determine that the employing organisation has not taken appropriate action. If the member continues to have reason to believe that the information is misleading, threats to compliance with the "Integrity and Objectivity Rule" and the fundamental principles would not be at an acceptable level. In such circumstances, the following further actions might be appropriate provided that the member remains alert to the "Acts Discreditable Rule" and fundamental principle of confidentiality:

- Consulting with:
  - A relevant professional body.
  - The internal or external auditor of the employing organisation.
  - Legal Counsel.
- Determining whether any requirements exist to communicate to:
  - Third parties, including users of the information.
  - Regulatory and oversight authorities.

R240.9 If after exhausting all feasible options, the member determines that appropriate action has not been taken and there is reason to believe that the information is still misleading, the member shall refuse to be or to remain associated with the information.

240.9 A1 In such circumstances, it might be appropriate for a member to resign from the employing organisation.

Documentation

240.10 A1 The member is encouraged to document:

- The facts.
- The accounting principles or other relevant professional standards involved.
- The communications and parties with whom matters were discussed.
- The courses of action considered.
- How the accountant attempted to address the matter(s).

Subordination of judgment

240.11 A1 The "Integrity and Objectivity Rule" and the fundamental principles prohibit a member from knowingly misrepresenting facts or subordinating their judgment when performing professional services for an employer or on a volunteer basis. This interpretation addresses differences of opinion between a member and their supervisor or any other person within the member's organisation.

240.11 A2 Self-interest, familiarity, and undue influence threats to the member's compliance with the "Integrity and Objectivity Rule" and the Integrity and Objectivity fundamental principles may exist when a member and their supervisor or any other person within the member's organisation have a difference of opinion relating to the application of accounting principles; auditing standards; or other relevant professional standards, including standards applicable to tax and consulting services or applicable laws or regulations.

240.11 A3 A member should evaluate the significance of any threats to determine if they are at an acceptable level. Threats are at an acceptable level if the member concludes that the position taken does not result in a material misrepresentation of fact or a violation of applicable laws or regulations.

240.11 A4 In evaluating threats, a member should determine, after appropriate research or consultation, whether the result of the position taken by the supervisor or other person

(a) Fails to comply with professional standards, when applicable;

(b) Creates a material misrepresentation of fact; or

(c) May violate applicable laws or regulations.

240.11 A5 If the member concludes that threats are at an acceptable level, the member should discuss their conclusions with the person taking the position. No further action would be needed under this interpretation.

240.11 A6 If the member concludes that the position results in a material misrepresentation of fact of a violation of applicable laws or regulations, then threats would not be at an acceptable level. In such circumstances, the member should discuss their concerns with the supervisor.

240.11 A7 If the difference of opinion is not resolved after discussing the concerns with the supervisor, the member should discuss their concerns with the appropriate higher level(s) of management with the member's organisation (for example, the supervisor's immediate superior, senior management, and those charged with governance).

240.11 A8 If after discussing the concerns with the supervisor and appropriate higher level(s) of management within the member's organisation, the member concludes that appropriate action was not taken, then the member might consider, in no specific order, the following safeguards to reduce threats to the member's compliance with the "Integrity and Objectivity Rule" and the Integrity and Objectivity fundamental principles to an acceptable level:

- Determine whether the organisation's internal policies and procedures have any additional requirements for reporting differences of opinion.

- Determine whether the member is responsible for communicating to third parties, such as regulatory authorities or the organisation's (former organisation's) external accountant. In considering such communications, the member should be cognizant of their obligations under Section 270.
- Consult with legal counsel regarding the member's responsibilities.
- Document the member's understanding of the facts, the accounting principles, auditing standards, or other relevant professional standards involved or applicable laws or regulations and the conversations and parties with whom these matters were discussed.

240.11 A9 If the member concludes that no safeguards can reduce the threats to an acceptable level or if the member concludes that appropriate action was not taken, then they should consider the continuing relationship with the member's organisation and take appropriate steps to eliminate their exposure to subordination of judgment.

240.11 A10 Nothing in this interpretation precludes a member from resigning from the organisation at any time. However, resignation may not relieve the member of responsibilities in the situation, including any responsibility to disclose concerns to third parties, such as regulatory authorities or the employer's (former employer's) external accountant.

240.11 A11 A member should use professional judgment and apply similar safeguards, as appropriate, to other situations involving a difference of opinion as described in this interpretation so that the member does not subordinate their judgment.

Obligation of a member to their employer's external accountant

240.12 A1 The "Integrity and Objectivity Rule" and the Integrity and Objectivity principles require a member to maintain objectivity and integrity in the performance of a professional service. When dealing with an employer's external accountant, a member must be candid and not knowingly misrepresent facts of knowingly fail to disclose material facts. This would include, for example, responding to specific inquiries for which the employer's external accountant requests written representation.

Section 250
Educational services

250.1 A1 Members who perform educational services, such as teaching full or part time at a university, teaching a continuing professional education course, or engaging in research and scholarship, are performing professional services and, therefore, are subject to the "Integrity and Objectivity Rule" and the Integrity and Objectivity principles.

Section 260
General standards / professional competence and due care

Introduction

R260.1 Members are required to comply with the General Standards Rule (AICPA) and the fundamental principle of Professional Competence and Due Care (CIMA) and apply the conceptual framework set out in Section 200 to identify, evaluate and address threats.

Requirements and application material

General

R260.2 A member shall not intentionally mislead an employing organisation as to the level of expertise or experience possessed.

General standards rule (AICPA)

R260.3 A member shall comply with the following standards and with any interpretations thereof by bodies designated by Council.

(a) Professional Competence. Undertake only those professional services that the member or the member's firm can reasonably expect to be completed with professional competence.

(b) Due Professional Care. Exercise due professional care in the performance of professional services.

(c) Planning and Supervision. Adequately plan and supervise the performance of professional services.

(d) Sufficient Relevant Data. Obtain sufficient relevant data to afford a reasonable basis for conclusions or recommendations in relation to any professional services performed.

Professional competence and due care principle (CIMA)

R260.4 A member shall comply with the fundamental principle of Professional Competence and Due Care, which imposes the following obligations on all members:

    (a) To attain and maintain professional knowledge and skill at the level required to ensure that a client or employing organisation receives competent professional service, based on current technical and professional standards and relevant legislation; and

    (b) To act diligently and in accordance with applicable technical and professional standards.

Interpretations under the "general standards rule" and "professional competence and due care principle

Application of the conceptual framework for members in business and ethical conflicts

260.5 A1 In the absence of an interpretation of the "General Standards Rule" and "Professional Competence and Due Care Principle" that addresses a particular relationship or circumstance, a member should apply the "Conceptual Framework for Members in Business" (200.3 – 200.4).

260.5 A2 A member would be considered in violation of the "General Standards Rule" and "Professional Competence and Due Care Principle" if the member cannot demonstrate that safeguards were applied that eliminated or reduced significant threats to an acceptable level.

260.5 A3 A member should consider the guidance in the "Ethical Conflicts" interpretation (210.1) when addressing ethical conflicts that may arise when the member encounters obstacles to following an appropriate course of action. Such obstacles may be due to internal or external pressures or to conflicts in applying relevant professional and legal standards, or both.

Professional competence and due care

260.6 A4 Competence, in this context, means that the member or member's staff possesses the appropriate technical qualifications to perform professional services and, as required, supervises and evaluates the quality of work performed. Competence encompasses knowledge of the profession's standards, the techniques and technical subject matter involved, and the ability to exercise sound judgment in applying such knowledge in the performance of professional services.

260.6 A5 A member's agreement to perform professional services implies that the member has the necessary competence to complete those services according to professional standards and to apply the member's knowledge and skill with reasonable care and diligence. However, the member does not assume a responsibility for infallibility of knowledge or judgment.

260.6 A6 The member may have the knowledge required to complete the services in accordance with professional standards prior to performance. A normal part of providing professional services involves performing additional research or consulting with others to gain sufficient competence.

260.6 A7 Threats to the member's compliance with the "General Standards Rule" and "Professional Competence and Due Care Principle" may exist if the member is performing professional services and the member has:

- Insufficient time for properly performing or completing the relevant duties;
- Incomplete, restricted or otherwise inadequate information for performing the duties properly;
- Insufficient experience, training or education, or both; or
- Inadequate resources for the proper performance of the duties.

260.6 A8 The significance of the threats will depend on factors such as the extent to which the member is working with others, relative seniority in the business, and the level of supervision and review applied to the work. The member should evaluate the significance of any threats and apply safeguards, when necessary, to eliminate or reduce the threats to an acceptable level. Examples of such safeguards include:

- Performing additional research or obtaining additional advice or training.
- Ensuring that there is adequate time available for performing the relevant duties.
- Obtaining assistance from someone with the necessary expertise.
- Consulting, where appropriate, with:
  - Superiors within the employing organisation;
  - Independent experts; or
  - A relevant professional body.

260.6 A9 If the member determines that the threats are so significant that no safeguards could eliminate or reduce the threats to an acceptable level, and therefore the member is unable to gain sufficient competence, the member should suggest the involvement of a competent person to perform the needed professional service, either independently or as an associate.

Submission of financial statements

R260.7 When a member is a stockholder, a partner, a director, an officer, or an employee of an entity and, in this capacity, prepares or submits the entity's financial statements to third parties, the member should clearly communicate, preferably in writing, the member's relationship to the entity and should not imply that the member is independent of the entity. In addition, if the communication states affirmatively that the financial statements are presented in conformity with the applicable financial reporting framework, the member should comply with the "Accounting Principles Rule" and the "Professional Competence and Due Care Principle".

260.7 A1 AICPA members should refer to the "Use of CPA Credential" interpretation (370.26) for additional guidance.

Compliance with standards / professional competence and due care

Compliance with standards rule (AICPA)

R260.8 A member who performs auditing, review, compilation, management consulting, tax, or other professional services shall comply with standards promulgated by bodies designated by Council.

Professional competence and due care principle (CIMA)

R260.9 A member shall comply with the fundamental principle of Professional Competence and Due Care, which imposes the following obligations on all members:

(a) To attain and maintain professional knowledge and skill at the level required to ensure that a client or employing organisation receives competent professional service, based on current technical and professional standards and relevant legislation; and

(b) To act diligently and in accordance with applicable technical and professional standards.

Interpretations under the compliance with standards rule and the professional competence and due care principle

Application of the conceptual framework for members in business and ethical conflicts

260.10 A1 In the absence of an interpretation of the "Compliance with Standards Rule" and the "Professional Competence and Due Care Principle" that addresses a particular relationship or circumstance, a member should apply the "Conceptual Framework for Members in Business" (300.2-300.3).

260.10 A2 A member would be considered in violation of the "Compliance with Standards Rule" and the "Professional Competence and Due Care Principle" if the member cannot demonstrate that safeguards were applied that eliminated or reduced significant threats to an acceptable level.

260.10 A3 A member should consider the guidance in the "Ethical Conflicts" interpretation (310.1) when addressing ethical conflicts that may arise when the member encounters obstacles to following an appropriate course of action. Such obstacles may be due to internal or external pressures or to conflicts in applying relevant professional or legal standards, or both.

Accounting principles

Accounting principles rule (AICPA)

R260.11 A member shall not:

(1) Express an opinion or state affirmatively that the financial statements or other financial data of any entity are presented in conformity with generally accepted accounting principles; or

(2) State that they are not aware of any material modifications that should be made to such statements or data in order for them to be in conformity with generally accepted accounting principles, if such statements or data contain any departure from an accounting principle promulgated by bodies designated by Council to establish such principles that has a material effect on the statements or data taken as a whole.

If, however, the statements or data contain such a departure and the member can demonstrate that due to unusual circumstances the financial statements or data would otherwise have been misleading, the member can comply with the rule by describing the departure, its approximate effects, if practicable, and the reasons why compliance with the principle would result in a misleading statement.

Professional competence and due care principle (CIMA)

R260.12 A member shall comply with the fundamental principle of Professional Competence and Due Care, which imposes the following obligations on all members:

(a) To attain and maintain professional knowledge and skill at the level required to ensure that a client or employing organisation receives competent professional service, based on current technical and professional standards and relevant legislation; and

(b) To act diligently and in accordance with applicable technical and professional standards.

Interpretations under the accounting principles rule and the professional competence and due care principles

Application of the conceptual framework for members in business and ethical conflicts

260.13 A1 In the absence of an interpretation of the "Accounting Principles Rule" and the "Professional Competence and Due Care Principle" that addresses a particular relationship or circumstance, a member should apply the "Conceptual Framework for Members in Business" (200.3 – 200.4).

260.13 A2 A member would be considered in violation of the "Accounting Principles Rule" and the "Professional Competence and Due Care Principle" if the member cannot demonstrate that safeguards were applied that eliminated or reduced significant threats to an acceptable level.

260.13 A3 A member should consider the guidance in the "Ethical Conflicts" interpretation (210.1) when addressing ethical conflicts that may arise when the member encounters obstacles to following an appropriate course of action. Such obstacles may be due to internal or external pressures or to conflicts in applying relevant professional or legal standards, or both.

Responsibility for affirming that financial statements are in conformity with the applicable financial reporting framework (AICPA)

R260.14 A member shall not state affirmatively that an entity's financial statements or other financial data are presented in conformity with generally accepted accounting principles (GAAP) if such statements or data contain any departure from an accounting principle promulgated by a body designated by Council to establish such principles. Members who affirm that financial statements or other financial data are presented in conformity with GAAP should comply with "Accounting Principles Rule". A member's representation in a letter or other communication that an entity's financial statements are in conformity with GAAP may be considered an affirmative statement within the meaning of this rule with respect to the member who signed the letter or other communication (for example, the member signed a report to a regulatory authority, a creditor, or an auditor).

Responsibility for affirming that financial statements are in conformity with the applicable financial reporting framework (CIMA)

R260.15 A member of CIMA who has responsibility for the preparation or approval of the general purpose financial statements of an employing organisation shall be satisfied that those financial statements are presented in accordance with the applicable financial reporting standards.

Status of financial accounting standards board, governmental accounting standards board, federal accounting standards advisory board, and international accounting standards board interpretations (AICPA)

260.16 A1 The "Accounting Principles Rule" authorises Council to designate bodies to establish accounting principles. Council has designated the U.S. Financial Accounting Standards Board (FASB) as such a body and has resolved that FASB Accounting Standards Codification® (ASC) constitutes accounting principles as contemplated in the rule. Council designated the U.S. Governmental Accounting Standards Board (GASB), with respect to Statements of Governmental Accounting Standards issued in July 1984 and thereafter, as the body to establish financial accounting principles for state and local governmental entities, pursuant to the "Accounting Principles Rule". Council designated the U.S. Federal Accounting Standards Advisory Board (FASAB), with respect to Statements of Federal Accounting Standards adopted and issued in March 1993 and subsequently, as the body to establish accounting principles for federal government entities, pursuant to the "Accounting Principles Rule". Council designated the International Accounting Standards Board (IASB) as an accounting body for purposes of establishing international financial accounting and reporting principles.

260.16 A2 Reference to GAAP in the "Accounting Principles Rule" means those accounting principles promulgated by bodies designated by Council, which are listed in paragraph .01 "Council Resolution Designating Bodies to Promulgate Technical Standards".

260.16 A3 The AICPA Professional Ethics Division will look to the codification or statements and any interpretations thereof issued by FASB, GASB, FASAB, or IASB in determining whether a member of the AICPA has departed from an accounting principle established by a designated accounting standard-setter in FASB ASC, a Statement of Governmental Accounting Standards, a Statement of Federal Accounting Standards, or International Financial Reporting Standards (IFRS).

Departures from generally accepted accounting principles (AICPA)

260.17 A1 It is difficult to anticipate all the circumstances in which accounting principles may be applied. However, there is a strong presumption that adherence to GAAP would, in nearly all instances, result in financial statements that are not misleading. The "Accounting Principles Rule" recognises that, upon occasion, there may be unusual circumstances when the literal application of GAAP would have the effect of rendering financial statements misleading. In such cases, the proper accounting treatment to apply is that which will not render the financial statements misleading.

260.17 A2 The question of what constitutes unusual circumstances, as referred to in the "Accounting Principles Rule" is a matter of professional judgment involving the ability to support the position that adherence to a promulgated principle within GAAP would be regarded generally by reasonable persons as producing misleading financial statements.

260.17 A3 Examples of circumstances that may justify a departure from GAAP include new legislation or evolution of a new form of business transaction. Examples of circumstances that would not justify departures from GAAP include an unusual degree of materiality or conflicting industry practices.

260.17 A4 If the statements or data contain such departures, see the "Accounting Principles Rule" for further guidance.

Financial statements prepared pursuant to financial reporting frameworks other than GAAP (AICPA)

260.18 A1 Reference to GAAP in the "Accounting Principles Rule" means those accounting principles promulgated by bodies designated by Council. The bodies designed by Council to promulgate accounting principles are
- FASAB,
- FASB,
- GASB, and
- IASB.

260.18 A2 Financial statements prepared pursuant to other accounting principles would be considered financial reporting frameworks other than GAAP within the context of the "Accounting Principles Rule".

260.18 A3 However, the "Accounting Principles Rule" does not preclude a member from preparing or reporting on financial statements that have been prepared pursuant to financial reporting frameworks other than GAAP, such as:

(a) financial reporting frameworks generally accepted in another country, including jurisdictional variations of IFRS such that the entity's financial statements do not meet the requirements for full compliance with IFRS, as promulgated by the IASB;

(b) financial reporting frameworks prescribed by an agreement or a contract; or

(c) other special purpose frameworks, including statutory financial reporting provisions required by law or a U.S. or foreign governmental regulatory body to whose jurisdiction the entity is subject.

In such circumstances, however, the financial statements or member's reports thereon should not purport that the financial statements are in accordance with GAAP and the financial statements or reports on those financial statements, or both, should clarify the financial reporting framework(s) used.

Section 270
Acts discreditable / professional behaviour / confidentiality

Introduction

270.1 Members are required to comply with the Acts Discreditable Rule (AICPA) and the fundamental principles of Professional Behaviour and Confidentiality (CIMA), and apply the conceptual framework set out in Section 200 to identify, evaluate and address threats.

Requirements and application material

General

Acts discreditable rule (AICPA)

R270.2 A member shall not commit an act discreditable to the profession.

Professional behaviour principle (CIMA)

R270.3 A member shall comply with the principle of professional behaviour, which requires a member to comply with relevant laws and regulations and avoid any conduct that the member knows or should know might discredit the profession. A member shall not knowingly engage in any business, occupation or activity that impairs or might impair the integrity, objectivity or good reputation of the profession, and as a result would be incompatible with the fundamental principles.

Confidentiality principle (CIMA)

R270.4   A member shall comply with the principle of confidentiality, which requires a member to respect the confidentiality of information acquired as a result of professional and business relationships. A member shall:

(a) Be alert to the possibility of inadvertent disclosure, including in a social environment, and particularly to a close business associate or an immediate or a close family relative;

(b) Maintain confidentiality of information within the firm or employing organisation;

(c) Maintain confidentiality of information disclosed by a prospective client or employing organisation;

(d) Not disclose confidential information acquired as a result of professional and business relationships outside the firm or employing organisation without proper and specific authority, unless there is a legal or professional duty or right to disclose;

(e) Not use confidential information acquired as a result of professional and business relationships for the personal advantage of the accountant or for the advantage of a third party;

(f) Not use or disclose any confidential information, either acquired or received as a result of a professional or business relationship, after that relationship has ended; and

(g) Take reasonable steps to ensure that personnel under the accountant's control, and individuals from whom advice and assistance are obtained, respect the accountant's duty of confidentiality.

Interpretations under the acts discreditable rule and professional behaviour and confidentiality principles

Application of the conceptual framework for members in business and ethical conflicts

270.5 A1   In the absence of an interpretation of the "Acts Discreditable Rule" and the Professional Behaviour and Confidentiality principles that addresses a particular relationship or circumstance, a member should apply the "Conceptual Framework for Members in Business" (200.3 – 200.4).

270.5 A2   A member would be considered in violation of the "Acts Discreditable Rule" and the Professional Behaviour and Confidentiality principles if the member cannot demonstrate that safeguards were applied that eliminated or reduced significant threats to an acceptable level.

270.5 A3   A member should consider the guidance in the "Ethical Conflicts" interpretation (310.1) when addressing ethical conflicts that may arise when the member encounters obstacles to follow an appropriate course of action. Such obstacles may be due to internal or external pressures or to conflicts in applying relevant professional standards or legal standards, or both.

Discrimination and harassment in employment practices

270.6 A1   A member would be presumed to have committed an act discreditable to the profession, in violation of the "Acts Discreditable Rule" and the "Professional Behaviour Principle" if a final determination, no longer subject to appeal, is made by a court or an administrative agency of competent jurisdiction that a member has violated any antidiscrimination laws of the country, state, or municipality, including those related to sexual and other forms of harassment.

Solicitation or disclosure of CPA/CIMA examination questions and answers

270.7 A1   A member who solicits or knowingly discloses the Uniform CPA Examination or the CIMA Examination question(s) or answer(s), or both, without the AICPA's or CIMA's respective written authorisation shall be considered to have committed an act discreditable to the profession, in violation of the "Acts Discreditable Rule" and the "Professional Behaviour Principle".

Failure to file a tax return or pay a tax liability

270.8 A1   A member who fails to comply with applicable federal, state, or local laws or regulations regarding:

(a) The timely filing of the member's personal tax returns or tax returns for the member's employer that the member has the authority to timely file; or

(b) The timely remittance of all payroll and other taxes collected on behalf of others may be considered to have committed an act discreditable to the profession, in violation of the "Acts Discreditable Rule" and the "Professional Behaviour Principle".

Negligence in the preparation of financial statements or records

270.9 A1 A member would be considered in violation of the "Acts Discreditable Rule" and the "Professional Behaviour Principle" if the member, by virtue of their negligence, does any of the following:

(a) Makes, or permits or directs another to make, materially false and misleading entries in the financial statements or records of an entity.

(b) Fails to correct an entity's financial statements that are materially false and misleading when the member has the authority to record an entry.

(c) Signs, or permits or directs another to sign, a document containing materially false and misleading information.

Governmental bodies, commissions, or other regulatory agencies

270.10 Many governmental bodies, commissions, or other regulatory agencies have established requirements, such as standards, guides, rules, and regulations that members are required to follow in the preparation of financial statements or related information.

R270.11 If a member prepares financial statements or related information (for example, management's discussion and analysis) for purposes of reporting to such bodies, commissions, or regulatory agencies, the member shall follow the requirements of such organisations in addition to the applicable financial reporting framework.

270.11 A1 A member's material departure from such requirements would be considered a violation of the "Acts Discreditable Rule" and the "Professional Behaviour Principle" unless the member discloses in the financial statements or related information that such requirements were not followed and the applicable reasons.

Indemnification and limitation of liability provisions

270.12 Certain governmental bodies, commissions, or other regulatory agencies (collectively, regulators) have established requirements through laws, regulations, or published interpretations that

(a) Prohibit entities subject to their regulation (regulated entity) from including certain types of indemnification and limitation of liability provisions in agreements for the performance of audit or other attest or assurance services on behalf of the employing organisation that are required by such regulators; or

(b) Provide that the existence of such provisions disqualifies a member from rendering such services to these entities.

R270.13 If a member enters into, or directs or knowingly permits another individual to enter into, a contract for the performance of audit or other attest or assurance services that are subject to the requirements of these regulators, the member should not include, or knowingly permit or direct another individual to include, an indemnification or limitation of liability provision that would cause the regulated entity or a member to be in violation of such requirements or disqualify a member from providing such services to the regulated entity.

270.13 A1 A member who enters into, or directs or knowingly permits another individual to enter into, such an agreement for the performance of audit or other attest services would be considered in violation of the "Acts Discreditable Rule" and the "Professional Behaviour Principle".

Confidential information obtained from employment or volunteer activities

R270.14 A member shall maintain the confidentiality of their employer's confidential information and should not use or disclose any confidential employer information obtained as a result of an employment relationship, such as discussions with the employer's vendors, customers, or lenders (for example, any confidential information pertaining to a current or previous employer, subsidiary, affiliate, or parent thereof, as well as any entities for which the member is working in a volunteer capacity).

270.14 A1 For purposes of this interpretation, confidential employer information is any proprietary information pertaining to the employer or any organisation for whom the member may work in a volunteer capacity that is not known to be available to the public and is obtained as a result of such relationships.

270.14 A2 A member should be alert to the possibility of inadvertent disclosure, particularly to a close business associate or close relative or immediate family relative. The member should also take reasonable steps to ensure that staff under their control or others within the employing organisation and persons from whom advice and assistance are obtained are aware of the confidential nature of the information.

270.14 A3 When a member changes employment, a member should not use confidential employer information acquired as a result of a prior employment relationship to their personal advantage or the advantage of a third party, such as a current or prospective employer. The requirement to maintain the confidentiality of an employer's confidential information continues even after the end of the relationship between a member and the employer. However, the member is entitled to use experience and expertise gained through prior employment relationships.

270.14 A4 A member would be considered in violation of the "Acts Discreditable Rule" and "Confidentiality Principle" if the member discloses or uses any confidential employer information acquired as a result of employment or volunteer relationships without the proper authority or specific consent of the employer or organisation for whom the member may work in a volunteer capacity, unless there is a legal or professional responsibility to use or disclose such information.

270.14 A5 The following are examples of situations in which members are permitted or may be required to disclose confidential employer information or when such disclosure may be appropriate:

(a) Disclosure is permitted by law and authorised by the employer.

(b) Disclosure is required by law, for example, to

• Comply with a validly issued and enforceable subpoena or summons or

• Inform the appropriate public authorities of violations of law that have been discovered.

(c) There is a professional responsibility or right to disclose information, when not prohibited by law, to

• Initiate a complaint with, or respond to any inquiry made by, the AICPA Professional Ethics Division or trial board of the AICPA or a duly constituted investigative or disciplinary body of a state CPA society, board of accountancy, or other regulatory body (AICPA) ;

• Initiate a complaint with, or respond to any inquiry made by, the CIMA Professional Conduct Department or a duly constituted investigative or disciplinary body of CIMA, or other regulatory body (CIMA);

• Protect the member's professional interests in legal proceedings;

• Comply with professional standards (for example, technical standards) and other ethics requirements; or

• Report potential concerns regarding questionable accounting, auditing, or other matters to the employer's confidential complaint hotline or those charged with governance.

(d) Disclosure is permitted on behalf of the employer to

• Obtain financing with lenders;

• Communicate with vendors and customers; or

• Communicate with the employer's external accountant, attorneys, regulators, and other business professionals.

270.14 A6 In deciding whether to disclose confidential employer information relevant factors to consider include the following:

(a) Whether all the relevant information is known and substantiated to the extent that it is practicable. When the situation involves unsubstantiated facts, incomplete information, or unsubstantiated conclusions, the member should use professional judgment in determining the type of disclosure to be made, if any.

(b) Whether the parties to whom the communication may be addressed are appropriate recipients.

270.14 A7 A member may wish to consult with legal counsel prior to disclosing, or determining whether to disclose, confidential employer information.

270.14 A8 Refer to the "Subordination of Judgment" interpretation (240.11) for additional guidance.

False, misleading, or deceptive acts in promoting or marketing professional services

R270.15 A member would be in violation of the "Acts Discreditable Rule" and the "Professional Behaviour Principle" if the member promotes or markets the member's abilities to provide professional services or makes claims about the member's experience or qualifications in a manner that is false, misleading, or deceptive.

270.15 A1 Promotional efforts would be false, misleading, or deceptive if they contain any claim or representation that would likely cause a reasonable person to be misled or deceived. This includes any representation about CPA licensure, CGMA credential or any other professional certification or accreditation that is not in compliance with the requirements of the relevant licensing authority or designating body.

Use of the CPA credential (AICPA)

270.16 A1   A member should refer to applicable state accountancy laws and board of accountancy rules and regulations for guidance regarding the use of the CPA credential.

270.16 A2   A member who fails to follow the accountancy laws, rules, and regulations on use of the CPA credential in any of the jurisdictions in which the CPA practices would be considered to have used the CPA credential in a manner that is false, misleading, or deceptive and in violation of the "Acts Discreditable Rule".

Section 280
Pressure to breach the rules / fundamental principles

Introduction

280.1   Members are required to comply with the rules and fundamental principles and apply the conceptual framework set out in Section 120 to identify, evaluate and address threats.

280.2   Pressure exerted on, or by, a member might create an intimidation or other threat to compliance with one or more of the fundamental principles or the rules, particularly the "Integrity and Objectivity Rule". This section sets out specific requirements and application material relevant to applying the conceptual framework in such circumstances.

Requirements and application material

General

R280.3   A member shall not:

    (a) Allow pressure from others to result in a breach of compliance with the rules, in particularly the "Integrity or Objectivity Rule", or the fundamental principles; or

    (b) Place pressure on others that the member knows, or has reason to believe, would result in the other individuals breaching the rules or the fundamental principles.

280.3 A1   A member may face pressure that could create threats to compliance with the rules, in particularly the "Integrity and Objectivity Rule", and the fundamental principles, for example an undue influence (intimidation) threat, when undertaking professional services. Pressure might be explicit or implicit and might come from:

- Within the employing organisation, for example, from a colleague or superior.
- An external individual or organisation such as a vendor, customer, or lender.
- Internal or external targets and expectations.

280.3 A2   Examples of pressure that might result in threats to compliance with the "Integrity and Objectivity Rule" and the fundamental principles include:

- Pressure related to conflicts of interest:
  - Pressure from a family relative bidding to act as a vendor to the member's employing organisation to select that vendor over another prospective vendor.

See also Section 220, Conflicts of Interest.

- Pressure to influence preparation or presentation of information:
  - Pressure to report misleading financial results to meet investor, analyst, or lender expectations.
  - Pressure from elected officials on public sector / government accountants to misrepresent programs or projects to voters.
  - Pressure from colleagues to misstate income, expenditure, or rates of return to bias decision-making on capital projects and acquisitions.
  - Pressure from superiors to approve or process expenditures that are not legitimate business expenses.
  - Pressure to suppress internal audit reports containing adverse findings.

See also Section 240, Preparation and Presentation of Information.

- Pressure to act without sufficient competence, expertise, or due care:
  - Pressure from superiors to inappropriately reduce the extent of work performed.
  - Pressure from superiors to perform a task without sufficient skills or training or within unrealistic deadlines.

See also Section 260, General Standards / Professional Competence and Due Care.

- Pressure related to financial interests:
  - Pressure from superiors, colleagues, or others, for example, those who might benefit from participation in compensation or incentive arrangements to manipulate performance indicators.

- Pressure related to inducements:
  - Pressure from others, either internal or external to the employing organisation, to offer inducements to influence inappropriately the judgment or decision-making process of an individual or organisation.

- Pressure from colleagues to accept a bribe or other inducement, for example to accept inappropriate gifts or entertainment from potential vendors in a bidding process.

See also Section 230, Inducements, Including Gifts and Hospitality.

280.3 A3 Factors that are relevant in evaluating the level of threats created by pressure include:

- The intent of the individual who is exerting the pressure and the nature and extent of the pressure.
- The application of laws, regulations, and professional standards to the circumstances.
- The culture and leadership of the employing organisation including the extent to which they reflect or emphasise the importance of ethical behaviour and the expectation that employees will act ethically. For example, a corporate culture that tolerates unethical behaviour might increase the likelihood that the pressure would result in a breach of the rules or threat to compliance with the fundamental principles.
- Policies and procedures, if any, that the employing organisation has established, such as ethics or human resources policies that address pressure.

280.3 A4 Discussing the circumstances creating the pressure and consulting with others about those circumstances might assist the member to evaluate the level of the threat. Such discussion and consultation, which requires being alert to the "Acts Discreditable Rule" (AICPA) and the fundamental principle of confidentiality (CIMA), might include:

- Discussing the matter with the individual who is exerting the pressure to seek to resolve it.
- Discussing the matter with the member's superior, if the superior is not the individual exerting the pressure.
- Escalating the matter within the employing organisation, including when appropriate, explaining any consequential risks to the organisation, for example with:
  - Higher levels of management.
  - Internal or external auditors.
  - Those charged with governance.
- Disclosing the matter in line with the employing organisation's policies, including ethics and whistleblowing policies, using any established mechanism, such as a confidential ethics hotline.
- Consulting with:
  - A colleague, superior, human resources personnel, or another member;
  - Relevant professional or regulatory bodies or industry associations; or
  - Legal Counsel.

280.3 A5 An example of an action that might eliminate threats created by pressure is the member's request for a restructure of, or segregation of, certain responsibilities and duties so that the member is no longer involved with the individual or entity exerting the pressure.

Documentation

280.4 A1 The member is encouraged to document:

- The facts.
- The communications and parties with whom these matters were discussed.
- The courses of action considered.
- How the matter was addressed.

Section 290
Responding to non-compliance with laws and regulations (CIMA only)

Introduction

290.1 This Section only applies to CIMA members, including:

(a) Professional accountants in business (CIMA); and

(b) An individual who is a professional accountant in public practice (CIMA) when performing professional activities pursuant to the accountant's relationship with the accountant's firm, whether as a contractor, employee or owner. More information on when Part 2 is applicable to professional accountants in public practice (CIMA) is set out in paragraphs R120.4, R300.5, and 300.5 A1.

This Section does NOT apply to AICPA members

290.2 Professional accountants are required to comply with the fundamental principles and apply the conceptual framework set out in Section 120 to identify, evaluate and address threats.

290.3 A self-interest or intimidation threat to compliance with the principles of integrity and professional behaviour is created when a professional accountant becomes aware of non-compliance or suspected non-compliance with laws and regulations.

290.4 A professional accountant might encounter or be made aware of non-compliance or suspected non-compliance in the course of carrying out professional activities. This section guides the accountant in assessing the implications of the matter and the possible courses of action when responding to non-compliance or suspected non-compliance with:

(a) Laws and regulations generally recognised to have a direct effect on the determination of material amounts and disclosures in the employing organisation's financial statements; and

(b) Others laws and regulations that do not have a direct effect on the determination of the amounts and disclosures in the employing organisation's financial statements, but compliance with which might be fundamental to the operating aspects of the employing organisation's business, to its ability to continue its business, or to avoid material penalties.

Objectives of the professional accountant in relation to non-compliance with laws and regulations

290.5 A distinguishing mark of the accountancy profession is its acceptance of the responsibility to act in the public interest. When responding to non-compliance or suspected non-compliance, the objectives of the professional accountant are:

(a) To comply with the principles of integrity and professional behaviour;

(b) By alerting management or, where appropriate, those charged with governance of the employing organisation, to seek to:

(i) Enable them to rectify, remediate or mitigate the consequences of the identified or suspected non-compliance; or

(ii) Deter the non-compliance where it has not yet occurred; and

(c) To take such further action as appropriate in the public interest.

Requirements and application material
General

290.6 A1 Non-compliance with laws and regulations ("non-compliance") comprises acts of omission or commission, intentional or unintentional, which are contrary to the prevailing laws or regulations committed by the following parties:

(a) The professional accountant's employing organisation;

(b) Those charged with governance of the employing organisation;

(c) Management of the employing organisation; or

(d) Other individuals working for or under the direction of the employing organisation.

290.6 A2 Examples of laws and regulations which this section addresses include those that deal with:

• Fraud, corruption and bribery.
• Money laundering, terrorist financing and proceeds of crime.
• Securities markets and trading.
• Banking and other financial products and services.
• Data protection.
• Tax and pension liabilities and payments.
• Environmental protection.
• Public health and safety.

290.6 A3 Non-compliance might result in fines, litigation or other consequences for the employing organisation, potentially materially affecting its financial statements. Importantly, such non-compliance might have wider public interest implications in terms of potentially substantial harm to investors, creditors, employees of the general public. For the purposes of this section, non-compliance that causes substantial harm is one that results in serious adverse consequences to any of these parties in financial or non-financial terms. Examples include the perpetration of a fraud resulting in significant financial losses to investors, and breaches of environmental laws and regulations endangering the health or safety of employees or the public.

R290.7 In some jurisdictions, there are legal or regulatory provisions governing how professional accountants are required to address non-compliance or suspected non-compliance. These legal or regulatory provisions might differ from or go beyond the provisions in this section. When encountering such non-compliance or suspected non-compliance, the accountant shall obtain an understanding of those legal or regulatory provisions and comply with them, including:

(a) Any requirement to report the matter to an appropriate authority; and

(b) Any prohibition on alerting the relevant party.

290.7 A1 A prohibition on alerting the relevant party might arise, for example, pursuant to anti-money laundering legislation.

40

290.8 A1 This section applies regardless of the nature of the employing organisation, including whether or not it is a public interest entity.

290.8 A2 A professional accountant who encounters or is made aware of matters that are clearly inconsequential is not required to comply with this section. Whether a matter is clearly inconsequential is to be judged with respect to its nature and its impact, financial or otherwise, on the employing organisation, its stakeholders and the general public.

290.8 A3 This section does not address:

(a) Personal misconduct unrelated to the business activities of the employing organisation; and

(b) Non-compliance by parties other than those specified in paragraph 290.6 A1.

The professional accountant might nevertheless find the guidance in this section helpful in considering how to respond in these situations

Responsibilities of the employing organisation's management and those charged with governance

290.9 A1 The employing organisation's management, with the oversight of those charged with governance, is responsible for ensuring that the employing organisation's business activities are conducted in accordance with laws and regulations. Management and those charged with governance are also responsible for identifying and addressing any non-compliance by:

(a) The employing organisation;

(b) An individual charged with governance of the employing organisation;

(c) A member of management; or

(d) Other individuals working for or under the direction of the employing organisation.

Responsibilities of all professional accountants

R290.10 If protocols and procedures exist within the professional accountant's employing organisation to address non-compliance or suspected non-compliance, the accountant shall consider them in determining how to respond to such non-compliance.

290.10 A1 Many employing organisations have established protocols and procedures regarding how to raise non-compliance or suspected non-compliance internally. These protocols and procedures include, for example, an ethics policy or internal whistle-blowing mechanism. Such protocols and procedures might allow matters to be reported anonymously through designated channels.

R290.11 Where a professional accountant becomes aware of a matter to which this section applies, the steps that the accountant takes to comply with this section shall be taken on a timely basis. For the purpose of taking timely steps, the accountant shall have regard to the nature of the matter and the potential harm to the interests of the employing organisation, investors, creditors, employees or the general public.

Responsibilities of senior professional accountants in business

290.12 A1 Senior professional accountants in business ("senior professional accountants") are directors, officers or senior employees able to exert significant influence over, and make decisions regarding, the acquisition, deployment and control of the employing organisation's human, financial, technological, physical and intangible resources. There is a greater expectation for such individuals to take whatever action is appropriate in the public interest to respond to non-compliance or suspected non-compliance that other professional accountants within the employing organisation. This is because of senior professional accountants' roles, positions and spheres of influence within the employing organisation.

Obtaining an understanding of the matter

R290.13 If, in the course of carrying out professional activities, a senior professional accountant becomes aware of information concerning non-compliance or suspected non-compliance, the accountant shall obtain an understanding of the matter. This understanding shall include:

(a) The nature of the non-compliance or suspected non-compliance and the circumstances in which it has occurred or might occur;

(b) The application of the relevant laws and regulations to the circumstances; and

(c) An assessment of the potential consequences to the employing organisation, investors, creditors, employees or the wider public.

290.13 A1 A senior professional accountant is expected to apply knowledge and expertise, and exercise professional judgment. However, the accountant is not expected to have a level of understanding of laws and regulations greater than that which is required for the accountant's role within the employing organisation. Whether an act constitutes non-compliance is ultimately a matter to be determined by a court of other appropriate adjudicative body.

290.13 A2 Depending on the nature and significance of the matter, the senior professional accountant might cause, or take appropriate steps to cause, the matter to be investigated internally. The accountant might also consult on a confidential basis with others within the employing organisation or a professional body, or with legal counsel.

Addressing the matter

R290.14 If the senior professional accountant identifies or suspects that non-compliance has occurred or might occur, the accountant shall, subject to paragraph R290.10, discuss the matter with the accountant's immediate superior, if any. If the accountant's immediate superior appears to be involved in the matter, the accountant shall discuss the matter with the next higher level of authority within the employing organisation.

290.14 A1 The purpose of the discussion is to enable a determination to be made as to how to address the matter.

R290.15 The senior professional accountant shall also take appropriate steps to:

(a) Have the matter communicated to those charged with governance;

(b) Comply with applicable laws and regulations, including legal or regulatory provisions governing the reporting of non-compliance or suspected non-compliance to an appropriate authority;

(c) Have the consequences of the non-compliance or suspected non-compliance rectified, remediated or mitigated;

(d) Reduce the risk of re-occurrence; and

(e) Seek to deter the commission of the non-compliance if it has not yet occurred.

290.15 A1 The purpose of communicating the matter to those charged with governance is to obtain their concurrence regarding appropriate actions to take to respond to the matter and to enable them to fulfill their responsibilities.

290.15 A2 Some laws and regulations might stipulate a period within which reports of non-compliance or suspected non-compliance are to be made to an appropriate authority.

R290.16 In addition to responding to the matter in accordance with the provisions of this section, the senior professional accountant shall determine whether disclosure of the matter to the employing organisation's external auditor, if any, is needed.

290.16 A1 Such disclosure would be pursuant to the senior professional accountant's duty or legal obligation to provide all information necessary to enable the auditor to perform the audit.

Determining whether further action is needed

R290.17 The senior professional accountant shall assess the appropriateness of the response of the accountant's superiors, if any, and those charged with governance.

290.17 A1 Relevant factors to consider in assessing the appropriateness of the response of the senior professional accountant's superiors, if any, and those charged with governance include whether:

• The response is timely.

• They have taken or authorised appropriate action to seek to rectify, remediate or mitigate the consequences of the non-compliance, or to avert the non-compliance if it has not yet occurred.

• The matter has been disclosed to an appropriate authority where appropriate and, if so, whether the disclosure appears adequate.

R290.18 In light of the response of the senior professional accountant's superiors, if any, and those charged with governance, the accountant shall determine if further action is needed in the public interest.

290.18 A1 The determination of whether further action is needed, and the nature and extent of it, will depend on various factors, including:

• The legal and regulatory framework.

• The urgency of the situation.

• The pervasiveness of the matter throughout the employing organisation.

• Whether the senior professional accountant continues to have confidence in the integrity of the accountant's superiors and those charged with governance.

• Whether the non-compliance or suspected non-compliance is likely to recur.

• Whether there is credible evidence of actual or potential substantial harm to the interests of the employing organisation, investors, creditors, employees or the general public.

290.18 A2 Examples of circumstances that might cause the senior professional accountant no longer to have confidence in the integrity of the accountant's superiors and those charged with governance include situations where:

• The accountant suspects or have evidence of their involvement or intended involvement in any non-compliance.

• Contrary to legal or regulatory requirements, they have not reported, or authorised the reporting of, the matter to an appropriate authority within a reasonable period.

R290.19 The senior professional accountant shall exercise professional judgment in determining the need for, and nature and extent of, further action. In making this determination, the accountant shall take into account whether a reasonable and informed third party would be likely to conclude that the accountant has acted appropriately in the public interest.

290.19 A1 Further action that the senior professional accountant might take includes:

- Informing the management of the parent entity of the matter if the employing organisation is a member of a group.
- Disclosing the matter to an appropriate authority even when there is no legal or regulatory requirements to do so.
- Resigning from the employing organisation.

290.19 A2 Resigning from the employing organisation is not a substitute for taking other actions that might be needed to achieve the senior professional accountant's objectives under this section. In some jurisdictions, however, there might be limitations as to the further actions available to the accountant. In such circumstances, resignation might be the only available course of action.

Seeking advice

290.20 A1 As assessment of the matter might involve complex analysis and judgments, the senior professional accountant might consider:

- Consulting internally.
- Obtaining legal advice to understand the accountant's options and the professional or legal implications of taking any particular course of action.
- Consulting on a confidential basis with a regulatory or professional body.

Determining whether to disclose the matter to an appropriate authority

290.21 A1 Disclosure of the matter to an appropriate authority would be precluded if doing so would be contrary to law or regulation. Otherwise, the purpose of making disclosure is to enable an appropriate authority to cause the matter to be investigated and action to be taken in the public interest.

290.21 A2 The determination of whether to make such a disclosure depends in particular on the nature and extent of the actual or potential harm that is or might be caused by the matter to investors, creditors, employees or the general public. For example, the senior professional accountant might determine that disclosure of the matter to an appropriate authority is an appropriate course of action if:

- The employing organisation is engaged in bribery (for example, of local or foreign government officials for purposes of securing large contracts).
- The employing organisation is regulated and the matter is of such significance as to threaten its license to operate.
- The employing organisation is listed on a securities exchange and the matter might result in adverse consequences to the fair and orderly market in the employing organisation's securities or pose a systemic risk to the financial markets.
- It is likely that the employing organisation would sell products that are harmful to public health or safety.
- The employing organisation is promoting a scheme to its clients to assist them in evading taxes.

290.21 A3 The determination of whether to make such a disclosure will also depend on external factors such as:

- Whether there is an appropriate authority that is able to receive the information, and cause the matter to be investigated and action to be taken. The appropriate authority will depend upon the nature of the matter. For example, the appropriate authority would be a securities regulator in the cause of fraudulent financial reporting or an environmental protection agency in the case of a breach of environmental laws and regulations.
- Whether there exists robust and credible protection from civil, criminal or professional liability or retaliation afforded by legislation or regulation, such as under whistle-blowing legislation or regulation.
- Whether there are actual or potential threats to the physical safety of the senior professional accountant or other individuals.

R290.22 If the senior professional accountant determines that disclosure of the matter to an appropriate authority is an appropriate course of action in the circumstances, that disclosure is permitted pursuant to paragraph R114.1 (d) of the Code. When making such disclosure, the accountant shall act in good faith and exercise caution when making statements and assertions.

Imminent breach

R290.23 In exceptional circumstances, the senior professional accountant might become aware of actual or intended conduct that the accountant has reason to believe would constitute an imminent breach of a law or regulation that would cause substantial harm to investors, creditors, employees or the general public. Having first considered whether it would be appropriate to discuss the matter with management or those charged with governance of the employing organisation, the accountant shall exercise professional judgment and determine whether to disclose the matter immediately to an appropriate authority in order to prevent or mitigate the consequences of such imminent breach. If disclosure is made, that disclosure is permitted pursuant to paragraph R114.1 (d) of the Code.

Documentation

290.24 A1 In relation to non-compliance or suspected non-compliance that falls within the scope of this section, the senior professional accountant is encouraged to have the following matters documented:

- The matter.
- The results of discussions with the accountant's superiors, if any, and those charged with governance and other parties.
- How the accountant's superiors, if any, and those charged with governance have responded to the matter.
- The courses of action the accountant considered, the judgments made and the decisions that were taken.
- How the accountant is satisfied that the accountant has fulfilled the responsibility set out in paragraph R290.18.

Responsibilities of professional accountants other than senior professional accountants

R290.25 If, in the course of carrying out professional activities, a professional accountant becomes aware of information concerning non-compliance or suspected non-compliance, the accountant shall seek to obtain an understanding of the matter. This understanding shall include the nature of the non-compliance or suspected non-compliance and the circumstances in which it has occurred or might occur.

290.25 A1 The professional accountant is expected to apply knowledge and expertise, and exercise professional judgment. However, the accountant is not expected to have a level of understanding of laws and regulations greater than that which is required for the accountant's role within the employing organisation. Whether an act constitutes non-compliance is ultimately a matter to be determined by a court or other appropriate adjudicative body.

290.25 A2 Depending on the nature and significance of the matter, the professional accountant might consult on a confidential basis with others within the employing organisation or a professional body, or with legal counsel.

R290. 26 If the professional accountant identifies or suspects that non-compliance has occurred or might occur, the accountant shall, subject to paragraph R290.10, inform an immediate superior to enable the superior to take appropriate action. If the accountant's immediate superior appears to be involved in the matter, the accountant shall inform the next higher level of authority within the employing organisation.

R290.27 In exceptional circumstances, the professional accountant may determine that disclosure of the matter to an appropriate authority is an appropriate course of action. If the accountant does so pursuant to paragraphs 290.21 A2 and A3, that disclosure is permitted pursuant to paragraph R114.1 (d) of the Code. When making such disclosure, the accountant shall act in good faith and exercise caution when making statements and assertions.

Documentation

290.28 A1 In relation to non-compliance or suspected non-compliance that falls within the scope of this section, the professional accountant is encouraged to have the following matters documented:

- The matter.
- The results of discussions with the accountant's superior, management and, where applicable, those charged with governance and other parties.
- How the accountant's superior has responded to the matter.
- The courses of action the accountant considered, the judgments made and the decisions that were taken.

Part 3
Professional accountants in public practice

Section 300

Applying the conceptual framework – professional accountants in public practice

Introduction

300.1   This Part of the Code sets out requirements and application material for professional accountants in public practice when applying the conceptual framework set out in Section 120. It does not describe all of the facts and circumstances, including professional activities, interests, and relationships, that could be encountered by professional accountants in public practice, which create or might create threats to compliance with the fundamental principles. Therefore, the conceptual framework requires professional accountants in public practice to be alert for such facts and circumstances.

300.2   The requirements and application material that apply to professional accountants in public practice are set out in:

   • Part 3 – Professional Accountants in Public Practice, Sections 300 to 399, which applies to all professional accountants in public practice, whether they provide assurance services or not.

   • International Independence Standards as follows:

   • Part 4A – Independence for Audit and Review Engagements, Sections 400 to 899, which applies to professional accountants in public practice when performing audit and review engagements.

   • Part 4B – Independence for Assurance Engagements Other than Audit and Review Engagements, Sections 900 to 999, which applies to professional accountants in public practice when performing assurance engagements other than audit or review engagements.

300.3   In this Part, the term "professional accountant" refers to individual professional accountants in public practice and their firms.

Requirements and application material

General

R300.4   A professional accountant shall comply with the fundamental principles set out in Section 110 and apply the conceptual framework set out in Section 120 to identify, evaluate and address threats to compliance with the fundamental principles.

R300.5   When dealing with an ethics issue, the professional accountant shall consider the context in which the issue has arisen or might arise. Where an individual who is a professional accountant in public practice is performing professional activities pursuant to the accountant's relationship with the firm, whether as a contractor, employee or owner, the individual shall comply with the provisions in Part 2 that apply to these circumstances.

300.5 A1   Examples of situations in which the provisions in Part 2 apply to a professional accountant in public practice include:

   • Facing a conflict of interest when being responsible for selecting a vendor for the firm when an immediate family member of the accountant might benefit financially from the contract. The requirements and application material set out in Section 220 apply in these circumstances.

   • Preparing or presenting financial information for the accountant's client or firm. The requirements and application material set out in Section 240 apply in these circumstances.

   • Being offered an inducement such as being regularly offered complimentary tickets to attend sporting events by a supplier of the firm. The requirements and application material set out in Section 230 apply in these circumstances.

   • Facing pressure from an engagement partner to report chargeable hours inaccurately for a client engagement. The requirements and application material set out in Section 280 apply in these circumstances.

Identifying threats

300.6 A1   Threats to compliance with the fundamental principles might be created by a broad range of facts and circumstances. The categories of threats are described in paragraph 120.6 A3. The following are examples of facts and circumstances within each of those categories of threats that might create threats for a professional accountant when undertaking a professional service:

(a) Self-interest Threats

   • A professional accountant having a direct financial interest in a client.

   • A professional accountant quoting a low fee to obtain a new engagement and the fee is so low that it might be difficult to perform the professional service in accordance with applicable technical and professional standards for that price.

   • A professional accountant having a close business relationship with a client.

   • A professional accountant having access to confidential information that might be used for personal gain.

- A professional accountant discovering a significant error when evaluating the results of a previous professional service performed by a member of the accountant's firm.

(b) Self-review Threats

- A professional accountant issuing an assurance report on the effectiveness of the operation of financial systems after implementing the systems.
- A professional accountant having prepared the original data used to generate records that are the subject matter of the assurance engagement.

(c) Advocacy Threats

- A professional accountant promoting the interests of, or shares in, a client.
- A professional accountant acting as an advocate on behalf of a client in litigation or disputes with third parties.
- A professional accountant lobbying in favour of legislation on behalf of a client.

(d) Familiarity Threats

- A professional accountant having a close or immediate family member who is a director or officer of the client.
- A director or officer of the client, or an employee in a position to exert significant influence over the subject matter of the engagement, having recently served as the engagement partner.
- An audit team member having a long association with the audit client.

(e) Intimidation Threats

- A professional accountant being threatened with dismissal from a client engagement or the firm because of a disagreement about a professional matter.
- A professional accountant feeling pressured to agree with the judgment of a client because the client has more expertise on the matter in question.
- A professional accountant being informed that a planned promotion will not occur unless the accountant agrees with an inappropriate accounting treatment.
- A professional accountant having accepted a significant gift from a client and being threatened that acceptance of this gift will be made public.

Evaluating threats

300.7 A1   The conditions, policies and procedures described in paragraph 120.6 A1 and 120.8 A2 might impact the evaluation of whether a threat to compliance with the fundamental principles is at an acceptable level. Such conditions, policies and procedures might relate to:

(a) The client and its operating environment; and

(b) The firm and its operating environment.

300.7 A2 The professional accountant's evaluation of the level of a threat is also impacted by the nature and scope of the professional service.

The client and its operating environment

300.7 A3   The professional accountant's evaluation of the level of a threat might be impacted by whether the client is:

(a) An audit client and whether the audit client is a public interest entity;

(b) An assurance client that is not an audit client; or

(c) A non-assurance client.

For example, providing a non-assurance service to an audit client that is a public interest entity might be perceived to result in a higher level of threat to compliance with the principle of objectivity with respect to the audit.

300.7 A4   The corporate governance structure, including the leadership of a client might promote compliance with the fundamental principles. Accordingly, a professional accountant's evaluation of the level of a threat might also be impacted by a client's operating environment. For example:

- The client requires appropriate individuals other than management to ratify or approve the appointment of a firm to perform an engagement.
- The client has competent employees with experience and seniority to make managerial decisions.
- The client has implemented internal procedures that facilitate objective choices in tendering non-assurance engagements.
- The client has a corporate governance structure that provides appropriate oversight and communications regarding the firm's services.

The firm and its operating environment

300.7 A5 A professional accountant's evaluation of the level of a threat might be impacted by the work environment within the accountant's firm and its operating environment. For example:

- Leadership of the firm that promotes compliance with the fundamental principles and establishes the expectation that assurance team members will act in the public interest.
- Policies or procedures for establishing and monitoring compliance with the fundamental principles by all personnel.
- Compensation, performance appraisal and disciplinary policies and procedures that promote compliance with the fundamental principles.
- Management of the reliance on revenue received from a single client.
- The engagement partner having authority within the firm for decisions concerning compliance with the fundamental principles, including decisions about accepting or providing services to a client.
- Educational, training and experience requirements.
- Processes to facilitate and address internal and external concerns or complaints.

Consideration of new information or changes in facts and circumstances

300.7 A6 New information or changes in facts and circumstances might:

(a) Impact the level of a threat; or

(b) Affect the professional accountant's conclusions about whether safeguards applied continue to address identified threats as intended.

In these situations, actions that were already implemented as safeguards might no longer be effective in addressing threats. Accordingly, the application of the conceptual framework requires that the professional accountant re-evaluate and address the threats accordingly. (Ref: Paras. R120.9 and R120.10).

300.7 A7 Examples of new information or changes in facts and circumstances that might impact the level of a threat include:

- When the scope of a professional service is expanded.
- When the client becomes a listed entity or acquires another business unit.
- When the firm merges with another firm.
- When the professional accountant is jointly engaged by two clients and a dispute emerges between the two clients.

- When there is a change in the professional accountant's personal or immediate family relationships.

Addressing threats

300.8 A1 Paragraphs R120.10 to 120.10 A2 set out requirements and application material for addressing threats that are not at an acceptable level.

Examples of safeguards

300.8 A2 Safeguards vary depending on the facts and circumstances. Examples of actions that in certain circumstances might be safeguards to address threats include:

- Assigning additional time and qualified personnel to required tasks when an engagement has been accepted might address a self-interest threat.
- Having an appropriate reviewer who was not a member of the team review the work performed or advise as necessary might address a self-review threat.
- Using different partners and engagement teams with separate reporting lines for the provision of non-assurance services to an assurance client might address self-review, advocacy or familiarity threats.
- Involving another firm to perform or re-perform part of the engagement might address self-interest, self-review, advocacy, familiarity or intimidation threats.
- Disclosing to clients any referral fees or commission arrangements received for recommending services or products might address a self-interest threat.
- Separating teams when dealing with matters of a confidential nature might address a self-interest threat.

300.8 A3 The remaining sections of Part 3 and International Independence Standards describe certain threats that might arise during the course of performing professional services and include examples of actions that might address threats.

Appropriate reviewer

300.8 A4 An appropriate reviewer is a professional with the necessary knowledge, skills, experience and authority to review, in an objective manner, the relevant work performed or service provided. Such an individual might be a professional accountant.

Communicating with those charged with governance

R300.9 When communicating with those charged with governance in accordance with the Code, a professional accountant shall determine the appropriate individual(s) within the entity's governance structure with whom to communicate. If the accountant communicates with a subgroup of those charged with governance, the accountant shall determine whether communication with all those charged with governance is also necessary so that they are adequately informed.

300.9 A1 In determining with whom to communicate, a professional accountant might consider:

(a) The nature and importance of the circumstances; and

(b) The matter to be communicated.

300.9 A2 Examples of a subgroup of those charged with governance include an audit committee or an individual member of those charged with governance.

R300.10 If a professional accountant communicates with individuals who have management responsibilities as well as governance responsibilities, the accountant shall be satisfied that communication with those individuals adequately informs all of those in a governance role with whom the accountant would otherwise communicate.

300.10 A1 In some circumstances, all of those charged with governance are involved in managing the entity, for example, a small business where a single owner manages the entity and no one else has a governance role. In these cases, if matters are communicated to individual(s) with management responsibilities, and those individual(s) also have governance responsibilities, the professional accountant has satisfied the requirement to communicate with those charged with governance.

Section 310

Conflicts of interest
Introduction

310.1 Professional accountants are required to comply with the fundamental principles and apply the conceptual framework set out in Section 120 to identify, evaluate and address threats.

310.2 A conflict of interest creates threats to compliance with the principle of objectivity and might create threats to compliance with other fundamental principles. Such threats might be created when:

(a) A professional accountant provides a professional service related to a particular matter for two or more clients whose interests with respect to that matter are in conflict; or

(b) The interests of a professional accountant with respect to a particular matter and the interests of the client for whom the accountant provides a professional service related to that matter are in conflict.

310.3 This section sets out specific requirements and application material relevant to applying the conceptual framework to conflicts of interest. When a professional accountant provides an audit, review or other assurance service, independence is also required in accordance with International Independence Standards.

Requirements and application material
General

R310.4 A professional accountant shall not allow a conflict of interest to compromise professional or business judgment.

310.4 A1 Examples of circumstances that might create a conflict of interest include:

• Providing a transaction advisory service to a client seeking to acquire an audit client, where the firm has obtained confidential information during the course of the audit that might be relevant to the transaction.

• Providing advice to two clients at the same time where the clients are competing to acquire the same company and the advice might be relevant to the parties' competitive positions.

• Providing services to a seller and a buyer in relation to the same transaction.

• Preparing valuations of assets for two parties who are in an adversarial position with respect to the assets.

• Representing two clients in the same matter who are in a legal dispute with each other, such as during divorce proceedings, or the dissolution of a partnership.

• In relation to a licence agreement, providing an assurance report for a licensor on the royalties due while advising the licensee on the amounts payable.

• Advising a client to invest in a business in which, for example, the spouse of the professional accountant has a financial interest.

• Providing strategic advice to a client on its competitive position while having a joint venture or similar interest with a major competitor of the client.

• Advising a client on acquiring a business which the firm is also interested in acquiring.

• Advising a client on buying a product or service while having a royalty or commission agreement with a potential seller of that product or service.

Conflict identification

General

R310.5 Before accepting a new client relationship, engagement, or business relationship, a professional accountant shall take reasonable steps to identify circumstances that might create a conflict of interest, and therefore a threat to compliance with one or more of the fundamental principles. Such steps shall include identifying:

(a) The nature of the relevant interests and relationships between the parties involved; and

(b) The service and its implication for relevant parties.

310.5 A1 An effective conflict identification process assists a professional accountant when taking reasonable steps to identify interests and relationships that might create an actual or potential conflict of interest, both before determining whether to accept an engagement and throughout the engagement. Such a process includes considering matters identified by external parties, for example, clients or potential clients. The earlier an actual or potential conflict of interest is identified, the greater the likelihood of the accountant being able to address threats created by the conflict of interest.

310.5 A2 An effective process to identify actual or potential conflicts of interest will take into account factors such as:

- The nature of the professional services provided.
- The size of the firm.
- The size and nature of the client base.
- The structure of the firm, for example, the number and geographic location of offices.

310.5 A3 More information on client acceptance is set out in Section 320, Professional Appointments.

Changes in circumstances

R310.6 A professional accountant shall remain alert to changes over time in the nature of services, interests and relationships that might create a conflict of interest while performing an engagement.

310.6 A1 The nature of services, interests and relationships might change during the engagement. This is particularly true when a professional accountant is asked to conduct an engagement in a situation that might become adversarial, even though the parties who engage the accountant initially might not be involved in a dispute.

Network firms

R310.7 If the firm is a member of a network, a professional accountant shall consider conflicts of interest that the accountant has reason to believe might exist or arise due to interests and relationships of a network firm.

310.7 A1 Factors to consider when identifying interests and relationships involving a network firm include:

- The nature of the professional services provided.
- The clients served by the network.
- The geographic locations of all relevant parties.

Threats created by conflicts of interest

310.8 A1 In general, the more direct the connection between the professional service and the matter on which the parties' interests conflict, the more likely the level of the threat is not at an acceptable level.

310.8 A2 Factors that are relevant in evaluating the level of a threat created by a conflict of interest include measures that prevent unauthorised disclosure of confidential information when performing professional services related to a particular matter for two or more clients whose interests with respect to that matter are in conflict. These measures include:

- The existence of separate practice areas for specialty functions within the firm, which might act as a barrier to the passing of confidential client information between practice areas.
- Policies and procedures to limit access to client files.
- Confidentiality agreements signed by personnel and partners of the firm.
- Separation of confidential information physically and electronically.
- Specific and dedicated training and communication.

310.8 A3 Examples of actions that might be safeguards to address threats created by a conflict of interest include:

- Having separate engagement teams who are provided with clear policies and procedures on maintaining confidentiality.
- Having an appropriate reviewer, who is not involved in providing the service or otherwise affected by the conflict, review the work performed to assess whether the key judgments and conclusions are appropriate.

Disclosure and consent

General

R310.9 A professional accountant shall exercise professional judgment to determine whether the nature and significance of a conflict of interest are such that specific disclosure and explicit consent are necessary when addressing the threat created by the conflict of interest.

310.9 A1 Factors to consider when determining whether specific disclosure and explicit consent are necessary include:

- The circumstances creating the conflict of interest.
- The parties that might be affected.
- The nature of the issues that might arise.
- The potential for the particular matter to develop in an unexpected manner.

310.9 A2 Disclosure and consent might take different forms, for example:

- General disclosure to clients of circumstances where, as is common commercial practice, the professional accountant does not provide professional services exclusively to any one client (for example, in a particular professional service and market sector). This enables the client to provide general consent accordingly. For example, an accountant might make general disclosure in the standard terms and conditions for the engagement.
- Specific disclosure to affected clients of the circumstances of the particular conflict in sufficient detail to enable the client to make an informed decision about the matter and to provide explicit consent accordingly. Such disclosure might include a detailed presentation of the circumstances and a comprehensive explanation of any planned safeguards and the risks involved.
- Consent might be implied by clients' conduct in circumstances where the professional accountant has sufficient evidence to conclude that clients know the circumstances at the outset and have accepted the conflict of interest if they do not raise an objection to the existence of the conflict.

310.9 A3 It is generally necessary:

(a) To disclose the nature of the conflict of interest and how any threats created were addressed to clients affected by a conflict of interest; and

(b) To obtain consent of the affected clients to perform the professional services when safeguards are applied to address the threat.

310.9 A4 If such disclosure or consent is not in writing, the professional accountant is encouraged to document:

(a) The nature of the circumstances giving rise to the conflict of interest;

(b) The safeguards applied to address the threats when applicable; and

(c) The consent obtained.

When explicit consent is refused

R310.10 If a professional accountant has determined that explicit consent is necessary in accordance with paragraph R310.9 and the client has refused to provide consent, the accountant shall either:

(a) End or decline to perform professional services that would result in the conflict of interest; or

(b) End relevant relationships or dispose of relevant interests to eliminate the threat or reduce it to an acceptable level.

Confidentiality

General

R310.11 A professional accountant shall remain alert to the principle of confidentiality, including when making disclosures or sharing information within the firm or network and seeking guidance from third parties.

310.11 A1 Subsection 114 sets out requirements and application material relevant to situations that might create a threat to compliance with the principle of confidentiality.

When disclosure to obtain consent would breach confidentiality

R310.12 When making specific disclosure for the purpose of obtaining explicit consent would result in a breach of confidentiality, and such consent cannot therefore be obtained, the firm shall only accept or continue an engagement if:

(a) The firm does not act in an advocacy role for one client in an adversarial position against another client in the same matter;

(b) Specific measures are in place to prevent disclosure of confidential information between the engagement teams serving the two clients; and

(c) The firm is satisfied that a reasonable and informed third party would be likely to conclude that it is appropriate for the firm to accept or continue the engagement because a restriction on the firm's ability to provide the professional service would produce a disproportionate adverse outcome for the clients or other relevant third parties.

310.12 A1 A breach of confidentiality might arise, for example, when seeking consent to perform:

- A transaction-related service for a client on a hostile takeover of another client of the firm.
- A forensic investigation for a client regarding a suspected fraud, where the firm has confidential information from its work for another client who might be involved in the fraud.

Documentation

R310.13 In the circumstances set out in paragraph R310.12, the professional accountant shall document:

(a) The nature of the circumstances, including the role that the accountant is to undertake;

(b) The specific measures in place to prevent disclosure of information between the engagement teams serving the two clients; and

(c) Why it is appropriate to accept or continue the engagement.

Section 320

Professional appointments

Introduction

320.1 Professional accountants are required to comply with the fundamental principles and apply the conceptual framework set out in Section 120 to identify, evaluate and address threats.

320.2 Acceptance of a new client relationship or changes in an existing engagement might create a threat to compliance with one or more of the fundamental principles. This section sets out specific requirements and application material relevant to applying the conceptual framework in such circumstances.

Requirements and application material

Client and engagement acceptance

General

320.3 A1 Threats to compliance with the principles of integrity or professional behaviour might be created, for example, from questionable issues associated with the client (its owners, management or activities). Issues that, if known, might create such a threat include client involvement in illegal activities, dishonesty, questionable financial reporting practices or other unethical behaviour.

320.3 A2 Factors that are relevant in evaluating the level of such a threat include:

- Knowledge and understanding of the client, its owners, management and those charged with governance and business activities.
- The client's commitment to address the questionable issues, for example, through improving corporate governance practices or internal controls.

320.3 A3 A self-interest threat to compliance with the principle of professional competence and due care is created if the engagement team does not possess, or cannot acquire, the competencies to perform professional services.

320.3 A4 Factors that are relevant in evaluating the level of such a threat include:

- An appropriate understanding of:
  - The nature of the client's business;
  - The complexity of its operations;
  - The requirements of the engagement; and
  - The purpose, nature and scope of the work to be performed.
- Knowledge of relevant industries or subject matter.
- Experience with relevant regulatory or reporting requirements.
- The existence of quality control policies and procedures designed to provide reasonable assurance that engagements are accepted only when they can be performed competently.

320.3 A5 Examples of actions that might be safeguards to address a self-interest threat include:

- Assigning sufficient engagement personnel with the necessary competencies.
- Agreeing on a realistic time frame for the performance of the engagement.
- Using experts where necessary.

Changes in a professional appointment

General

R320.4 A professional accountant shall determine whether there are any reasons for not accepting an engagement when the accountant:

(a) Is asked by a potential client to replace another accountant;

(b) Considers tendering for an engagement held by another accountant; or

(c) Considers undertaking work that is complementary or additional to that of another accountant.

320.4 A1 There might be reasons for not accepting an engagement. One such reason might be if a threat created by the facts and circumstances cannot be addressed by applying safeguards. For example, there might be a self-interest threat to compliance with the principle of professional competence and due care if a professional accountant accepts the engagement before knowing all the relevant facts.

320.4 A2 If a professional accountant is asked to undertake work that is complementary or additional to the work of an existing or predecessor accountant, a self-interest threat to compliance with the principle of professional competence and due care might be created, for example, as a result of incomplete information.

320.4 A3 A factor that is relevant in evaluating the level of such a threat is whether tenders state that, before accepting the engagement, contact with the existing or predecessor accountant will be requested. This contact gives the proposed accountant the opportunity to inquire whether there are any reasons why the engagement should not be accepted.

320.4 A4 Examples of actions that might be safeguards to address such a self-interest threat include:

- Asking the existing or predecessor accountant to provide any known information of which, in the existing or predecessor accountant's opinion, the proposed accountant needs to be aware before deciding whether to accept the engagement. For example, inquiry might reveal previously undisclosed pertinent facts and might indicate disagreements with the existing or predecessor accountant that might influence the decision to accept the appointment.
- Obtaining information from other sources such as though inquiries of third parties or background investigations regarding senior management or those charged with governance of the client.

Communicating with the existing or predecessor accountant

320.5 A1 A proposed accountant will usually need the client's permission, preferably in writing, to initiate discussions with the existing or predecessor accountant.

R320.6 If unable to communicate with the existing or predecessor accountant, the proposed accountant shall take other reasonable steps to obtain information about any possible threats.

Communicating with the proposed accountant

R320.7 When an existing or predecessor accountant is asked to respond to a communication from a proposed accountant, the existing or predecessor accountant shall:

(a) Comply with relevant laws and regulations governing the request; and

(b) Provide any information honestly and unambiguously.

320.7 A1 An existing or predecessor accountant is bound by confidentiality. Whether the existing or predecessor accountant is permitted or required to discuss the affairs of a client with a proposed accountant will depend on the nature of the engagement and:

(a) Whether the existing or predecessor accountant has permission from the client for the discussion; and

(b) The legal and ethics requirements relating to such communications and disclosure, which might vary by jurisdiction.

320.7 A2 Circumstances where a professional accountant is or might be required to disclose confidential information, or when disclosure might be appropriate, are set out in paragraph 114.1 A1 of the Code.

Changes in audit or review appointments

R320.8 In the case of an audit or review of financial statements, a professional accountant shall request the existing or predecessor accountant to provide known information regarding any facts or other information of which, in the existing or predecessor accountant's opinion, the proposed accountant needs to be aware before deciding whether to accept the engagement. Except for the circumstances involving non-compliance or suspected non-compliance with laws and regulations set out in paragraphs R360.21 and R360.22:

(a) If the client consents to the existing or predecessor accountant disclosing any such facts or other information, the existing or predecessor accountant shall provide the information honestly and unambiguously; and

(b) If the client fails or refuses to grant the existing or predecessor accountant permission to discuss the client's affairs with the proposed accountant, the existing or predecessor accountant shall disclose this fact to the proposed accountant, who shall carefully consider such failure or refusal when determining whether to accept the appointment.

Client and engagement continuance

R320.9 For a recurring client engagement, a professional accountant shall periodically review whether to continue with the engagement.

320.9 A1 Potential threats to compliance with the fundamental principles might be created after acceptance which, had they been known earlier, would have caused the professional accountant to decline the engagement. For example, a self-interest threat to compliance with the principle of integrity might be created by improper earnings management or balance sheet valuations.

Using the work of an expert

R320.10 When a professional accountant intends to use the work of an expert, the accountant shall determine whether the use is warranted.

320.10 A1 Factors to consider when a professional accountant intends to use the work of an expert include the reputation and expertise of the expert, the resources available to the expert, and the professional and ethics standards applicable to the expert. This information might be gained from prior association with the expert or from consulting others.

Section 321

Second opinions

Introduction

321.1 Professional accountants are required to comply with the fundamental principles and apply the conceptual framework set out in Section 120 to identify, evaluate and address threats.

321.2 Providing a second opinion to an entity that is not an existing client might create a self-interest threat to compliance with one or more of the fundamental principles. This section sets out specific requirements and application material relevant to applying the conceptual framework in such circumstances.

Requirements and application material

General

321.3 A1 A professional accountant might be asked to provide a second opinion on the application of accounting, auditing, reporting or other standards or principles to (a) specific circumstances, or (b) transactions by or on behalf of a company or an entity that is not an existing client. A threat, for example, a self-interest threat to compliance with the principle of professional competence and due care, might be created if the second opinion is not based on the same facts that the existing or predecessor accountant had, or is based on inadequate evidence.

321.3 A2 A factor that is relevant in evaluating the level of such a self-interest threat is the circumstances of the request and all the other available facts and assumptions relevant to the expression of a professional judgment.

321.3 A3 Examples of actions that might be safeguards to address such a self-interest threat include:

- With the client's permission, obtaining information from the existing or predecessor accountant.
- Describing the limitations surrounding any opinion in communications with the client.
- Providing the existing or predecessor accountant with a copy of the opinion.

When permission to communicate is not provided

R321.4 If an entity seeking a second opinion from a professional accountant will not permit the accountant to communicate with the existing or predecessor accountant, the accountant shall determine whether the accountant may provide the second opinion sought.

Section 330

Fees and other types of remuneration

General

330.1 Professional accountants are required to comply with the fundamental principles and apply the conceptual framework set out in Section 120 to identify, evaluate and address threats.

330.2 The level and nature of fee and other remuneration arrangements might create a self-interest threat to compliance with one or more of the fundamental principles. This section sets out specific application material relevant to applying the conceptual framework in such circumstances.

Application material

Level of fees

330.3 A1 The level of fees quoted might impact a professional accountant's ability to perform professional services in accordance with professional standards.

330.3 A2 A professional accountant might quote whatever fee is considered appropriate. Quoting a fee lower than another accountant is not in itself unethical. However, the level of fees quoted creates a self-interest threat to compliance with the principle of professional competence and due care if the fee quoted is so low that it might be difficult to perform the engagement in accordance with applicable technical and professional standards.

330.3 A3 Factors that are relevant in evaluating the level of such a threat include:

- Whether the client is aware of the terms of the engagement and, in particular, the basis on which fees are charged and which professional services the quoted fee covers.
- Whether the level of the fee is set by an independent third party such as a regulatory body.

330.4 A4 Examples of actions that might be safeguards to address such a self-interest threat include:

- Adjusting the level of fees or the scope of the engagement.
- Having an appropriate reviewer review the work performed.

Contingent fees

330.4 A1 Contingent fees are used for certain types of non-assurance services. However, contingent fees might create threats to compliance with the fundamental principles, particularly a self-interest threat to compliance with the principle of objectivity, in certain circumstances.

330.4 A2 Factors that are relevant in evaluating the level of such threats include:

- The nature of the engagement.
- The range of possible fee amounts.
- The basis for determining the fee.
- Disclosure to intended users of the work performed by the professional accountant and the basis of remuneration.
- Quality control policies and procedures.
- Whether an independent third party is to review the outcome or result of the transaction.
- Whether the level of the fee is set by an independent third party such as a regulatory body.

330.4 A3 Examples of actions that might be safeguards to address such a self-interest threat include:

- Having an appropriate reviewer who was not involved in performing the non-assurance service review the work performed by the professional accountant.
- Obtaining an advance written agreement with the client on the basis of remuneration.

330.4 A4 Requirements and application material related to contingent fees for services provided to audit or review clients and other assurance clients are set out in International Independence Standards.

Referral fees or commissions

330.5 A1 A self-interest threat to compliance with the principles of objectivity and professional competence and due care is created if a professional accountant pays or receives a referral fee or receives a commission relating to a client. Such referral fees or commissions include, for example:

- A fee paid to another professional accountant for the purposes of obtaining new client work when the client continues as a client of the existing accountant but requires specialist services not offered by that accountant.

- A fee received for referring a continuing client to another professional accountant or other expert where the existing accountant does not provide the specific professional service required by the client.
- A commission received from a third party (for example, a software vendor) in connection with the sale of goods or services to a client.

330.5 A2 Examples of actions that might be safeguards to address such a self-interest threat include:

- Obtaining an advance agreement from the client for commission arrangements in connection with the sale by another party of goods or services to the client might address a self-interest threat.
- Disclosing to clients any referral fees or commission arrangements paid to, or received from, another professional accountant or third party for recommending services or products that might address a self-interest threat.

Purchase or Sale of a Firm

330.6 A1 A professional accountant may purchase all or part of another firm on the basis that payments will be made to individuals formerly owning the firm or to their heirs or estates. Such payments are not referral fees or commissions for the purposes of this section.

Section 340

Inducements, including gifts and hospitality

Introduction

340.1 Professional accountants are required to comply with the fundamental principles and apply the conceptual framework set out in Section 120 to identify, evaluate and address threats.

340.2 Offering or accepting inducements might create a self-interest, familiarity or intimidation threat to compliance with the fundamental principles, particularly the principles of integrity, objectivity, and professional behaviour.

340.3 This section sets out requirements and application material relevant to applying the conceptual framework in relation to the offering and accepting of inducements when performing professional services that does not constitute non-compliance with laws and regulations. This section also requires a professional accountant to comply with relevant laws and regulations when offering or accepting inducements.

Requirements and application material

General

340.4 A1 An inducement is an object, situation, or action that is used as a means to influence another individual's behaviour, but not necessarily with the intent to improperly influence that individual's behaviour. Inducements can range from minor acts of hospitality between professional accountants and existing or prospective clients to acts that result in non-compliance with laws and regulations. An inducement can take many different forms, for example:

- Gifts.
- Hospitality.
- Entertainment.
- Political or charitable donations.
- Appeals to friendship and loyalty.
- Employment or other commercial opportunities.
- Preferential treatment, rights or privileges.

Inducements prohibited by laws and regulations

R340.5 In many jurisdictions, there are laws and regulations, such as those related to bribery and corruption, that prohibit the offering or accepting of inducements in certain circumstances. The professional accountant shall obtain an understanding of relevant laws and regulations and comply with them when the accountant encounters such circumstances.

Inducements not prohibited by laws and regulations

340.6 A1 The offering or accepting of inducements that is not prohibited by laws and regulations might still create threats to compliance with the fundamental principles.

Inducements with intent to improperly influence behaviour

R340.7 A professional accountant shall not offer, or encourage others to offer, any inducement that is made, or which the accountant considers a reasonable and informed third party would be likely to conclude is made, with the intent to improperly influence the behaviour of the recipient or of another individual.

R340.8 A professional accountant shall not accept, or encourage others to accept, any inducement that the accountant concludes is made, or considers a reasonable and informed third party would be likely to conclude is made, with the intent to improperly influence the behaviour of the recipient or of another individual.

340.9 A1 An inducement is considered as improperly influencing an individual's behaviour if it causes the individual to act in an unethical manner. Such improper influence can be directed either towards the recipient or towards another individual who has some relationship with the recipient. The fundamental principles are an appropriate frame of reference for a professional accountant in considering what constitutes unethical behaviour on the part of the accountant and, if necessary by analogy, other individuals.

340.9 A2 A breach of the fundamental principle of integrity arises when a professional accountant offers or accepts, or encourages others to offer or accept, an inducement where the intent is to improperly influence the behaviour of the recipient or of another individual.

340.9 A3 The determination of whether there is actual or perceived intent to improperly influence behaviour requires the exercise of professional judgment. Relevant factors to consider might include:

- The nature, frequency, value and cumulative effect of the inducement.

- Timing of when the inducement is offered relative to any action or decision that it might influence.

- Whether the inducement is a customary or cultural practice in the circumstances, for example, offering a gift on the occasion of a religious holiday or wedding.

- Whether the inducement is an ancillary part of a professional activity, for example, offering or accepting lunch in connection with a business meeting.

- Whether the offer of the inducement is limited to an individual recipient or available to a broader group. The broader group might be internal or external to the employing organisation, such as other suppliers to the client.

- The roles and positions of the individuals at the firm or the client offering or being offered the inducement.

- Whether the professional accountant knows, or has reason to believe, that accepting the inducement would breach the policies and procedures of the client.

- The degree of transparency with which the inducement is offered.

- Whether the inducement was required or requested by the recipient.

- The known previous behaviour or reputation of the offeror.

Consideration of further actions

340.10 A1 If the professional accountant becomes aware of an inducement offered with actual or perceived intent to improperly influence behaviour, threats to compliance with the fundamental principles might still be created even if the requirements in paragraphs R340.7 and R340.8 are met.

340.10 A2 Examples of actions that might be safeguards to address such threats include:

- Informing senior management of the firm or those charged with governance of the client regarding the offer.

- Amending or terminating the business relationship with the client.

Inducements with no intent to improperly influence behaviour

340.11 A1 The requirements and application material set out in the conceptual framework apply when a professional accountant has concluded there is no actual or perceived intent to improperly influence the behaviour of the recipient or of another individual.

340.11 A2 If such an inducement is trivial and inconsequential, any threats created will be at an acceptable level.

340.11 A3 Examples of circumstances where offering or accepting such an inducement might create threats even if the professional accountant has concluded there is no actual or perceived intent to improperly influence behaviour include:

- Self-interest threats
  - A professional accountant is offered hospitality from the prospective acquirer of a client while providing corporate finance services to the client.

- Familiarity threats
  - A professional accountant regularly takes an existing or prospective client to sporting events.

- Intimidation threats
  - A professional accountant accepts hospitality from a client, the nature of which could be perceived to be inappropriate were it to be publicly disclosed.

340.11 A4 Relevant factors in evaluating the level of such threats created by offering or accepting such an inducement include the same factors set out in paragraph 340.9 A3 for determining intent.

340.11 A5 Examples of actions that might eliminate threats created by offering or accepting such an inducement include:

- Declining or not offering the inducement.

- Transferring responsibility for the provision of any professional services to the client to another individual who the professional accountant has no reason to believe would be, or would be perceived to be, improperly influenced when providing the services.

340.11 A6 Examples of actions that might be safeguards to address such threats created by offering or accepting such an inducement include:

- Being transparent with senior management of the firm or of the client about offering or accepting an inducement.

- Registering the inducement in a log monitored by senior management of the firm or another individual responsible for the firm's ethics compliance or maintained by the client.

- Having an appropriate reviewer, who is not otherwise involved in providing the professional service, review any work performed or decisions made by the professional accountant with respect to the client from which the accountant accepted the inducement.

- Donating the inducement to charity after receipt and appropriately disclosing the donation, for example, to a member of senior management of the firm or the individual who offered the inducement.

- Reimbursing the cost of the inducement, such as hospitality, received.

- As soon as possible, returning the inducement, such as a gift, after it was initially accepted.

Immediate or close family relatives

R340.12 A professional accountant shall remain alert to potential threats to the accountant's compliance with the fundamental principles created by the offering of an inducement:

(a) By an immediate or close family member of the accountant to an existing or prospective client of the accountant; or

(b) To an immediate or close family member of the accountant by an existing or prospective client of the accountant.

R340.13 Where the professional accountant becomes aware of an inducement being offered to or made by an immediate or close family member and concludes there is intent to improperly influence the behaviour of the accountant or of an existing or prospective client of the accountant, or considers a reasonable and informed third party would be likely to conclude such intent exists, the accountant shall advise the immediate or close family member not to offer or accept the inducement.

340.13 A1 The factors set out in paragraph 340.9 A3 are relevant in determining whether there is actual or perceived intent to improperly influence the behaviour of the professional accountant or of the existing or prospective client. Another factor that is relevant is the nature or closeness of the relationship, between:

(a) The accountant and the immediate or close family member;

(b) The immediate or close family member and the existing or prospective client; and

(c) The accountant and the existing or prospective client.

For example, the offer of employment, outside of the normal recruitment process, to the spouse of the accountant by a client for whom the accountant is providing a business valuation for a prospective sale might indicate such intent.

340.13 A2 The application material in paragraph 340.10 A2 is also relevant in addressing threats that might be created when there is actual or perceived intent to improperly influence the behaviour of the professional accountant, or of the existing or prospective client even if the immediate or close family member has followed the advice given pursuant to paragraph R340.13.

Application of the conceptual framework

340.14 A1 Where the professional accountant becomes aware of an inducement offered in the circumstances addressed in paragraph R340.12, threats to compliance with the rules and fundamental principles might be created where:

(a) The immediate or close family member offers or accepts the inducement contrary to the advice of the accountant pursuant to paragraph R340.13; or

(b) The accountant does not have reason to believe an actual or perceived intent to improperly influence the behaviour of the accountant or of the existing or prospective client exists.

340.14 A2 The application material in paragraphs 340.11 A1 to 340.11 A6 is relevant for the purposes of identifying, evaluating and addressing such threats. Factors that are relevant in evaluating the level of threats in these circumstances also include the nature or closeness of the relationships set out in paragraph 340.13 A1.

Other considerations

340.15 A1 If a professional accountant encounters or is made aware of inducements that might result in non-compliance or suspected non-compliance with laws and regulations by a client or individuals working for or under the direction of the client, the requirements and application material in Section 360 apply.

340.15 A2 If a firm, network firm or an audit team member is being offered gifts or hospitality from an audit client, the requirement and application material set out in Section 420 apply.

340.15 A3 If a firm, network firm or an audit team member is being offered gifts or hospitality from an assurance client, the requirement and application material set out in Section 906 apply.

Section 350
Custody of client assets
Introduction

350.1 Professional accountants are required to comply with the fundamental principles and apply the conceptual framework set out in Section 120 to identify, evaluate and address threats.

350.2 Holding client assets creates a self-interest or other threat to compliance with the principles of professional behaviour and objectivity. This section sets out specific requirements and application material relevant to applying the conceptual framework in such circumstances.

Requirements and application material

Before taking custody

R350.3 A professional accountant shall not assume custody of client money or other assets unless permitted to do so by law and in accordance with any conditions under which such custody may be taken.

R350.4 As part of client and engagement acceptance procedures related to assuming custody of client money or assets, a professional accountant shall:

(a) Make inquiries about the source of the assets; and

(b) Consider related legal and regulatory obligations.

350.4 A1 Inquiries about the source of client assets might reveal, for example, that the assets were derived from illegal activities, such as money laundering. In such circumstances, a threat would be created and the provisions of Section 360 would apply.

After taking custody

R350.5 A professional accountant entrusted with money or other assets belonging to others shall:

(a) Comply with the laws and regulations relevant to holding and accounting for the assets;

(b) Keep the assets separately from personal or firm assets;

(c) Use the assets only for the purpose for which they are intended; and

(d) Be ready at all times to account for the assets and any income, dividends, or gains generated, to any individuals entitled to that accounting.

Section 360
Responding to non-compliance with laws and regulations
Introduction

360.1 Professional accountants are required to comply with the fundamental principles and apply the conceptual framework set out in Section 120 to identify, evaluate and address threats.

360.2 A self-interest or intimidation threat to compliance with the principles of integrity and professional behaviour is created when a professional accountant becomes aware of non-compliance or suspected non-compliance with laws and regulations.

360.3 A professional accountant might encounter or be made aware of non-compliance or suspected non-compliance in the course of providing a professional service to a client. This section guides the accountant in assessing the implications of the matter and the possible courses of action when responding to non-compliance or suspected non-compliance with:

(a) Laws and regulations generally recognised to have a direct effect on the determination of material amounts and disclosures in the client's financial statements; and

(b) Other laws and regulations that do not have a direct effect on the determination of the amounts and disclosures in the employing organisation's financial statements, but compliance with which might be fundamental to the operating aspects of the employing organisation's business, to its ability to continue its business, or to avoid material penalties.

Objectives of the professional accountant in relation to non-compliance with laws and regulations

360.4 A distinguishing mark of the accountancy profession is its acceptance of the responsibility to act in the public interest. When responding to non-compliance or suspected non-compliance, the objectives of the professional accountant are:

(a) To comply with the principles of integrity and professional behaviour;

(b) By alerting management or, where appropriate, those charged with governance of the employing organisation, to seek to:

(i) Enable them to rectify, remediate or mitigate the consequences of the identified or suspected non-compliance; or

(ii) Deter the non-compliance where it has not yet occurred; and

(c) To take such further action as appropriate in the public interest.

Requirements and application material

General

360.5 A1 Non-compliance with laws and regulations ("non-compliance") comprises acts of omission or commission, intentional or unintentional, which are contrary to the prevailing laws or regulations committed by the following parties:

(a) A client;

(b) Those charged with governance of a client;

(c) Management of a client; or

(d) Other individuals working for or under the direction of a client.

360.5 A2 Examples of laws and regulations which this section addresses include those that deal with:

• Fraud, corruption and bribery.

• Money laundering, terrorist financing and proceeds of crime.

• Securities markets and trading.

• Banking and other financial products and services.

• Data protection.

• Tax and pension liabilities and payments.

• Environmental protection.

• Public health and safety

360.5 A3 Non-compliance might result in fines, litigation or other consequences for the client, potentially materially affecting its financial statements. Importantly, such non-compliance might have wider public interest implications in terms of potentially substantial harm to investors, creditors, employees of the general public. For the purposes of this section, an act that causes substantial harm is one that results in serious adverse consequences to any of these parties in financial or non-financial terms. Examples include the perpetration of a fraud resulting in significant financial losses to investors, and breaches of environmental laws and regulations endangering the health or safety of employees or the public.

R360.6 In some jurisdictions, there are legal or regulatory provisions governing how professional accountants should address non-compliance or suspected non-compliance. These legal or regulatory provisions might differ from or go beyond the provisions in this section. When encountering such non-compliance or suspected non-compliance, the accountant shall obtain an understanding of those legal or regulatory provisions and comply with them, including:

(a) Any requirement to report the matter to an appropriate authority; and

(b) Any prohibition on alerting the client.

360.6 A1 A prohibition on alerting the client might arise, for example, pursuant to anti-money laundering legislation.

360.7 A1 This section applies regardless of the nature of the client, whether or not it is a public interest entity.

360.7 A2 A professional accountant who encounters or is made aware of matters that are clearly inconsequential is not required to comply with this section. Whether a matter is clearly inconsequential is to be judged with respect to its nature and its impact, financial or otherwise, on the client, its stakeholders and the general public.

360.7 A3   This section does not address:

(a) Personal misconduct unrelated to the business activities of the client; and

(b) Non-compliance by parties other than those specified in paragraph 360.5 A1. This includes, for example, circumstances where a professional accountant has been engaged by a client to perform a due diligence assignment on a third party entity and the identified or suspected non-compliance has been committed by that third-party.

The accountant might nevertheless find the guidance in this section helpful in considering how to respond in these situations.

Responsibilities of management and those charged with governance

360.8 A1   Management, with the oversight of those charged with governance, is responsible for ensuring that the client's business activities are conducted in accordance with laws and regulations. Management and those charged with governance are also responsible for identifying and addressing any non-compliance by:

(a) The client;

(b) An individual charged with governance of the entity;

(c) A member of management; or

(d) Other individuals working for or under the direction of the client.

Responsibilities of all professional accountants

R360.9   Where a professional accountant becomes aware of a matter to which this section applies, the steps that the accountant takes to comply with this section shall be taken on a timely basis. In taking timely steps, the accountant shall have regard to the nature of the matter and the potential harm to the interests of the entity, investors, creditors, employees or the general public.

Audits of financial statements

Obtaining an understanding of the matter

R360.10   If a professional accountant engaged to perform an audit of financial statements becomes aware of information concerning non-compliance or suspected non-compliance, the accountant shall obtain an understanding of the matter. This understanding shall include the nature of the non-compliance or suspected non-compliance and the circumstances in which it has occurred or might occur.

360.10 A1   The professional accountant might become aware of the non-compliance or suspected non-compliance in the course of performing the engagement or through information provided by other parties.

360.10 A2   The professional accountant is expected to apply knowledge and expertise, and exercise professional judgment. However, the accountant is not expected to have a level of knowledge of laws and regulations greater than that which is required to undertake the engagement. Whether an act constitutes non-compliance is ultimately a matter to be determined by a court or other appropriate adjudicative body.

360.10 A3   Depending on the nature and significance of the matter, the professional accountant might consult on a confidential basis with others within the firm, a network firm or a professional body, or with legal counsel.

R360.11   If the professional accountant identifies or suspects that non-compliance has occurred or might occur, the accountant shall discuss the matter with the appropriate level of management and, where appropriate, those charged with governance.

360.11 A1   The purpose of the discussion is to clarify the professional accountant's understanding of the facts and circumstances relevant to the matter and its potential consequences. The discussion also might prompt management or those charged with governance to investigate the matter.

360.11 A2   The appropriate level of management with whom to discuss the matter is a question of professional judgment. Relevant factors to consider include:

• The nature and circumstances of the matter.

• The individuals actually or potentially involved.

• The likelihood of collusion.

• The potential consequences of the matter.

• Whether that level of management is able to investigate the matter and take appropriate action.

360.11 A3   The appropriate level of management is usually at least one level above the individual or individuals involved or potentially involved in the matter. In the context of a group, the appropriate level might be management at an entity that controls the client.

360.11 A4 The professional accountant might also consider discussing the matter with internal auditors where applicable.

R360.12 If the professional accountant believes that management is involved in the non-compliance or suspected non-compliance, the accountant shall discuss the matter with those charged with governance.

Addressing the matter

R360.13 In discussing the non-compliance or suspected non-compliance with management and, where appropriate, those charged with governance, the professional accountant shall advise them to take appropriate and timely actions, if they have not already done so, to:

(a) Rectify, remediate or mitigate the consequences of the non-compliance;

(b) Deter the commission of the non-compliance where it has not yet occurred; or

(c) Disclose the matter to an appropriate authority where required by law or regulation or where considered necessary in the public interest.

R360.14 The professional accountant shall consider whether management and those charged with governance understand their legal or regulatory responsibilities with respect to the non-compliance or suspected non-compliance.

360.14 A1 If management and those charged with governance do not understand their legal or regulatory responsibilities with respect to the matter, the professional accountant might suggest appropriate sources of information or recommend that they obtain legal advice.

R360.15 The professional accountant shall comply with applicable:

(a) Laws and regulations, including legal or regulatory provisions governing the reporting of non-compliance or suspected non-compliance to an appropriate authority; and

(b) Requirements under auditing standards, including those relating to:

• Identifying and responding to non-compliance, including fraud.

• Communicating with those charged with governance.

• Considering the implications of the non-compliance or suspected non-compliance for the auditor's report.

360.15 A1 Some laws and regulations might stipulate a period within which reports of non-compliance or suspected non-compliance are to be made to an appropriate authority.

Communication with respect to groups

R360.16 Where a professional accountant becomes aware of non-compliance or suspected non-compliance in relation to a component of a group in either of the following two situations, the accountant shall communicate the matter to the group engagement partner unless prohibited from doing so by law or regulation:

(a) The accountant is, for purposes of an audit of the group financial statements, requested by the group engagement team to perform work on financial information related to the component; or

(b) The accountant is engaged to perform an audit of the component's financial statements for purposes other than the group audit, for example, a statutory audit.

The communication to the group engagement partner shall be in addition to responding to the matter in accordance with the provisions of this section.

360.16 A1 The purpose of the communication is to enable the group engagement partner to be informed about the matter and to determine, in the context of the group audit, whether and, if so, how to address it in accordance with the provisions in this section. The communication requirement in paragraph R360.16 applies regardless of whether the group engagement partner's firm or network is the same as or different from the professional accountant's firm or network.

R360.17 Where the group engagement partner become aware of non-compliance or suspected non-compliance in the course of an audit of group financial statements, the group engagement partner shall consider whether the matter might be relevant to one or more components:

(a) Whose financial information is subject to work for purposes of the audit of the group financial statements; or

(b) Whose financial statements are subject to audit for purposes other than the group audit, for example, a statutory audit.

This consideration shall be in addition to responding to the matter in the context of the group audit in accordance with the provisions of this section.

R360.18 If the non-compliance or suspected non-compliance might be relevant to one or more of the components specified in paragraph R360.17 (a) and (b), the group engagement partner shall take steps to have the matter communicated to those performing work at the components, unless prohibited from doing so by law or regulation.
If necessary, the group engagement partner shall arrange for appropriate inquiries to be made (either of management or from publicly available information) as to whether the relevant component(s) specified in paragraph R360.17(b) is subject to audit and, if so, to ascertain to the extent practicable the identity of the auditor.

360.18 A1 The purpose of the communication is to enable those responsible for work at the components to be informed about the matter and to determine whether and, if so, how to address it in accordance with the provisions in this section. The communication requirement applies regardless of whether the group engagement partner's firm or network is the same as or different from the firms or networks of those performing work at the components.

Determining whether further action is needed

R360.19 A1 The professional accountant shall assess the appropriateness of the response of management and, where applicable, those charged with governance.

360.19 A1 Relevant factors to consider in assessing the appropriateness of the response of management and, where applicable, those charged with governance include whether:

- The response is timely.
- The non-compliance or suspected non-compliance has been adequately investigated.
- Action has been, or is being, taken to rectify, remediate or mitigate the consequences of any non-compliance.
- Action has been, or is being, taken to deter the commission of any non-compliance where it has not yet occurred.
- Appropriate steps have been, or are being, taken to reduce the risk of re-occurrence, for example, additional controls or training.

- The non-compliance or suspected non-compliance has been disclosed to an appropriate authority where appropriate and, if so, whether the disclosure appears adequate.

R360.20 In light of the response of management and, where applicable, those charged with governance, the professional accountant shall determine if further action is needed in the public interest.

360.20 A1 The determination of whether further action is needed, and the nature and extent of it, will depend on various factors, including:

- The legal and regulatory framework.
- The urgency of the situation.
- The pervasiveness of the matter throughout the client.
- Whether the professional accountant continues to have confidence in the integrity of management and, where applicable, those charged with governance.
- Whether the non-compliance or suspected non-compliance is likely to recur.
- Whether there is credible evidence of actual or potential substantial harm to the interests of the entity, investors, creditors, employees or the general public

360.20 A2 Examples of circumstances that might cause the professional accountant no longer to have confidence in the integrity of management and, where applicable, those charged with governance include situations where:

- The accountant suspects or has evidence of their involvement or intended involvement in any non-compliance.
- The accountant is aware that they have knowledge of such non-compliance and, contrary to legal or regulatory requirements, have not reported, or authorised the reporting of, the matter to an appropriate authority within a reasonable period.

R360.21 The professional accountant shall exercise professional judgment in determining the need for, and nature and extent of, further action. In making this determination, the accountant shall take into account whether a reasonable and informed third party would be likely to conclude that the accountant has acted appropriately in the public interest.

360.21 A1 Further action that the senior professional accountant might take includes:

Disclosing the matter to an appropriate authority even when there is no legal or regulatory requirement to do so.

Withdrawing from the engagement and the professional relationship where permitted by law or regulation.

360.21 A2 Withdrawing from the engagement and the professional relationship is not a substitute for taking other actions that might be needed to achieve the professional accountant's objectives under this section. In some jurisdictions, however, there might be limitations as to the further actions available to the accountant. In such circumstances, withdrawal might be the only available course of action.

R360.22 Where the professional accountant has withdrawn from the professional relationship pursuant to paragraphs R360.20 and 360.21 A1, the accountant shall, on request by the proposed accountant pursuant to paragraph R320.8, provide all relevant facts and other information concerning the identified or suspected non-compliance to the proposed accountant. The predecessor accountant shall do so, even in the circumstances addressed in paragraph R320.8 (b) where the client fails or refuses to grant the predecessor accountant permission to discuss the client's affairs with the proposed accountant, unless prohibited by law or regulation.

360.22 A1 The facts and other information to be provided are those that, in the predecessor accountant's opinion, the proposed accountant needs to be aware of before deciding whether to accept the audit appointment. Section 320 addresses communications from proposed accountants.

R360.23 If the proposed accountant is unable to communicate with the predecessor accountant, the proposed accountant shall take reasonable steps to obtain information about the circumstances of the change of appointment by other means.

360.23 A1 Other means to obtain information about the circumstances of the change of appointment include inquiries of third parties or background investigations of management or those charged with governance.

360.24 A1 As assessment of the matter might involve complex analysis and judgments, the senior professional accountant might consider:

- Consulting internally.
- Obtaining legal advice to understand the accountant's options and the professional or legal implications of taking any particular course of action.
- Consulting on a confidential basis with a regulatory or professional body.

Determining whether to disclose the matter to an appropriate authority

360.25 A1 Disclosure of the matter to an appropriate authority would be precluded if doing so would be contrary to law or regulation. Otherwise, the purpose of making disclosure is to enable an appropriate authority to cause the matter to be investigated and action to be taken in the public interest.

360.25 A2 The determination of whether to make such a disclosure depends in particular on the nature and extent of the actual or potential harm that is or might be caused by the matter to investors, creditors, employees or the general public. For example, the professional accountant might determine that disclosure of the matter to an appropriate authority is an appropriate course of action if:

- The entity is engaged in bribery (for example, of local or foreign government officials for purposes of securing large contracts).
- The entity is regulated and the matter is of such significance as to threaten its license to operate.
- The entity is listed on a securities exchange and the matter might result in adverse consequences to the fair and orderly market in the entity's securities or pose a systemic risk to the financial markets.
- It is likely that the entity would sell products that are harmful to public health or safety.
- The entity is promoting a scheme to its clients to assist them in evading taxes.

360.25 A3 The determination of whether to make such a disclosure will also depend on external factors such as:

- Whether there is an appropriate authority that is able to receive the information, and cause the matter to be investigated and action to be taken. The appropriate authority will depend upon the nature of the matter. For example, the appropriate authority would be a securities regulator in the cause of fraudulent financial reporting or an environmental protection agency in the case of a breach of environmental laws and regulations.

- Whether there exists robust and credible protection from civil, criminal or professional liability or retaliation afforded by legislation or regulation, such as under whistle-blowing legislation or regulation.
- Whether there are actual or potential threats to the physical safety of the senior professional accountant or other individuals.

R360.26 If the professional accountant determines that disclosure of the non-compliance or suspected non-compliance to an appropriate authority is an appropriate course of action in the circumstances, that disclosure is permitted pursuant to paragraph R114.1 (d) of the Code. When making such disclosure, the accountant shall act in good faith and exercise caution when making statements and assertions. The accountant shall also consider whether it is appropriate to inform the client of the accountant's intentions before disclosing the matter.

Imminent breach

R360.27 In exceptional circumstances, the professional accountant might become aware of actual or intended conduct that the accountant has reason to believe would constitute an imminent breach of a law or regulation that would cause substantial harm to investors, creditors, employees or the general public. Having first considered whether it would be appropriate to discuss the matter with management or those charged with governance of the employing organisation, the accountant shall exercise professional judgment and determine whether to disclose the matter immediately to an appropriate authority in order to prevent or mitigate the consequences of such imminent breach. If disclosure is made, that disclosure is permitted pursuant to paragraph R114.1 (d) of the Code.

Documentation

R360.28 In relation to non-compliance or suspected non-compliance that falls within the scope of this section, the professional accountant shall document:

- How management and, where applicable, those charged with governance have responded to the matter.
- The courses of action the accountant considered, the judgments made and the decisions that were taken, having regard to the reasonable and informed third party test.
- How the accountant is satisfied that the accountant has fulfilled the responsibility set out in paragraph R360.20.

360.28 A1 This documentation is in addition to complying with the documentation requirements under applicable auditing standards. ISAs, for example, require a professional accountant performing an audit of financial statements to:

- Prepare documentation sufficient to enable an understanding of significant matters arising during the audit, the conclusions reached, and significant professional judgments made in reaching those conclusions;
- Document discussions of significant matters with management, those charged with governance, and others, including the nature of the significant matters discussed and when and with whom the discussions took place; and
- Document identified or suspected non-compliance, and the results of discussion with management and, where applicable, those charged with governance and other parties outside the entity.

Professional services other than audits of financial statements

Obtaining an understanding of the matter and addressing it with management and those charged with governance

R360.29 If a professional accountant engaged to provide a professional service other than an audit of financial statements becomes aware of information concerning non-compliance or suspected non-compliance, the accountant shall seek to obtain an understanding of the matter. This understanding shall include the nature of the non-compliance or suspected non-compliance and the circumstances in which it has occurred or might occur.

360.29 A1 The professional accountant is expected to apply knowledge and expertise, and exercise professional judgment. However, the accountant is not expected to have a level of understanding of laws and regulations beyond that which is required for the professional service for which the accountant was engaged. Whether an act constitutes actual non-compliance is ultimately a matter to be determined by a court or other appropriate adjudicative body.

360.29 A2 Depending on the nature and significance of the matter, the professional accountant might consult on a confidential basis with others within the firm, a network firm or a professional body, or with legal counsel.

R360.30 If the professional accountant identifies or suspects that non-compliance has occurred or might occur, the accountant shall discuss the matter with the appropriate level of management. If the accountant has access to those charged with governance, the accountant shall also discuss the matter with them where appropriate.

360.30 A1 The purpose of the discussion is to clarify the professional accountant's understanding of the facts and circumstances relevant to the matter and its potential consequences. The discussion also might prompt management or those charged with governance to investigate the matter.

360.30 A2 The appropriate level of management with whom to discuss the matter is a question of professional judgment. Relevant factors to consider include:

- The nature and circumstances of the matter.
- The individuals actually or potentially involved.
- The likelihood of collusion.
- The potential consequences of the matter.
- Whether that level of management is able to investigate the matter and take appropriate action.

Communicating the matter to the entity's external auditor

R360.31 If the professional accountant is performing a non-audit service for:

(a) An audit client of the firm; or

(b) A component of an audit client of the firm,

the accountant shall communicate the non-compliance or suspected non-compliance within the firm, unless prohibited from doing so by law or regulation. The communication shall be made in accordance with the firm's protocols or procedures. In the absence of such protocols and procedures, it shall be made directly to the audit engagement partner.

R360.32 If the professional accountant is performing a non-audit service for:

(a) An audit client of a network firm; or

(b) A component of an audit client of a network firm,

the accountant shall consider whether to communicate the non-compliance or suspected non-compliance to the network firm. Where the communication is made, it shall be made in accordance with the network's protocols and procedures. In the absence of such protocols and procedures, it shall be made directly to the audit engagement partner.

R360.33 If the professional accountant is performing a non-audit service for a client that is not:

(a) An audit client of the firm or a network firm; or

(b) A component of an audit client of the firm or a network firm,

the accountant shall consider whether to communicate the non-compliance or suspected non-compliance to the firm that is the client's external auditor, if any.

Relevant factors to consider

360.34 A1 Factors relevant to considering the communication in accordance with paragraphs R360.31 to R360.33 include:

- Whether doing so would be contrary to law or regulation.
- Whether there are restrictions about disclosure imposed by a regulatory agency or prosecutor in an ongoing investigation into the non-compliance or suspected non-compliance.
- Whether the purpose of the engagement is to investigate potential non-compliance within the entity to enable it to take appropriate action.
- Whether management or those charged with governance have already informed the entity's external auditor about the matter.
- The likely materiality of the matter to the audit of the client's financial statements or, where the matter relates to a component of a group, its likely materiality to the audit of the group financial statements.

Purpose of communication

360.35 A1 In the circumstances addressed in paragraphs R360.31 to R360.33, the purpose of the communication is to enable the audit engagement partner to be informed about the non-compliance or suspected non-compliance and to determine whether and, if so, how to address it in accordance with the provisions in this section.

Considering whether further action is needed

R360.36 The professional accountant shall also consider whether further action is needed in the public interest.

360.36 A1 Whether further action is needed, and the nature and extent of it, will depend on factors such as:

- The legal and regulatory framework.
- The appropriateness and timeliness of the response of management and, where applicable, those charged with governance.
- The urgency of the situation.
- The involvement of management or those charged with governance in the matter.
- The likelihood of substantial harm to the interests of the client, investors, creditors, employees or the general public.

360.36 A2 Further action by the professional accountant might include:

- Disclosing the matter to an appropriate authority even when there is no legal or regulatory requirement to do so.
- Withdrawing from the engagement and the professional relationship where permitted by law or regulation.

360.36 A3 In considering whether to disclose to an appropriate authority, relevant factors to take into account include:

- Whether doing so would be contrary to law or regulation.
- Whether there are restrictions about disclosure imposed by a regulatory agency or prosecutor in an ongoing investigation into the non-compliance or suspected non-compliance.
- Whether the purpose of the engagement is to investigate potential non-compliance within the entity to enable it to take appropriate action.

R360.37 If the professional accountant determines that disclosure of the non-compliance or suspected non-compliance to an appropriate authority is an appropriate course of action in the circumstances, that disclosure is permitted pursuant to paragraph R114.1 (d) of the Code. When making such disclosure, the accountant shall act in good faith and exercise caution when making statements and assertions. The accountant shall also consider whether it is appropriate to inform the client of the accountant's intentions before disclosing the matter.

Imminent breach

R360.38 In exceptional circumstances, the professional accountant might become aware of actual or intended conduct that the accountant has reason to believe would constitute an imminent breach of a law or regulation that would cause substantial harm to investors, creditors, employees or the general public. Having first considered whether it would be appropriate to discuss the matter with management or those charged with governance of the entity, the accountant shall exercise professional judgment and determine whether to disclose the matter immediately to an appropriate authority in order to prevent or mitigate the consequences of such imminent breach of law or regulation. If disclosure is made, that disclosure is permitted pursuant to paragraph 114.1 (d) of the Code.

Seeking advice

360.39 A1 The professional accountant might consider:

- Consulting internally.
- Obtaining legal advice to understand the professional or legal implications of taking any particular course of action.
- Consulting on a confidential basis with a regulatory or professional body.

Documentation

360.40 A1 In relation to non-compliance or suspected non-compliance that falls within the scope of this section, the professional accountant is encouraged to document:

- The matter.
- The results of discussions with management and, where applicable, those charged with governance and other parties.
- How management and, where applicable, those charged with governance have responded to the matter.
- The courses of action the accountant considered, the judgments made and the decisions that were taken.
- How the accountant is satisfied that the accountant has fulfilled the responsibility set out in paragraph R360.36.

Glossary

Glossary (Parts 1, 3, 4a and 4b)

In Parts 1 and 3 of the CIMA Code of Ethics for Professional Accountants, the following expressions have the following meanings assigned to them: Please see the next section for definitions applicable to Part 2 of the Code.

Acceptable level	A level at which a professional accountant using the reasonable and informed third party would likely conclude that the accountant complies with the fundamental principles.
Advertising	The communication to the public of information as to the services or skills provided by professional accountants in public practice with a view to procuring professional business.
Appropriate reviewer	An appropriate reviewer is a professional with the necessary knowledge, skills, experience and authority to review, in an objective manner, the relevant work performed or service provided. Such an individual might be a professional accountant. This term is described in paragraph 300.8 A4.
Assurance client	The responsible party that is the person (or persons) who: (a) In a direct reporting engagement, is responsible for the subject matter; or (b) In an assertion-based engagement, is responsible for the subject matter information and may be responsible for the subject matter.
Assurance engagement	An engagement in which a professional accountant in public practice expresses a conclusion designed to enhance the degree of confidence of the intended users other than the responsible party about the outcome of the evaluation or measurement of a subject matter against criteria. (For guidance on assurance engagements see the International Framework for Assurance Engagements issued by the International Auditing and Assurance Standards Board. The International Framework for Assurance Engagements describes the elements and objectives of an assurance engagement and identifies engagements to which International Standards on Auditing (ISAs), International Standards on Review Engagements (ISREs) and International Standards on Assurance Engagements (ISAEs) apply).
Assurance team	(a) All members of the engagement team for the assurance engagement; (b) All others within a firm who can directly influence the outcome of the assurance engagement, including: (i) Those who recommend the compensation of, or who provide direct supervisory, management or other oversight of the assurance engagement partner in connection with the performance of the assurance engagement; (ii) Those who provide consultation regarding technical or industry specific issues, transactions or events for the assurance engagement; and (iii) Those who provide quality control for the assurance engagement, including those who perform the engagement quality control review for the assurance engagement.

Audit	In Part 4A, the term "audit" applies equally to "review".
Audit client	An entity in respect of which a firm conducts an audit engagement. When the client is a listed entity, audit client will always include its related entities. When the audit client is not a listed entity, audit client includes those related entities over which the client has direct or indirect control (See also paragraph R400.20). In Part 4A, the term "audit client" applies equally to "review client".
Audit engagement	A reasonable assurance engagement in which a professional accountant in public practice expresses an opinion whether financial statements are prepared, in all material respects (or give a true and fair view or are presented fairly, in all material respects,), in accordance with an applicable financial reporting framework, such as an engagement conducted in accordance with International Standards on Auditing. This includes a Statutory Audit, which is an audit required by legislation or other regulation. In Part 4A, the term "audit engagement" applies equally to "review engagement".
Audit report	In Part 4A, the term "audit report" applies equally to "review report".

Audit team	(a) All members of the engagement team for the audit engagement;
	
	(b) All others within a firm who can directly influence the outcome of the audit engagement, including:
	  (i) Those who recommend the compensation of, or who provide direct supervisory, management or other oversight of the engagement partner in connection with the performance of the audit engagement including those at all successively senior levels above the engagement partner through to the individual who is the firm's Senior or Managing Partner (Chief Executive or equivalent);
	  (ii) Those who provide consultation regarding technical or industry-specific issues, transactions or events for the engagement; and
	  (iii) Those who provide quality control for the engagement, including those who perform the engagement quality control review for the engagement; and
	
	(c) All those within a network firm who can directly influence the outcome of the audit engagement.
	
	In Part 4A, the term "audit team" applies equally to "review team".

Close family	A parent, child or sibling who is not an immediate family member. (See also definition of "immediate family")
Conceptual framework	This term is described in Section 120.
Contingent fee	A fee calculated on a predetermined basis relating to the outcome of a transaction or the result of the services performed by the firm. A fee that is established by a court or other public authority is not a contingent fee.
Cooling-off period	This term is described in paragraph R540.5 for the purposes of paragraphs R540.11 to R540.19.

Direct financial interest	A financial interest:
	  (a) Owned directly by and under the control of an individual or entity (including those managed on a discretionary basis by others); or
	  (b) Beneficially owned through a collective investment vehicle, estate, trust or other intermediary over which the individual or entity has control, or the ability to influence investment decisions.

Director or officer	Those charged with the governance of an entity, or acting in an equivalent capacity, regardless of their title, which may vary from jurisdiction to jurisdiction.

Eligible audit engagement	This term is described in paragraph 800.2 for the purposes of Section 800.
Eligible assurance engagement	This term is described in paragraph 990.2 for the purposes of Section 990.
Engagement partner	The partner or other person in the firm who is responsible for the engagement and its performance, and for the report that is issued on behalf of the firm, and who, where required, has the appropriate authority from a professional, legal or regulatory body.
Engagement period (Audit and Review Engagements	The engagement period starts when the audit team begins to perform the audit. The engagement period ends when the audit report is issued. When the engagement is of a recurring nature, it ends at the later of the notification by either party that the professional relationship has ended or the issuance of the final audit report.
Engagement period (Assurance engagements other than audit and review engagements)	The engagement period starts when the assurance team begins to perform assurance services with respect to the particular engagement. The engagement period ends when the assurance report is issued. When the engagement is of a recurring nature, it ends at the later of the notification by either party that the professional relationship has ended or the issuance of the final assurance report.
Engagement quality control review	A process designed to provide an objective evaluation, on or before the report is issued, of the significant judgments the engagement team made and the conclusions it reached in formulating the report.
Engagement team	All partners and staff performing the engagement, and any individuals engaged by the firm or a network firm who perform assurance procedures on the engagement. This excludes external experts engaged by the firm or a network firm. The term "engagement team" also excludes individuals within the client's internal audit function who provide direct assistance on an audit engagement when the external auditor complies with the requirements of ISA 610 (Revised 2013) Using the Work of Internal Auditors.[2]
Existing accountant	A professional accountant in public practice currently holding an audit appointment or carrying out accounting, taxation, consulting or similar professional services for a client.
External expert	An individual (who is not a partner or a member of the professional staff, including temporary staff, of the firm or a network firm) or organisation possessing skills, knowledge and experience in a field other than accounting or auditing, whose work in that field is used to assist the professional accountant in obtaining sufficient appropriate evidence.
Financial interest	An interest in an equity or other security, debenture, loan or other debt instrument of an entity, including rights and obligations to acquire such an interest and derivatives directly related to such interest.
Financial statements	A structured representation of historical financial information, including related notes, intended to communicate an entity's economic resources or obligations at a point in time or the changes therein for a period of time in accordance with a financial reporting framework. The related notes ordinarily comprise a summary of significant accounting policies and other explanatory information. The term can relate to a complete set of financial statements, but it can also refer to a single financial statement, for example, a balance sheet, or a statement of revenues and expenses, and related explanatory notes.

---

[2] ISA 610 (Revised 2013) establishes limits on the use of direct assistance. It also acknowledges that the external auditor may be prohibited by law or regulation from obtaining direct assistance from internal auditors. Therefore, the use of direct assistance is restricted to situations where it is permitted.

Firm	(a) A sole practitioner, partnership or corporation of professional accountants;
	(b) An entity that controls such parties, through ownership, management or other means; and
	(c) An entity controlled by such parties, through ownership, management or other means.
	Paragraphs 400.4 and 900.3 explain how the word "firm" is used to address the responsibility of professional accountants and firms for compliance with Parts 4A and 4B, respectively.
Fundamental principles	This term is described in paragraph 110.1 A1. Each of the fundamental principles is, in turn, described in the following paragraphs:
	Integrity R111.1
	Objectivity R112.1
	Professional competence and due care R113.1
	Confidentiality R114.1
	Professional behaviour R115.1
Historical financial information	Information expressed in financial terms in relation to a particular entity, derived primarily from that entity's accounting system, about economic events occurring in past time periods or about economic conditions or circumstances at points in time in the past.
Immediate family	A spouse (or equivalent) or dependent.
Independence	Independence is:
	(a) Independence of mind – the state of mind that permits the expression of a conclusion without being affected by influences that compromise professional judgment, thereby allowing an individual to act with integrity, and exercise objectivity and professional skepticism
	(b) Independence in appearance – the avoidance of facts and circumstances that are so significant that a reasonable and informed third party would be likely to conclude, weighing all the specific facts and circumstances, that a firm's, or a member of the audit or assurance team's, integrity, objectivity or professional skepticism has been compromised.
	As set out in paragraphs 400.5 and 900.4, references to an individual or firm being "independent" mean that the individual or firm has complied with Parts 4A and 4B, as applicable.
Indirect financial interest	A financial interest beneficially owned through a collective investment vehicle, estate, trust or other intermediary over which the individual or entity has no control or ability to influence investment decisions.
Inducement	An object, situation, or action that is used as a means to influence another individual's behaviour, but not necessarily with the intent to improperly influence that individual's behaviour.
	Inducements can range from minor acts of hospitality between business colleagues (for professional accountants in business and Members in Business), or between professional accountants in public practice, to acts that result in non-compliance with laws and regulations. An inducement can take many different forms, for example:
	• Gifts.
	• Hospitality.
	• Entertainment.
	• Political or charitable donations.
	• Appeals to friendship and loyalty.
	• Employment or other commercial opportunities.
	• Preferential treatment, rights or privileges.

Key audit partner	The engagement partner, the individual responsible for the engagement quality control review, and other audit partners, if any, on the engagement team who make key decisions or judgments on significant matters with respect to the audit of the financial statements on which the firm will express an opinion. Depending upon the circumstances and the role of the individuals on the audit, "other audit partners" may include, for example, audit partners responsible for significant subsidiaries or divisions.
Listed entity	An entity whose shares, stock or debt are quoted or listed on a recognised stock exchange, or are marketed under the regulations of a recognised stock exchange or other equivalent body.
May	This term is used in the Code to denote permission to take a particular action in certain circumstances, including as an exception, to a requirement. It is not used to denote possibility.
Might	This term is used in the Code to denote the possibility of a matter arising, an event occurring or a course of action being taken. The term does not ascribe any particular level of possibility or likelihood when used in conjunction with a threat, as the evaluation of the level of a threat depends on the facts and circumstances of any particular matter, event or course of action.
Network	A larger structure: (a) That is aimed at co-operation; and (b) That is clearly aimed at profit or cost sharing or shares common ownership, control or management, common quality control policies and procedures, common business strategy, the use of a common brand-name, or a significant part of professional resources.
Network firm	A firm or entity that belongs to a network. For further information, see paragraphs 400.50 A1 to 400.54 A1.
Non-compliance with laws and regulations	Non-compliance with laws and regulations ("non-compliance") comprises acts of omission or commission, intentional or unintentional, which are contrary to the prevailing laws or regulations committed by the following parties: (a) A client; (b) Those charged with governance of a client; (c) Management of a client; or (d) Other individuals working for or under the direction of a client This term is described in paragraph 360.5 A1.
Office	A distinct sub-group, whether organised on geographical or practice lines.
Predecessor accountant	A professional accountant in public practice who most recently held an audit appointment or carried out accounting, tax, consulting or similar professional services for a client, where there is no existing accountant.
Professional accountant	An individual who is a member of an IFAC member body. In Part 1, the term "professional accountant" refers to individual professional accountants in business and to professional accountants in public practice and their firms. In Parts 3, 4A and 4B, the term "professional accountant" refers to professional accountants in public practice and their firms.
Professional accountant in business	A professional accountant working in areas such as commerce, industry, service, the public sector, education, the not for profit sector, or in regulatory bodies or professional bodies, who might be an employee, contractor, partner, director (executive or non-executive), owner-manager or volunteer.

Professional accountant in public practice	A professional accountant, irrespective of functional classification (for example, audit, tax or consulting) in a firm that provides professional services.
	The term "professional accountant in public practice" is also used to refer to a firm of professional accountants in public practice.
Professional activity	An activity requiring accountancy or related skills undertaken by a professional accountant, including accounting, auditing, taxation, management consulting, and financial management.
Professional services	Professional activities performed for clients.
Proposed accountant	A professional accountant in public practice who is considering accepting an audit appointment or an engagement to perform accounting, tax, consulting or similar professional services for a prospective client (or in some cases, an existing client).
Public interest entity	(a) A listed entity; and
	(b) An entity:
	(i) Defined by regulation or legislation as a public interest entity; or
	(ii) For which the audit is required by regulation or legislation to be conducted in compliance with the same independence requirements that apply to the audit of listed entities. Such regulation may be promulgated by any relevant regulator, including an audit regulator.
	Other entities might also be considered to be public interest entities, as set out in paragraph 400.8.
Reasonable and informed third party	The reasonable and informed third party test is a consideration by the professional accountant about whether the same conclusions would likely be reached by another party. Such consideration is made from the perspective of a reasonable and informed third party, who weighs all the relevant facts and circumstances that the accountant knows, or could reasonably be expected to know, at the time that the conclusions are made. The reasonable and informed third party does not need to be an accountant, but would possess the relevant knowledge and experience to understand and evaluate the appropriateness of the accountant's conclusions in an impartial manner.
	The terms are described in paragraph R120.5 A4.
Related entity	An entity that has any of the following relationships with the client:
	(a) An entity that has direct or indirect control over the client if the client is material to such entity;
	(b) An entity with a direct financial interest in the client if that entity has significant influence over the client and the interest in the client is material to such entity;
	(c) An entity over which the client has direct or indirect control;
	(d) An entity in which the client, or an entity related to the client under (c) above, has a direct financial interest that gives it significant influence over such entity and the interest is material to the client and its related entity in (c); and
	(e) An entity which is under common control with the client (a "sister entity") if the sister entity and the client are both material to the entity that controls both the client and sister entity.
Review client	An entity in respect of which a firm conducts a review engagement.

Review engagement	(a) All members of the engagement team for the review engagement; and
	(b) All others within a firm who can directly influence the outcome of the review engagement, including:
	(i) Those who recommend the compensation of, or who provide direct supervisory, management or other oversight of the engagement partner in connection with the performance of the review engagement including those at all successively senior levels above the engagement partner through to the individual who is the firm's Senior or Managing Partner (Chief Executive or equivalent);
	(ii) Those who provide consultation regarding technical or industry specific issues, transactions or events for the engagement; and
	(iii) Those who provide quality control for the engagement, including those who perform the engagement quality control review for the engagement; and
	(c) All those within a network firm who can directly influence the outcome of the review engagement.
Safeguards	Safeguards are actions, individually or in combination that the professional accountant takes that effectively reduce threats to compliance with the fundamental principles to an acceptable level.
	This term is described in paragraph 120.10 A2.
Substantial harm	This term is described in paragraph 360.
Special purpose financial statements	Financial statements prepared in accordance with a financial reporting framework designed to meet the financial information needs of specified users.
Those charged with governance	The person(s) or organisation(s) (for example, a corporate trustee) with responsibility for overseeing the strategic direction of the entity and obligations related to the accountability of the entity. This includes overseeing the financial reporting process.
	For some entities in some jurisdictions, those charged with governance may include management personnel, for example, executive members of a governance board of a private or public sector entity, or an owner-manager.
Threats	This term is described in paragraph 120.6 A3 and includes the following categories:
	Self-interest 120.6 A3(a)
	Self-review 120.6 A3(b)
	Advocacy 120.6 A3(c)
	Familiarity 120.6 A3(d)
	Intimidation 120.6 A3(e)
Time-on period	This term is described in paragraph R540.5

Glossary (Part 2)

In Part 2 of the CIMA Code of Ethics for Professional Accountants, the following expressions have the following meanings assigned to them:

Acceptable level	A level at which a professional accountant using the reasonable and informed third party test would likely conclude that the accountant complies with the fundamental principles.
Client	Any person or entity, other than the member's employer, that engages a member or member's firm to perform professional services and, if different, the person or entity with respect to which professional services are performed. For purposes of this definition for AICPA members, the term employer does not include the following: (a) Person or entity engaged in public practice. (b) Federal, state, and local government or component unit thereof, provided that the member performing professional services with respect to the entity is (i) directly elected by voters of the government or component unit thereof with respect to which professional services are performed; (ii) an individual who is (1) appointed by a legislative body and (2) subject to removal by a legislative body; or (iii) appointed by someone other than the legislative body, so long as the appointment is confirmed by the legislative body and removal is subject to oversight or approval by the legislative body.
Close relative	A parent, sibling, or nondependent child.
Council	The AICPA Council.
Employing organisation	Any entity that employs the member or engages the member on a contractual or volunteer basis in an executive, a staff, a governance, an advisory, or an administrative capacity to provide professional services.
Financial interest	An ownership interest in an equity or a debt security issued by an entity, including rights and obligations to acquire such an interest and derivatives directly related to such interest.
Financial statements	A presentation of financial data, including accompanying disclosures, if any, intended to communicate an entity's economic resources or obligations, or both, at a point in time or the changes therein for a period of time, in accordance with the applicable financial reporting framework. Tax returns and supporting schedules do not, for this purpose, constitute financial statements. The statement, affidavit, or signature of preparers required on tax returns neither constitutes an opinion on financial statements nor requires a disclaimer of such opinion.
Fundamental principles	The fundamental principles are integrity, objectivity, professional competence and due care, confidentiality, and professional behaviour.
Immediate family	A spouse, spousal equivalent, or dependent (regardless of whether the dependent is related).

Inducement	An object, situation, or action that is used as a means to influence another individual's behaviour, but not necessarily with the intent to improperly influence that individual's behaviour.
	Inducements can range from minor acts of hospitality between business colleagues (for professional accountants in business and Members in Business), or between professional accountants in public practice, to acts that result in non-compliance with laws and regulations. An inducement can take many different forms, for example:
	• Gifts.
	• Hospitality.
	• Entertainment.
	• Political or charitable donations.
	• Appeals to friendship and loyalty.
	• Employment or other commercial opportunities.
	• Preferential treatment, rights or privileges.
Institute	The AICPA or CIMA.
Interpretation	Pronouncements issued by the AICPA and CIMA to provide guidelines concerning the scope and application of the rules of conduct and fundamental principles.
Member	A member of the AICPA is a member, an associate or affiliate member or international associate of the AICPA. A member of CIMA is a Fellow or Associate of the Institute, and includes, for the purposes of the disciplinary powers and procedures of the Institute, a person who ceased to be a member on or after June 14, 2003. When used in this Code, the term member means a member in business or professional accountant in business and who is a CGMA (or entitled to use the designation CGMA).
Member(s) in business or professional accountant(s) in business	A member who is employed or engaged on a contractual or volunteer basis in a(n) executive, staff, governance, advisory, or administrative capacity in such areas as industry, the public sector, education, the not-for-profit sector, and regulatory or professional bodies. This does not include a member engaged in public practice.
Professional services	Include all services requiring accountancy or related skills that are performed by a member for an employer, or on a volunteer basis. These services include, but are not limited to accounting, tax, bookkeeping, management consulting, financial management, corporate governance, business valuation and educational services. For AICPA members, it also includes those services for which standards are promulgated by bodies designated by AICPA Council.
Public interest entity(ies)	Public interest entities are (a) all listed entities, including entities whose shares, stock, or debt are quoted or listed on a recognised stock exchange or marketed under the regulations of a recognised stock exchange or other equivalent body, and (b) any entity for which an audit is required by regulation or legislation to be conducted in compliance with the same independence requirements that apply to an audit of listed entities. Members may wish to consider whether additional entities should also be treated as public interest entities because they have a large number and wide range of stakeholders. Factors to be considered may include (a) the nature of the business, such as the holding of assets in a fiduciary capacity for a large number of stakeholders; (b) size; and (c) number of employees.
Public practice	Consists of the performance of professional services for a client by a member or member's firm.
Rules	The AICPA Code of Professional Conduct.

Safeguards	Actions or other measures that may eliminate a threat or reduce a threat to an acceptable level.
Those charged with governance	The person(s) or organisation(s) (for example, a corporate trustee) with responsibility for overseeing the strategic direction of the entity and the obligations related to the accountability of the entity. This includes overseeing the financial reporting process. Those charged with governance may include management personnel (for example, executive members of a governance board or an owner-manager).
	When an interpretation requires communicating with those charged with governance, the member should determine, considering the nature and importance of the particular circumstances and matter to be communicated, the appropriate person(s) within the entity's governance structure with whom to communicate. If the member communicates with a subgroup of those charged with governance (for example, an audit committee or an individual), the member should determine whether communication with all of those charged with governance is also necessary, so that they are adequately informed.
Threat(s)	Relationships or circumstances that could compromise a member's compliance with the rules or fundamental principles.

Notes

Chartered Institute of
Management Accountants
The Helicon
One South Place
London EC2M 2RB
United Kingdom
T. +44 (0) 20 8849 2251
E. cima.contact@cimaglobal.com
W. cimaglobal.com

Index

Index